GALLIPOLI
THEN AND NOW

If I should die, think only this of me:
That there's some corner of a foreign field
That is forever England.

RUPERT BROOKE

This book is dedicated to all those who lie buried at Gallipoli
including the many thousands who have no known grave.

GALLIPOLI
THEN AND NOW
STEVE NEWMAN

AN
AFTER THE
BATTLE
PUBLICATION

GALLIPOLI THEN & NOW

ISBN: 1 870067 29 0
© Steve Newman/*After the Battle* 2000
Designed by Gordon Ramsey

PUBLISHERS
Battle of Britain International Limited,
Church House, Church Street, London
E15 3JA
Telephone: (020) 8534 8833
PRINTERS
Printed in Great Britain by Heronsgate
Ltd., Basildon, Essex

FRONT COVER
The 9.4 inch gun destroyed by HMS
Queen Elizabeth in the fort behind V
Beach — then and now.
REAR COVER
The dead still lie on the battlefield *Top:*
The French cemetery at Morto Bay;
below: Lancashire Landing Cemetery.
FRONT ENDPAPER
The *River Clyde* abandoned on V Beach.
(IWM)
REAR ENDPAPER
Preparing for the evacuation of W Beach.
(IWM)
FRONTISPIECE
Snapshot taken of the front line trenches
held by the Herts Yeomanry in the Suvla
sector.
Chapter 1
Section from Keith Johnston's 1861 map
of the Eastern Mediterranean, showing
Italy, Greece and its islands ('Archipel-
ago'), the enlarged Turkish empire as it
then was, with the Gallipoli peninsula in
the eastern Aegean. The Dardanelles —
the infamous 'narrows' — lead to the Sea
of Marmara and the capital of Turkey,
Constantinople (today Istanbul).
Chapter 2
British and French shipping at Mudros
Harbour. (IWM)
Chapter 3
Burial of the dead on the field of battle.
(IWM)
Chapter 4
Men of the Sharpshooters ashore on
August 20. (Sharpshooters Museum)

Chapter 5
North Beach, Anzac, after the August
offensive with No. 1 Australian Station-
ary Hospital in the foreground. (IWM)
Chapter 6
Suvla — guns being evacuated by raft.
(IWM)
Chapter 7
Remains of the unidentified fallen laid
out for burial at Chunuk Bair Cemetery in
1919. (IWM)
Chapter 8
Captain Richard Wills depicted in an
artist's impression of his VC exploit
during the landing on W Beach.
Chapter 9
Anzac Cove today.

PHOTOGRAPHS

Australian War Memorial: Page 21 top left G905, bottom left A3785, 22 bottom left P1287/11/08, 26 top left
P1075/51/45, 27 top left C2168, 49 left A3868, 56 top left
G981, 70 top C01079, 72 left H16894, 73 left C01491, 76
top G988, 77 top H03920, 78 left A03114, 79 top
C02207, 95 left A848, 99 top C1812, 118 A05778, 119
A02025, 121 left J02660, 122 left JO2444, 158 bottom
left H02779, 168 left G01063, 172 bottom right J02405,
177 top C1621, 180 top left G1287, bottom left G01291,
181 top J02522, 183 left H03486.

Bedford Museum: Page 155 left, 163 top.

Bundesarchiv: Page 10, 11, 12 left, 13, 16, 17, 57
right, 68, 116 left.

Commonwealth War Graves Commission: Page 93 top
right.

Hulton Getty: Page 15 bottom right.

Imperial War Museum: Page 16, 35 top right, 38 bottom
left, 39 top, 40 top right, 41 left, 44, 47 left, 48, 51
top left, top right, 52 left, 54 top, 60 top, 61 left, 62 left,
63 left, 66 left, 67 top, 71 left, 80 left, 81 bottom left, 85
top, 86 left, 87 left, 93 left, 94 left, 96, 97 bottom left, 98
top left, bottom left, 102 top, 112 bottom left, 113 top,
114 top, 116 top right, 117 top, 125 top, 128 top, 129 left,
130 top, 131 left, 134 left, 140 right, 144 left, 146 left,
147, 157 top, 158 top left, 159 top right, 160, 162 top left,
bottom left, 167 left, 169 top, 170 left, 171 top, 172 left,
173 left, 176, 178 top right, 179 left, 182 left, 184 top,
bottom left, bottom right, 185 left, 186 left, 187, 188 left,
190 left, 194, 197 top, 200 top left, 201.

Keep Museum: Page 151 top, 156 left.

Kent and Sharpshooters' Museum: Page 101, 108, 132
left, 136 top left, top right, 148 left, 149 top, 153 top left,
166 left, 174 left, 175 left.

John Murphy: Page 26 top right, 55 left, 56 bottom left.

National Army Museum: Page 42, 58, 164 top, 191 left.

National Maritime Museum: Page 45 top right.

Royal British Legion: Page 150 top left, 152 top left, top
right, bottom left, bottom right.

Royal Engineers Museum: Page 178 left, 199 left.

Royal Fusiliers Museum: Page 34 right, 35 top left, 36
top left.

Royal London Hospital: Page 224 left.

Tameside Local Studies Library: Page 104 top.

Acknowledgements

It is not possible to complete such a project without help from many
different sources. Without doubt the hardest part was trying to find as
many unpublished pictures as possible, and for his help on this front, and
in so many other aspects of this work, I must first thank my good friend
Pierce Noonan of the London auctioneers Dix Noonan and Webb.

Also in London I was very fortunate in finding a veritable gold mine
of Gallipoli pictures at the Kent and Sharpshooters' Museum in Croydon,
and special thanks must go to Guy Farrage, Brian Mulcock, BEM, and
Boris Mollo who allowed me not only to copy the photographs I needed
but also to open the museum in their own time to assist me.

My first port of call in my quest for illustrations was the Imperial War
Museum in London and the Australian War Memorial in Canberra where
Jillian Brankin was very helpful. Other museums which have given assis-
tance with pictures or with help and advice are the National Army Mus-
eum; Ian Hook at the Essex Regiment Museum, Chelmsford; Stuart East-
wood at the Border Regiment Museum, Carlisle; Helen Mackie at the
Tameside Library Service, Stalybridge; Maggie Magnusson at the Royal
Engineers Library, Chatham; Nigel Lutt at the Bedfordshire and Luton
Archives; Joseph Warden at the Royal Logistic Corps Museum; Jim Kelle-
her of the Royal Fusiliers Museum; Mr G. Edgerly-Harris at the Gurkha's
Museum; Major J. McQHallam and his staff at the Lancashire Fusiliers
Museum, and Mr G. Wilson, a member of the Gallipoli Association.

Other people I have to thank are John Murphy for the use of a number
of pictures in his private collection as well as being able to use his CD data-
base 'Murphys Register' of the records of individual soldiers which also
assisted me in tracking down photographs of particular men. My thanks
also to Carolyn Parker for her excellent maps and Stan Noyce for his work
in copying and enhancing some very poor black and white pictures. I
would also like to thank Patrick Tootal, OBE, of the Royal British Legion
who through a chance encounter with my father allowed me to use some
unique shots of the campaign taken by a Yeomanry officer. Finally I extend
my appreciation to all the members of the Gallipoli Association who go so
far to preserving the memories of those who served on the peninsula.

I am specially indebted to Sir Martin Gilbert, Winston's Churchill's
biographer, and to his publishers HarperCollins for allowing me to include
a lengthy extract from his book *In Search of Churchill* in Chapter 9.

Whilst at the Dardanelles, few cannot be moved, not only by the
beauty of the surroundings but for the immaculate way in which all the
cemeteries and memorials are maintained by the sterling efforts of the
Commonwealth War Gaves Commission. My appreciation is extended to
Kim Clarke of the CWGC who, when I was having difficulty with accom-
modation when let down at the last moment, saved the day by allowing
me to use the CWGC 'cottage' on the Anzac coast, which gave me a most
peaceful and productive week. I would also like to thank Winston Ramsey
at *After the Battle* who has helped and supported me throughout.

Finally, I must say a big thank you to my family, both my mum and
dad who have taken the time to read through any number of proofs and
offer suggestions and help, whilst my brother Ross has often 'covered' for
me at my place of work to allow me the time needed to finish the project.

STEVE NEWMAN, 2000

CONTENTS

INTRODUCTION

I first visited Gallipoli in 1990 for the 75th anniversary of the landings. I went as someone interested in the First World War and came back as someone deeply moved and almost addicted to this infamous peninsula and the men who fought there. Since then, Gallipoli has become more than an interest and I have often tried to find a way to record the heroism and endurance of the men who served at places such as Chunuk Bair, Lone Pine, The Nek, Quinn's Post, Scimitar Hill and Sedd-el-Bahr; all names that are forever etched in both blood and military legend. This work is my contribution to their courage and sacrifice.

Since 1915, most people have viewed the campaign as a tragic side-show to the Western Front and even at the end of hostilities, the idea of a Gallipoli campaign medal was shelved because 'We don't issue medals for defeats'. If they had issued them for living under constant shelling, the risk of snipers, plagues of flies, extremes of hot and cold and often being needlessly sacrificed by unbelievably incompetent leadership, then every man that ever stepped onto that narrow strip of land would surely have received more than one.

This book, though, is not about apportioning blame, for many far more qualified people than myself have written about the 'what if's' that form an integral part of the Gallipoli legend.

The Gallipoli campaign is of particular historical significance to Australia and New Zealand in that it was the first time that these countries had committed themselves to such an extent in any military operations. At this time both these countries were still relatively young, and the perceived glories of the initial landings and the inevitable casualties suffered over the next eight months served to establish Gallipoli as an extremely important part of their national identities. Even today in the southern hemisphere April 25 is commemorated as a national holiday known as Anzac Day. I wonder in Britain how many school children or even adults would know the significance or possibly have even heard of Gallipoli? For these reasons, it is understandable that many of the published works available to historians are written with, shall we say, a 'pro-colonial' stance with many of the books about the campaign almost ignoring the fact that British troops were even there. It is only when there is some finger-pointing to be done, usually at the inept leadership, that British troops get a mention and this is often only derogatory. Even more forgotten however must be the French who lost nearly 10,000 of their men at Gallipoli and who rarely get a mention in many books on the subject. It is for these reasons I would like to offer the following casualty statistics so that one might gain some sort of perspective of the cost to human life: Australia 8,709; Britain 21,255; France 9,874; India 7,594; New Zealand 2,701; Turkey 86,692 (as quoted by the Australian War Memorial Canberra *see* Epilogue). Remember that each one of these figures represents a mother who has lost a son or perhaps a child who lost his father and you can easily imagine just how many lives were irreversibly altered by a campaign so far from home.

Whatever your views of the leadership, politicians or strategy, what must not be forgotten is that thousands of men of all nationalities suffered hardships and died on this barren landscape.

Today, Gallipoli is not the most easily reached place in the world, particularly for people travelling from Australia and New Zealand, whose forefathers died here in their thousands and from whose suffering and sacrifice were born proud nations. It is however a quiet reflective place, the sun beats down over the distant plains of Troy and then sets majestically behind the Aegean Sea, lighting up the sky with a beauty that has to be seen to be believed.

On the former battlefields today, few people live and work and, but for some farmers and Commonwealth War Graves gardeners, the place might easily be a wilderness. The stillness all adds to the ghostly mystique that still haunts this most beautiful, yet inhospitable of places . . . of lost friends . . . heroism . . . suffering . . . missed opportunities . . . and . . . ultimately . . . defeat and death.

I am proud to add *Gallipoli Then and Now* to the trilogy of First World War volumes by the late John Giles covering the Western Front that have already been published by *After the Battle*. However, one of the biggest trials in this project was procuring enough photographs that were either accurately captioned or distinct enough to find their location today to be able to take the comparison shot. I have tried to include as many previously unpublished photos as possible and I am indebted to the many regimental museums and private collections which allowed me to troll through and use pictures that they held. I hope above all that the pictorial comparisons and the almost diary format of the main events, that have been brought together here, will bring to life some of the much-read-about place names that present day pilgrims, researchers and medal collectors will all know.

One of the most striking factors about the campaign is the dignity of the troops who, right up until their withdrawal, remained determined and disciplined. This dignity surely deserves our respect today. As Brigadier-General Aspinall-Oglander noted at the time: 'Up to the very last, the men were visiting the cemeteries, erecting new crosses, or tidying up the grave of a dead friend. Pointing to one of the cemeteries one of them said to General Birdwood: " I hope they won't hear us marching back to the beach".'

Nearly 85 years on I hope they did hear us return.
(α 94 years on)
STEVE NEWMAN, 2000

THE ROAD TO GALLIPOLI

When the Archduke Franz Ferdinand and his wife were assassinated in Sarajevo on June 28, 1914, the destinies of millions of men were also sealed, and Europe blundered its way into a war that in both misery and scale it could not begin to imagine.

The Germans' famous Schlieffen Plan called for the quick advance and encircling of Paris, that it was hoped would force the French, who had a pact with the Russians, to capitulate. With the French out of the battle, this would then leave the Germans free to look east towards the Russians who they believed would not launch any attack until they were fully mobilised. According to the strictly-timetabled Schlieffen Plan, this gave them roughly six weeks to knock out the French before having to seriously worry about the threat from the east.

When German forces violated Belgian neutrality in their advance towards France, Britain, which had an agreement to protect Belgium, was sucked into the unstoppable chain of events that were quickly leading to a global conflict.

Late August saw the first clashes in France and Belgium, with both the French Fifth Army and the British Expeditionary Force (BEF) fighting successful delaying actions. These stretched the German lines of supply but did not halt the relentless advance on Paris. However, due to the lie of the roads in northern France and Belgium, the units that should have had the French capital directly in front of them were being pushed further and further west. If they persisted on this course, the walled fortress of Paris would split the attackers in two and possibly leave them vulnerable to being surrounded by the reserve garrisons of that city.

General Alexander von Kluck turned his First Army southeastwards. This took his forces to the east of Paris and, whilst regaining contact with the now static Second Army, he exposed his flank for a distance of 100 miles. This change of direction was quickly spotted by the airmen of the Royal Flying Corps and duly reported. The Generals at GHQ in Paris, quickly realising the opportunity that had presented itself, ordered an attack along the entire 100-mile front. The Battle of the Marne had begun.

The fighting raged for four days although, on the scale of things to come it was not a massive battle, it did serve to change

Early battles in France: French infantry on the offensive at the Marne (above) and German dugouts on the Aisne (below).

the entire course of events. Whereas before, the German troops had swept aside all in their path, they were now not only being met by defensive fire but were also being heavily attacked by French forces on a wide front. Meanwhile, the small yet well-trained BEF were exploiting the weak link between the German First and Second Armies. A decision was made by the German High Command to retreat back to the River Aisne, dig in and reform before re-launching their offensive. The retreat was carried out in good heart and an orderly front line was maintained throughout. As the German retreat continued, their lines of supply shortened, allowing reinforcements to reach them quickly. Added to this they were also picking up stragglers which thickened their numbers. The result was that the French and British, keen to keep pushing the Germans back, followed on to attack the defences of the Aisne and in doing so gained nothing more than heavy casualties.

Taken on August 10, 1914, this German snapshot shows the stern of the *Goeben* shadowed by a Turkish MTB in the Dardanelles. The breakout of *Goeben* and *Breslau* from Messina, and their arrival in Constantinople, coupled with Baron von Wangenheim's expert political manoeuverings as German ambassador there, ensured Turkey's full co-operation in the war.

With deadlock in the south, everyone looked to the north for the big breakthrough. The British rushed fresh troops to the area whilst the Germans sent a volunteer force consisting mainly of patriotic students. The Germans got their troops in place first and attacked near the Belgian town of Ypres. A more fierce baptism of fire could not have awaited them as the well-trained British infantrymen, firing 15 rounds a minute, took a terrible toll amongst the inexperienced troops. It was, however, impossible for the British to counter-attack with much hope of success as the Germans could hold out by sheer weight of numbers alone. The entire Western Front stalemate was now complete. From Nieuwpoort on the North Sea to neutral Switzerland, defensive fortifications were established along a front which would remain almost entirely static for the next four years.

It was from this stalemate and mutual destruction that the British and French sought an escape and the taking of Constantinople offered exactly that.

Turkey, which was led by a government known colloquially as the Young Turks, was not keen on war. However, a game of diplomatic chess had been taking place in both Berlin and Constantinople for quite some time and by the outbreak of hostilities in August 1914 the Germans had all but won it.

Turkey had ordered two warships from Britain, which had been paid for mainly by donations from the public and there was a great sense of expectation and national pride surrounding these vessels. However, on the eve of war — August 3, 1914 to be precise — with a crew of Turkish sailors already in England to deliver the first ship, Winston Churchill, the then First Lord of the Admiralty, announced that in the interest of national security, these ships were being requisitioned for the Royal Navy. The disappointment of the Turks was obviously huge and Baron von Wangenheim, the German Ambassador in Constantinople, took little time in exploiting the situation for national advantage. He stressed that this proved what he had said all along; the British were not to be trusted. The Germans were the Turks true friends and they would make good the losses Turkey had suffered by sending two of their own warships to Constantinople at once.

The two ships that Germany decided to send were, by luck or by design, already in the Mediterranean. The *Goeben*, a 22,640-ton battle-cruiser and her attendant light cruiser the *Breslau*.

Throughout August 4, the two German ships were shadowed by HMS *Indomitable* and *Indefatigable*. These ships, which could have easily outgunned and sunk the *Goeben*, were however banned from doing so because Britain's ultimatum to Germany did not expire until midnight.

Whilst some members of the Admiralty were still keen to sink the *Goeben* before nightfall, politics dictated that nothing could be done that would provoke a situation that was already far beyond a peaceful settlement. During the night, the *Goeben* and *Breslau* increased speed and by morning had vanished from the sight of the following British ships. It was nearly two days later that the missing German vessels were tracked down to Messina in Italy having had to stop for coal. The British, expecting the two ships to try and break out through the Straits of Gibraltar, positioned themselves to the west. They were not to have known that the German captain had received a signal to proceed eastwards, directly to Constantinople.

After waiting at the mouth of the Dardanelles for permission to proceed, both the *Goeben* and *Breslau* were allowed to enter whilst the pursuing British ships were denied access. Once at Constantinople, the German sailors on board both ships exchanged their naval caps for fezzes and became part of the still neutral Turkish Navy.

Germany's hold over Turkey was by now virtually complete. However, Germany had little interest at this stage in seeing Turkey directly involved in the war as she was still confident of success in the west and any support from Turkey would have to be reciprocated at a later date. Anyway, as a friendly neutral, she was serving a more than useful purpose in tying up the British flotilla that was still waiting for the *Goeben* to exit the Dardanelles.

However, as the Battle of the Marne proved, German forces in the west were not unstoppable and by late September Germany was becoming more keen to have Turkey as a full ally. On September 26, a Turkish patrol boat was stopped at the mouth of the Dardanelles by the British squadron positioned there and, on finding out there were German crew members on board, the ship was ordered back to Constantinople. This singularly unimportant act was about to have grave consequences. The German officer commanding the fortifications at the narrows made the decision to close the passage which was contrary to international law and

was, in itself, an act of war. Mines were laid across the entrance to the narrows and, with the closing of the passage, so went Russia's supply line to the west. The Turks, who knew nothing of this beforehand, were angry but by now though almost all of Turkey's military forces were under German command and, whatever they threatened, they were too reliant on Germany to have much say over their own destiny.

The next few weeks were spent by German technicians and sailors furiously readying everything for war. They did not have long to wait. On October 29, the *Goeben* and *Breslau* shelled Russian ports and sunk Russian merchantmen in the Black Sea. The Turkish Minister for Marine Affairs denied any knowledge of this action but it was too late. Turkey had been successfully manoeuvred into the ever-widening world war.

Immediately Britain found itself at war with Turkey, plans were made to re-open the narrows. This was primarily so that help

This rare photograph taken on August 4, 1914 from *Goeben* shows the smoke from the two pursuing British warships HMS *Indomitable* and HMS *Indefatigable* during the chase from Africa towards Messina. Following *Goeben*'s halt there for coal, instructions were given to proceed to Constantinople. Whilst the Germans received Turkish permission to proceed up the Dardanelles, the British did not so the hunt was at a stalemate with the 'Big Is' shut outside the straits.

could be sent to the Russians who, through both lack of fuel, food and munitions, were suffering some worrying defeats and were particularly fearful of a Turkish offensive in the oil-rich Caucasus area. On November 3, British ships shelled the forts at Kum Kale and Sedd-el-Bahr. Lasting only about 30 minutes, and with no follow up action planned, this ill-conceived action only served to reinforce what the Germans and Turks already knew; they had to strengthen their defences along the Dardanelles and particularly the Gallipoli peninsula.

Meanwhile in London, politicians and military men were considering the various options. The Western Front was now just a killing ground where, in the first three months alone, the Allies had suffered over a million casualties. However, the outdated leadership still insisted on full frontal attacks against deep redoubts housing machine guns with overlapping fields of fire and which were secure behind virtually impregnable barbed wire.

With this as a backdrop, the idea of a limited naval assault against Turkey looked like a cheap and easy way to knock out an ally of Germany whilst at the same time strengthening Russia's position. In the longer term, it would also give the Allies a base from which to attack Austria, Hungary and even Germany itself. As one British officer at the time enthusiastically noted, ' It is the ultimate outflanking manoeuvre' and so it could have been if enough troops had been landed quickly. But, as with so many things during the entire Gallipoli campaign, things did not go smoothly.

Politicians and the military heirarchy were divided into two camps. The 'Westerners' were convinced that the only place to win the war was in France and Belgium and that any troops deployed anywhere else were wasted as they were not directly involved in the killing of Germans, whereas the 'Easterners' favoured a landing in the east to outflank the German forces, a link up with the Russians to then attack Germany itself.

The wreck of the Turkish ship *Messudieh* (above), torpedoed by Lieutenant Norman Holbrook (right) on Sunday, December 13, 1914. Lieutenant Holbrook's submarine, *B11*, managed to enter the straits at dawn just after the Turkish searchlights were extinguished. Finding his way gingerly through the minefields, four hours later Holbrook was surveying the twin-funnelled *Messudieh* at anchor in Sari Sigla Bay through his periscope. Firing his torpedoes from 600 yards, Holbrook waited just long enough to see their effect before diving steeply to bump along the bed of the Dardanelles and out to the open sea. This action earned Norman Holbrook the Victoria Cross.

The green light was finally given for a naval assault to open up the narrows following a meeting of the War Council on January 13, 1915. No troops were to be landed, other than some Royal Marines, who would go ashore to complete the destruction of anything not destroyed by the ships' guns.

The plan was put into action on the morning of February 19, but, due to bad weather, it had to be suspended until the 25th. Commodore Roger Keyes sent a message to the Admiralty saying that, given favourable weather conditions, he thought the forts at the entrance to the narrows could be dealt with within a day.

By March 2 things were still looking good. No ships had been lost; casualties were minimal, and the Royal Marines that had been landed were roaming on both the Asian and European side of the narrows, destroying equipment and guns. It was now anticipated that the Navy should be off of Constantinople within 14 days.

As was to be expected, the Turks soon got over their initial fear and, with the help of the German commanders who had been sent to the narrows, they started to hit back. They quickly learned that it was almost impossible for the ships to knock out the small field guns and mobile howitzers they were operating if they were moved on a regular basis. These small guns were not a problem to the thickly armour-plated battleships but they were causing chaos amongst the civilian-crewed minesweepers that were little more than converted tugs. The British and French navies found themselves in a 'Catch 22' position; the minesweepers couldn't clear the mines until the guns were knocked out and the battleships couldn't get in close enough to destroy the guns until the mines were cleared.

March 18 proved to be the key day in the naval engagement. On the one hand, the Turkish gunners were now in a desperate situation, having been shelled all day. They were short of ammunition; less than half of their guns were still serviceable, and almost all of their communications had been cut. The successes they had witnessed during the day, including the sinking of the French warship *Bouvet* by a mine, were all but forgotten that night as they anxiously awaited first light and what most believed would be the day that the Allied ships passed the narrows on their way to Constantinople.

The British and French naval officers did not realise at the time that Turkey only had a few dozen mines left. Any serious

A Turkish-manned 'heavy' fires on the British observation post on Rabbit Island, a small land mass facing the intended French diversionary landing sites of Kum Kale and Yeni Shehr. Well camouflaged, these guns (as well as mobile light howitzers) were very difficult for the British seaborne artillery to destroy.

attempt to sweep the mouth of the narrows now would inevitably lead to a passage being cleared, giving the battleships a clear run to Constantinople. On board the Allied ships, everyone was worried about the continuing threat of mines that had inflicted the worst of the day's losses in an area that was thought to have been already swept clear of mines. Indeed, it had been cleared once but the Turks, noticing that the Allied ships were constantly manoeuvring in this area, had floated 20 mines down on the current, from a converted fishing boat called the *Nousret*.

The Navy had always been keen to have an army force land on the Gallipoli peninsula and in the middle of February, the 29th Division, which was at the time sitting idle in England, was earmarked for the job. If it had left immediately and been able to land during the naval engagement on March 18, undoubtedly the whole campaign would have had a different outcome. However it was not to be. The 'Westerners' did not want to see this highly-experienced force go anywhere else other than to the 'real war' which they claimed could only be won in France. Instead it was decided to send the new forces of Australians and New Zealanders who were presently in Egypt. It was also hoped that the Greeks would provide three divisions but the government in Greece was overthrown and replaced by a pro-German regime so replacements had to be found elsewhere. The choice fell again on the 29th Division so all the packing of stores, assembly of ships, and the other complications associated with moving thousands of fighting men, had to be undertaken a second time. All the while, this inordinate loss of time was giving the Turks chances to regroup and reorganise their defences; the delay would be paid for dearly later.

By late March, the Allied ships carrying troops and supplies were starting to arrive at the Greek island of Lemnos, which,

despite the Greeks' more pro-German views, they still allowed the Allies to use against their natural enemy, the Turks. It was only now that it was realised that the ships had been loaded very haphazardly and would have to be repacked into some kind of order before any landing could take place. Unfortunately, this could not be done at Lemnos as it did not possess the necessary facilities to undertake such a massive operation, so the decision had to be taken to send the entire fleet back to Alexandria. Further delay was inevitable. General Sir Ian Hamilton, the appointed Commander-in-Chief, expected the ships to be loaded and ready to go in approximately three weeks, so the date for the landings was loosely set for April 14. However, security was proving to be another problem faced by the Allies. Letters were actually arriving for soldiers marked the 'Constantinople Expeditionary Force' and Turkish spies in Egypt were regularly able to pass back similar information.

Prior to the Gallipoli Landings, the troops of the Anzac force (Australian and New Zealand Army Corps — Anzac) had been based in Egypt. The largest camp was here at Mena, overlooked by the Pyramids of ancient Egypt. Conditions under canvas in the desert were unenviable and most of the men were relieved to quit this tiresome camp with its endless cycle of training exercises (besides some odd skirmishes near the Suez Canal).

Final stop on the road to Gallipoli was Mudros harbour on the Greek island of Lemnos, some 50 miles east of the Gallipoli peninsula. Here, the material necessary to land and keep an attacking force in action was assembled — somewhat inauspiciously at first when the initial consignment of troops and supplies had to return to Alexandria for repacking! In this shot, some of the boats used in putting the troops ashore are visible.

Meanwhile, excitement amongst the Allied troops increased, amongst them was a young scholar Rupert Brooke whose literary works, first from Rugby and then Cambridge, are still much read today. Perhaps the most famous verse by which he is known, written shortly before he was due to land at Gallipoli, is the one that includes these memorable words:

If I should die think only this of me:
That there's some corner of a foreign field
That is forever England.

However, for Rupert Brooke, fate was to deny him his chance of fulfilling his childhood ambition of a military campaign against Constantinople. On April 17, accompanied by many other well-known names who were also serving in the Hood Battalion of the Royal Naval Division, they landed on the Greek island of Skyros. For the next few days they eagerly explored this small island where Theseus is supposed to be buried. By April 21, however, Brooke fell ill and he was transferred to a French hospital ship where they treated him for the blood poisoning that he had contracted as a result of an insect bite. Alas there was little they could do and on April 23 he passed away.

His burial on Skyros was just how he would have wanted it. Naval ratings standing every 20 feet lit the way with candles while his close friends followed the coffin to an olive grove where, in the warm Aegean night, he was laid to rest. Of his friends in attendance, only two would survive the war, Arthur Asquith, the Prime Minister's son, and Bernard Freyburg, who, during the course of two world wars, would be awarded a Victoria Cross and the Distinguished Service Order with three bars before being appointed Governor General of New Zealand.

Meanwhile, as the assembled men from many different units were packing up to leave these small islands, the Turkish defences on the mainland were being strengthened. Finally, after so many delays to make sure everything was in order, the operation was set for April 25, 1915 but, unfortunately for the troops soon to land, the Turks were now also quite ready to repel them.

Rupert Brooke's grave on Skyros, depicted in 1915 (top) and after the war (below). Brooke (inset) is remembered more for 'what might have been' as an unfulfilled potential than for the poetry he managed to produce in his tragically short life.

THE LANDINGS

THE ANZAC SECTOR

By the early morning of April 25 the Turkish headquarters were receiving numerous confused messages reporting landings and imminent landings from the toe of the peninsula to the neck and on both the European and Asian sides of the Dardanelles.

General Otto Liman von Sanders (German commander of Turkish forces on the peninsula) was fully aware that the British, Commonwealth and French troops could not possibly hope to reinforce all these landings and that some were therefore feints. His problem was deciding which were which.

The reports that most worried General von Sanders, were those of heavy shelling and an imminent landing at the neck of the peninsula near Bulair. To suffer defeat here at the northern end where the peninsula is at its narrowest would mean entrapment for the rest of his forces further south. He was not to know that the Bulair 'landing' was, along with the French landing at Kum Kale on the Asian side of the Dardanelles, purely a diversion. This was to aid the actual landings which were taking place near Cape Helles and Gaba Tepe on the Gallipoli peninsula proper.

General Otto Liman von Sanders' HQ at Galata on the east coast

General von Sanders was originally Inspector of the Turkish Army — a kind of advisory role in helping to train the Turks along Western lines. Appointed in 1913, he was able to second German officers to senior Turkish army commands. In March 1915, von Sanders was made Commander-in-Chief of the Turkish Fifth Army, raised for the defence of the Gallipoli peninsula, so giving the Turks an experienced commander to combat a Western invasion force. He was destined to fight the British again with Turkish troops — in Palestine against General Allenby in 1917 — though this time he lost!

For once, an Allied plan was having its desired effect. For most of the day, British ships had been manoeuvring in Bakka Bay, shelling Turkish positions, and by late afternoon Turkish spotters could clearly see men being loaded into cutters and towed towards the shore. However, in line with the Allied diversion plan, as soon as darkness fell, these men were returned to the transport ships which they had just left. When no troops landed shortly after nightfall, Liman von Sanders, who had been watching the Bulair coast and who was originally convinced that this was to be the main landing, was now equally and correctly convinced that this was purely a diversionary attack.

However, so worried was he about an attack here that it would not be until early the next day that he would allow any troops to be moved further south. It was April 27 before he permitted the bulk of his reserves that were being desperately requested by his commanders to the south, to be released.

Taken aboard SS *Triad* in April 1915, this picture shows the main players in both the Naval and Army spheres of the Allied command. L-R: Commodore Roger Keyes was Chief-of-Staff to Vice-Admiral John de Robeck (second left), the commander of all naval forces in the Dardanelles. General Sir Ian Hamilton (with hand on pole) was the Army Commander-in-Chief and Major-General Walter Braithwaite (right) his Chief-of-Staff.

The aim of this diversionary landing was to allow the Australian and New Zealand forces consisting of the 1st, 2nd, 3rd and 4th Australian Brigades, as well as a New Zealand Brigade, to get ashore to the north of Gaba Tepe and capture the high ground before Turkish reinforcements could arrive. The Australian troops had had it drummed into them that they were to get off the beaches and push inland towards Maidos as soon as they could. This plan made a lot of sense: land on a lightly defended beach and then push inland quickly. The left flank was being covered as

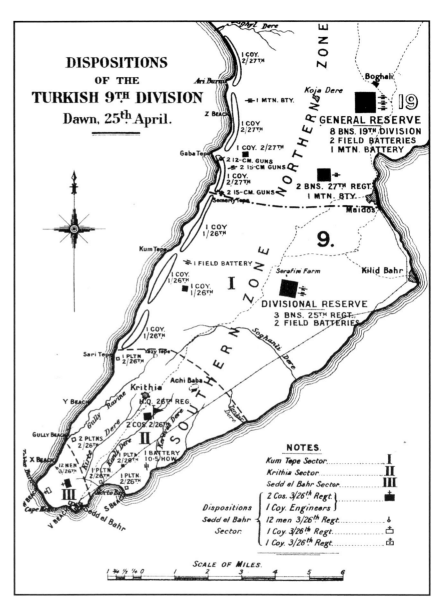

The disposition of the Turkish defences reproduced from the British official history published in 1929.

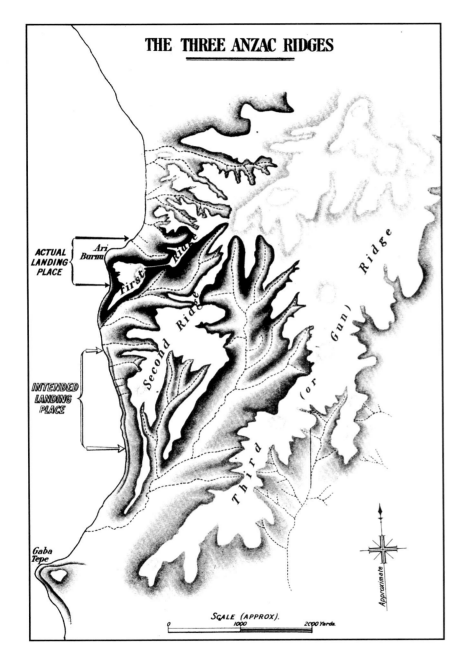

THE THREE ANZAC RIDGES

Ari Burnu

ACTUAL
LANDING
PLACE

First Ridge

Second Ridge

INTENDED
LANDING
PLACE

Third (or Gun) Ridge

Gaba
Tepe

SCALE (APPROX).
1000   2000 Yards.

Approximate

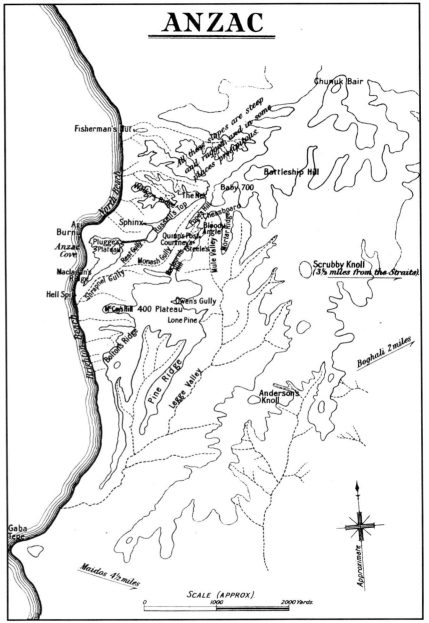

ANZAC

Chunuk Bair

Fisherman's Hut

All these slopes are steep and rugged and in some places precipitous.

Battleship Hill

Baby 700

The Nek

Walker's Ridge

North Beach

Russell's Top

Sphinx

Ari
Burnu

Plugge's
Plateau

Anzac
Cove

Rest Gully

Maclagan's
Ridge

Shrapnel Gully

Hell Spit

Pope's Hill
The Chessboard
Bloody
Angle
Quinn's Post
Courtney's
Steele's
Mortar Ridge
Monash Gully
Mule Valley

Scrubby Knoll
(3½ miles from the Straits)

M'Cay's Hill   400 Plateau
Owen's Gully
Lone Pine

Brighton Beach

Bolton's Ridge

Pine Ridge

Legge Valley

Anderson's
Knoll

Boghali 2 miles

Gaba
Tepe

Maidos 4½ miles

SCALE (APPROX).
1000   2000 Yards.

Approximate

19

Left: 'D-Day' at Gallipoli. Troops landing in a somewhat leisurely manner near Hell Spit on April 25, 1915. The curve of the beach is a distinctive landmark, and today (right) with the remnants of old landing jetties (constructed after April 25) and later Turkish defences still in evidence, it is not hard to imagine the nervous excitement of the first troops landing here in the half light of dawn.

much by the inhospitable landscape as by the troops. The capture of the Third Ridge (or Gun Ridge as it became known) would then allow the left flank to sweep up towards and capture the heights of Sari Bair. Meanwhile, the main thrust would push across the peninsula towards Maidos. Once the heights were captured, Turkish reinforcements would find it virtually impossible to reach the British landings at the toe of the peninsula. This would pave the way for the British to fight up the peninsula and link with the Australians and New Zealanders. This they desperately tried to do but they had been landed in the wrong place thus the impassable terrain that was supposed to be protecting their flank now faced them. There was no time to try and disembark the troops at the correct beach; with both the Divisional and the Commander-in-Chief aboard ships and not in direct communication, the Gallipoli jinx had struck early.

The 4,000 men landed by 0500 hours started to push inland and, had they landed in the correct place, there is little doubt that they would have taken most of their objectives. If this had been the case, then many of the places that were soon to become household names in the southern hemisphere would never have held any significance.

By 0700 hours nearly 8,000 men had been put ashore but, due to the terrain and confusion of having been landed at the wrong beach, the going was slow. The First Ridge had been captured and fighting on the Second Ridge was now dying out as the Australians pushed on. Capture of the Third Ridge would all but control the peninsula and indeed some men had already reached it. Lieutenant Noel Loutit and some scouts from the 10th (South Australia) Battalion had penetrated as far as Scrubby Knoll from where they could see the waters of the narrows less than three miles away. Only a few times in the entire campaign would Allied troops be able to see the shimmering waters of the narrows and here on the first day were some men as near to that goal as would happen again. Once again the ubiquitous Gallipoli question of 'what if' has to be asked. If the commanders had realised the importance of this moment, and been able to get reinforcements to the area quickly enough, the campaign might well have taken an entirely different course. However it was not to be and the opportunity to take control of the sparsely defended high ground of Gun Ridge was rapidly ticking away.

Due to the unexpected terrain now faced by the Australian and New Zealand Army Corps, the battle was taking turns for

Left: Troops landing at Anzac Cove on April 25. The horse boats (with the ramps down), which have just landed mules of 26th (Jacob's) Indian Mountain Battery, are not dissimilar to the landing craft of World War II. The battleship close in is the *Bacchante.*

Right: Today, if you do by chance meet someone at Anzac Cove, they are just as likely to be foreign visitors who in many cases have come half way around the world to wander along these famous shores.

Left: Anzac Cove at 1100 hours on April 25. The beach is almost deserted except for a small party of troops in the background, contrasting with the frenzied activities which took place later in the campaign on this narrow stretch of sand. Also missing are the large stacks of stores and supplies which accumulated here

shortly after the landings. Right: Once again Anzac Cove has regained that quiet desolate feeling, undisturbed by humans. The shape of Ari Burnu has changed somewhat over the years as has the bank which still erodes from time to time as evidenced by the latest landslide to the right.

which no commander could plan. Near 400 Plateau, Colonel Ewen Sinclair-MacLagan, commanding the 3rd Australian Brigade, had seen his troops become separated from one another whilst fighting isolated skirmishes on a wide front. He was completely unaware that other troops were already on the Third Ridge and so he chose to hold the Second Ridge as a covering area until further forces could reinforce them.

On the left of Sinclair-MacLagan's men, things were if not more, then at least equally confused. A small group led by Captain Eric Tulloch of the 11th Battalion had crossed the Nek and were on the lower slopes of Baby 700 not far from Battleship Hill and the strategically important heights of Chunuk Bair. They, too, were fighting against an unseen enemy who was hiding in the thick undergrowth, firing and then changing position, slowing their progress but not being able to halt it. It has to be remembered that the Turks had made no plans for defending this area of the peninsula, as they had considered it impossible to land troops here, so it was left to a few Turkish snipers, outnumbered by five or six to one, to fight a desperate rearguard action.

Looking down towards Ari Burnu from Walker's Ridge with the Sphinx on the left. An idea of the difficulties in climbing this hillside under fire on April 25 can be gauged from this view. The Turks had not expected this area to come under attack; consequently very few troops were defending it though the terrain lent itself to almost guerilla-type warfare with concealment and high ground being the key components. Anzac Cove itself lies just out of sight to the left of the Ari Burnu headland that is visible in the background.

Australians of the 6th and 7th Battalions leave the transport ship *Galeka* on the morning of April 25. Many of these men were unfortunate enough to come ashore too far north, close by the Turkish position around Fisherman's Hut, where they were decimated.

Meanwhile a disaster had struck the 7th (Victoria) Battalion which was supposed to be reinforcing this important left flank. They had arrived offshore at 0445 hours in the transport ship *Galeka* but unfortunately no cutters had arrived to ferry the troops ashore. The captain of the ship decided he could not sit so close to the beach, under heavy shrapnel fire with the decks crowded with troops, so he took the decision to use his own lifeboats. However, due to the confusion caused by the original mistake in landing at the wrong beach, no one was quite sure where exactly the left flank was. They were shortly to find out.

The boats approached the shore too far to the north, near an area called Fisherman's Hut. This position was still in Turkish

A panoramic view taken from near Outpost No. 2 looking towards the area of Fisherman's Hut. It was here that men of the 7th Battalion of the Australian Imperial Forces (AIF) were caught by the guns of a Turkish strong point after having been landed too far to the north.

hands and as the troops neared the beach they were greeted by rapid fire. Of the 140 men on board these six small boats, only 18 would rejoin their battalion at the end of the day. On the other hand, the Turks defending the coastline here soon retreated to the high ground that was rapidly becoming the key to victory.

It was at this moment that fate took another unfortunate swipe at the Allies. A 34-year-old Turkish Lieutenant-Colonel by the name of Mustafa Kemal, commanding a battalion of reserves that had just been released to resist the Anzac landings, arrived at the summit of Chunuk Bair. He instantly grasped what no other commander so far had seen: that the success or failure of the entire battle lay not with number of troops, or the number of guns, but with the possession of the hills of the Sari Bair range and Chunuk

Architect of Turkey's victory: Lieutenant-Colonel Mustafa Kemal,

Today the Turkish 57th Regiment Cemetery on the Northern Apex near Quinn's Post is one of the most visited places on the peninsula, particularly at weekends when the solitude and peace is somewhat shattered by the throngs of tourists who make the pilgrimage. Nevertheless, much of the old battlefield remains peacefully quiet where one can reflect and contemplate the awful carnage which once took place on the very soil beneath one's feet. The burial ground is one of only two formal Turkish cemeteries, compared to the 31 maintained by Commonwealth War Graves Commission (CWGC) for the Allies (see page 226).

Bair in particular. Whosoever controlled these would control the battlefield and would be certain of eventual victory.

Kemal now took things into his own hands. On meeting some fleeing Turkish soldiers who were desperately low on ammunition and being pursued by an advanced party of Anzacs, he ordered them to lie down and fix bayonets. This seemingly small event forced the Anzacs to take cover, giving Kemal the chance to bring up the rest of his battalion who were sheltering on the other side of the ridge. Upon their arrival, they quickly swept the few Anzacs off the hill and Chunuk Bair was a step closer to remaining in Turkish hands. Thus, the initial chance of taking the high ground cheaply had now slipped from the Allies grasp; over the next eight months, some 50,000 men from all nationalities were to die in bitter fighting around these barren hills.

Kemal now ordered the Turkish 57th Regiment and an Arab regiment up into the fight. As a divisional commander he had no right to do this but, as the battle intensified, his superiors had little choice but to give him further reinforcements as he requested them. The ingredients were now all in place for wholesale slaughter with both sides being reinforced and both dead set on attacking. The Turks now believed they could push the Anzacs into the sea, whilst the Anzacs still believed one more push might see them through.

After a brief slackening in the fighting, it erupted with new fury at around 1600 hours. The men of the 57th Regiment were ordered by Kemal 'not only to attack but to die' and this they obligingly did. They charged head-on into fierce Anzac rifle and machine-gun fire in an assault, that, for futility, even the Western Front generals would have been justly proud.

The Turkish attacks continued. Fighting raged around The Nek with first one side on top and then the other. The same was true at Baby 700 and 400 Plateau.

Holes were now appearing in the Anzac lines. Some were plugged by the more recently-landed New Zealanders whilst others went unexploited by the equally exhausted and confused Turks.

Another hugely worrying problem for the Allied commanders was the landing of supplies and the evacuation of the wounded. Whereas the logistics men had been promised a long sandy beach nearly a mile long, they were actually faced with a small cove that was surrounded by cliffs and still under both small-arms fire and random shelling. Under these conditions, it was impossible to land stores in anything other than a confused jumble. Adding to the confusion on the beach were now hundreds of lost and weary men who, having been separated from their units, were returning to the only familiar place they knew. The feeling on the beach at this crucial stage was one of uneasiness that extreme fatigue and constant shelling was only heightening.

General William Birdwood (General Officer Commanding, Australian and New Zealand Army Corps) discussed the options with his two divisional generals, Major-General Alexander Godley (Australian and New Zealand Division) and Major-General William Bridges (1st Australian) who would die of wounds on May 18. Birdwood then sent a message to the Commander-in-Chief Sir Ian

Anzacs on the lookout for snipers shortly after the landing on April 25. It is interesting to note that whilst two men lie dead in the foreground, and two more are sheltering by them, the two soldiers coming back down the paths seem completely oblivious to any danger.

With the bush in the foreground once again separating two slightly less obvious paths, it is difficult to imagine the deadly game once played out here. In the far distance can be seen the memorials around Quinn's Post.

The *AE2* was the only Australian submarine to take part in the Gallipoli campaign. This picture taken at Gosport, Hampshire, in 1914, shows Lieutenant-Commander Henry Stoker and his crew at the time of collecting the vessel for wartime operations.

Hamilton who was still on board the battleship *Queen Elizabeth*. In short, the message informed Hamilton that the troops, including the most recently landed New Zealanders, had all suffered heavy casualties and were both demoralised and worn out. It was also feared by Birdwood that if the Turks resumed shelling and attacking in greater numbers the following day, a fiasco could be expected. He ended this downbeat message by declaring that 'if we are to re-embark it must be at once'.

The Turks, too, had suffered terribly and even the inspirational Kemal could not produce fresh soldiers out of thin air and any thought of a heavy counter-attack tomorrow was quite beyond his capability. Naturally Sir Ian was not privy to this information and he was not about to be rushed into making a hasty decision about the future of the Anzac beach-head. Even after speaking to Rear-Admiral Cecil Thursby (who was in charge of naval activities connected to the Anzac sector), and who told him it would take at

least two days to evacuate the sector, he would still not commit himself. It was not until a message was received from the Australian submarine *AE2* stating that it had reached the Sea of

Early in the morning of April 25, *AE2* slipped through the entrance to the Dardanelles — the 'narrows' — having left Mudros harbour on the island of Lemnos. It reached the Sea of Marmara the same day, thus being able to threaten Turkish shipping bringing supplies and reinforcements to their front. Near midnight the news of its successful infiltration reached Sir Ian aboard his HQ ship *Queen Elizabeth* at the precise moment when he was being urged by Generals Bridges and Godley (commanding the two Anzac divisions) to contemplate the evacuation of their forces. Commodore Keyes handed General Hamilton the message with the comment: 'Tell them this. It is an omen — an Australian submarine has done the finest feat in submarine history, and is going to torpedo all the ships bringing reinforcements into Gallipoli'. The impeccable timing of Lieutenant-Commander Stoker's news was to steady nerves and bolster confidences at a critical juncture on the first day. As for Stoker and his crew, they played hide-and-seek with Turkish gun-boats for several days until on April 30 a faulty main ballast tank forced *AE2* to the surface and surrender. After being taken to Gallipoli town (now Gelibolu), where General von Sanders inspected the crew, they were sent via Constantinople to a POW camp in Anatolia (in the Turkish interior in Asia Minor).

Top left: Most of the cemeteries in Gallipoli contain the graves of men from the same units who fought and died together. Taken by Lieutenant J. Stubbs, this photo shows the original graves of members of the 10th Battalion of the Australian Imperial Forces who were killed in action on April 25. Note how the 10th AIF graves are all together. Below left: Today, Lieutenant Albert Byrne and Major Edward Oldham still lie side by side in the beautiful and immaculately-maintained Beach Cemetery. Above left: Albert Byrne was born on September 21, 1890 at Thackaringa, New South Wales. He volunteered for active service and was offered a commission in the 10th Battalion. Lieutenant Byrne was seriously wounded at around 4 p.m. during the Gaba Tepe landings, succumbing to his injuries the following day. Above right: Edward Oldham, born at Gawler, South Australia, on August 8, 1876, was commissioned in the Australian Army in 1905. He had been selected as one of the few Colonial officers to study British tactics in India from 1909-10, only one Australian officer from each state being chosen for this posting. Major Oldham was also killed at Gaba Tepe at the close of the first day's operations.

These two snapshots from a private collection show the bottom end of Shrapnel Gully, the top picture taken looking away from Brighton Beach south of Hell Spit. The original caption to the lower picture states: 'Australian Corporal looking over the battlefield after the first day's fighting'. In both shots, the rugged terrain over which the Anzacs had to climb on April 25 is painfully evident.

Marmara that Hamilton finally made up his mind. He replied as follows:

'Your news is indeed serious. But there is nothing else for it but to dig yourselves in and stick it out. It would take at least two days to re-embark you as Admiral Thursby will explain to you. Meanwhile, an Australian submarine has got up through the narrows and has torpedoed a gunboat at Cunuk (Chanak). Hunter-Weston despite his heavy losses will be advancing tomorrow which should divert pressure from you. Make a personal appeal to your men and Godley's to make supreme effort to hold your ground.

Ian Hamilton

P.S You have got through the difficult business, now you have only to dig, dig, dig, until you are safe.

Ian H'.

The Anzacs received Hamilton's message as the last organised Turkish counter-attacks died away. Despite the fact that most of them had little more than inadequate entrenching tools to start digging (all the heavier implements were at present among the confusion of supplies on the beach), the message at least ended the agonising wait for orders. So throughout the night with renewed purpose, the Anzacs set about digging in and it was from this action that their nickname 'diggers' is said to have been born.

Despite the day's disappointing results, the inexperienced Anzac troops had behaved better than anyone had dared hope. They had been landed on terrain that no military commander would have ever chosen and proved themselves to be incredibly brave and resilient under terrible conditions. On the first day the Anzac legend had been born.

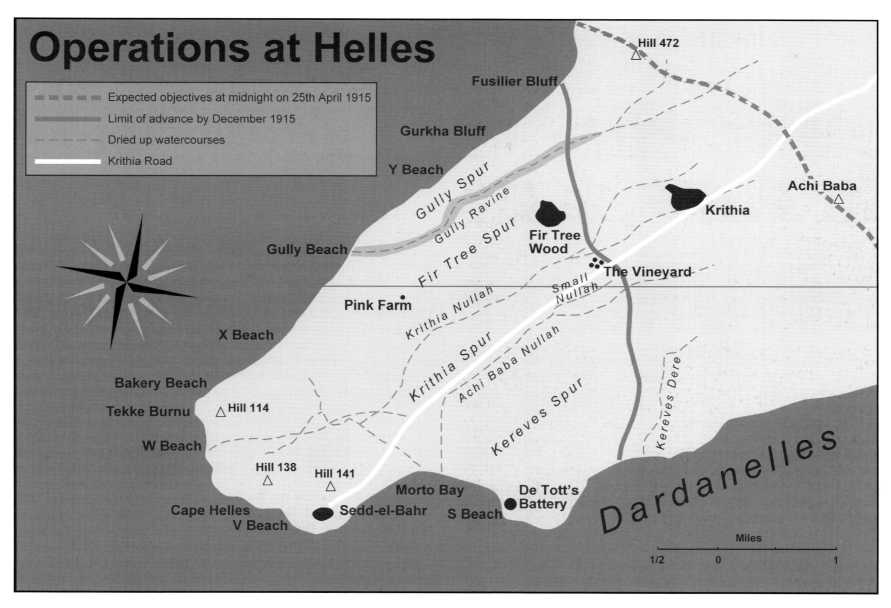

Operations at Helles

Legend:
- Expected objectives at midnight on 25th April 1915
- Limit of advance by December 1915
- Dried up watercourses
- Krithia Road

Hill 472

Fusilier Bluff

Gurkha Bluff

Y Beach

Achi Baba

Gully Spur

Gully Ravine

Krithia

Fir Tree Spur

Fir Tree Wood

Gully Beach

The Vineyard

Small Nullah

Pink Farm

Krithia Nullah

X Beach

Krithia Spur

Achi Baba Nullah

Kereves Dere

Bakery Beach

Kereves Spur

Tekke Burnu

Hill 114

W Beach

Hill 138

Hill 141

Morto Bay

De Tott's Battery

Dardanelles

Cape Helles

Sedd-el-Bahr

S Beach

V Beach

Miles

1/2   0   1

Specially drawn by Carolyn Cornwall-Jones to illustrate the Helles sector (as the relevant plans in the British official history are split over several separate maps), this composite view gives the reader a better overview of British operations.

THE HELLES SECTOR

Y BEACH

If things had not gone well in the Anzac sector, events on the British sector some 15 miles to the south were not going smoothly either. Here the plan was to land troops at five different beaches, coded Y, X, W, V, and S. The most northerly of these landings was at Y Beach, nearly four miles north of the main landings at Sedd-el-Bahr.

The terrain around Y Beach generally consists of steep cliffs but during the naval engagement of March 18, Sir Ian Hamilton had spotted this small beach and correctly surmised that it was only lightly defended.

A rare find indeed — a Royal Marines Light Infantry cap badge discovered near the Helles Memorial in the mid-1990s.

PERSONAL NOTE

FROM

MAJOR-GENERAL AYLMER HUNTER-WESTON, C.B., D.S.O.,

TO EACH MAN OF THE 29th DIVISION

ON THE OCCASION OF THEIR FIRST

GOING INTO ACTION TOGETHER.

The Major-General Commanding congratulates the Division on being selected for an enterprise the success of which will have a decisive effect on the War.

The eyes of the World are upon us and your deeds will live in history.

To us now is given an opportunity of avenging our friends and relatives who have fallen in France and Flanders. Our comrades there willingly gave their lives in thousands and tens of thousands for our King and Country, and by their glorious courage and dogged tenacity they defeated the invaders and broke the German offensive.

We also must be prepared to suffer hardships, privations, thirst, and heavy losses, by bullets, by shells, by mines, by drowning. But if each man feels, as is true, that on him individually, however small or however great his task, rests the success or failure of the Expedition, and therefore the honour of the Empire and the welfare of his own folk at home, we are certain to win through to a glorious victory.

In Nelson's time it was England, now it is the whole British Empire, which expects that each man of us will do his duty.

A. H-W.

There was no preliminary bombardment and the operation was almost entirely reliant on surprise. The troops to be landed here included the experienced and well disciplined regulars of the 1st Battalion King's Own Scottish Borderers (KOSB) under Lieu- tenant-Colonel Archibald Koe and a company of the 2nd Battalion South Wales Borderers.

Following them ashore were to be the men of the Plymouth Battalion Royal Marine Light Infantry (RMLI) under Lieutenant-

Contemporary snapshot looking north from the area around Y Beach (apparently completely devoid of life), which was captured successfully on April 25 but then lost because of an unauthorised evacuation.

The thick prickly scrub and a sheer drop today make the Y Beach area difficult to negotiate to take an exact comparison. This shot, however, is quite clearly the same place, looking north towards the Turkish lines.

Colonel Godfrey Matthews. These men, who in many cases were inadequately trained, had originally been scheduled to make up the first wave. This oversight had been spotted late but had been changed so that the regulars would land in the first wave whilst the men of the Plymouth Battalion would land later on in the day. However, the unfortunate consequence of this was that no one was really sure of who was in command of this operation. Lieutenant-Colonel Matthews had received verbal instructions from Major-General Aylmer Hunter-Weston, (General Officer Commanding, 29th Division) giving him a vague idea of what was expected of him. This also led him to believe that he was in command. GHQ however, firmly believed that Lieutenant-Colonel Koe was in charge but, having been unable to attend the meeting with Hunter-Weston, Koe had received no direct orders. This confusion in the chain of command therefore fatally undermined the landing at Y Beach before a single soldier had been put ashore. It was all the more galling because the Y Beach landing was probably the best opportunity to present itself in the opening 24 hours.

The first troops got ashore unopposed at approximately 0445 hours and by 0545 the entire regular force and the Plymouth Battalion were all on dry land without a shot being fired. After an early skirmish with four gendarmes (two of whom were killed and two captured), scouts were sent out and reported that there were no more enemy in the vicinity. It now only remained to carry out Hunter-Weston's orders but once again this was not an easy proposition. The instructions had been vague and Lieutenant-Colonel Matthews had asked surprisingly few pertinent questions. The orders were to capture a Turkish gun, 'believed to be in the area' and interfere with reinforcements heading towards Cape Helles and Sedd-el-Bahr before linking up with the Royal Fusiliers who had landed at nearby X Beach. When the main force drew level with them, they were then to join in on the advance towards the high ground of the Achi Baba feature.

It was confidently predicted, that Achi Baba would be captured by nightfall on the first day but in reality it remained in Turkish hands throughout the entire campaign. So what went wrong?

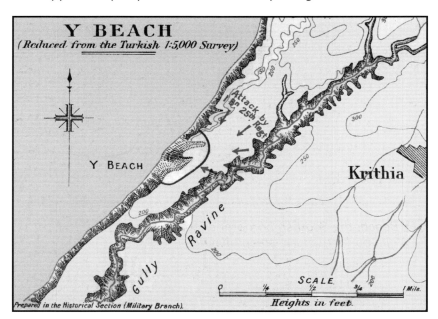

The Turkish counter-attacks at 'Y' Beach from the official history.

A British entrenching tool found on Y Beach by Steve Newman.

Troops and their supplies had been landed with ease, no Turkish guns had been encountered and Lieutenant-Colonel Matthews had himself crossed over Gully Ravine and approached to within 500 yards of the deserted village of Krithia. Nevertheless, one of the many golden opportunities that were to consistently present themselves to the Allies throughout the campaign was lost. At the ghostly quiet Y Beach, the troops just sat around at the top of the hills awaiting the order to advance. Sir Ian, realising that here was an opportunity to cut the enemy off, wired Hunter-Weston asking if he would like to send further troops ashore at Y Beach. In his message, however, he failed to explain the crucial point: that they had landed with no resistance and were clear to push inland if more troops could be made available. As Commander-in-Chief, he would have been fully within his rights to order troops ashore but, in an almost fatal politeness, he made only the suggestion leaving the decision to his subordinate. Hunter-Weston did not reply to the message and time was now working inexorably against the Allies.

Lieutenant-Colonel Matthews was unsure of what to do next as he was hearing heavy firing from the direction of V and W Beaches and was becoming concerned that the advance from the south had been held up. He eventually established contact with the Royal Fusiliers at X Beach inquiring, of all things, whether he should post a guard on his ammunition supplies. Why he should ask such a strange question at such a critical time almost defies belief. Shortly after this unexplained incident, he took the decision to withdraw his troops from the vicinity of Krithia and Gully Ravine, ordering them to dig in at the top of the cliffs, only yards from the water's edge. It is tragic that whilst hundreds of men to the south were dying trying to get off the beaches, here under no pressure at all, they were retreating back to the beach!

Digging in was no easy task as the entrenching tools were wholly inadequate for the stony ground. By mid-afternoon the little scrapes and small trenches that the men had managed to excavate were about to be tested as the Turkish 9th Division, led by Sami Bey, started a series of head-on attacks . Throughout the night the assaults became heavier as more Turkish reinforcements arrived and it is a credit to the men that they held the line as well as they did for most of their trenches were not more than 18 inches deep.

As dawn was breaking on the 26th, the Turks retreated for fear of being shelled by the fleet with hideous losses so once again the way to Krithia and Achi Baba lay open. However, a strange confusion and panic now took over many of those present and an impromptu evacuation started to take place. The signallers were also caught up in this wave of hysteria and started sending messages like 'desperate situation' and 'will hold ridge until wounded evacuated, send boats now'. Amidst this confusion, rumours and panic started to spread. On seeing more and more men leaving with the boats that were sent for the wounded, the men in the trenches overlooking the beach started trickling down believing that an evacuation had been ordered. Lieutenant-Colonel Matthews, who was now confirmed as the commander at Y Beach since Lieutenant-Colonel Koe had died of wounds during the night, knew nothing of this evacuation until he inspected the very poorly-held lines. The Navy was sending more boats to take the men off and Matthews had little choice now but to continue the evacuation. So it was that just 29 hours after the first landing at Y Beach, the whole landing site was abandoned much as it was found, without a shot fired and with the way to Achi Baba and victory still open.

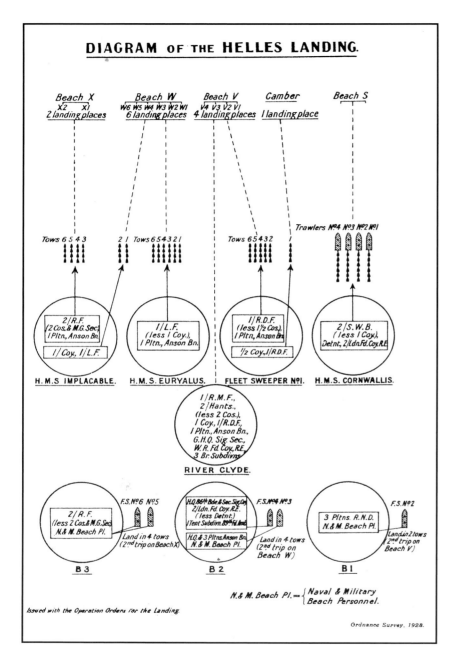

DIAGRAM OF THE HELLES LANDING.

Beach X	Beach W	Beach V	Camber	Beach S
X2 X1	W6 W5 W4 W3 W2 W1	V4 V3 V2 V1	1 landing place	
2 landing places	6 landing places	4 landing places		

Tows 6 5 4 3 | 2 1 | Tows 6 5 4 3 2 1 | Tows 6 5 4 3 2 | | Trawlers Nº4 Nº3 Nº2 Nº1

2/R.F.
(2 Cos.& M.G.Sec.)
1 Pltn, Anson Bn.
1/ Coy, 1/ L.F.

1/L.F.
(less 1 Coy.)
1 Pltn., Anson Bn.

1/R.D.F.
(less 1½ Cos.)
1 Pltn., Anson Bn.
½ Coy, 1/R.D.F.

2/S.W.B.
(less 1 Coy.)
Detnt, 2/Ldn.Fd.Coy.R.E.

H.M.S. IMPLACABLE.   **H.M.S. EURYALUS.**   **FLEET SWEEPER Nº1.**   **H.M.S. CORNWALLIS.**

1/R.M.F.,
2/Hants.,
(less 2 Cos.),
1 Coy, 1/R.D.F.
1 Pltn, Anson Bn.,
G.H.Q. Sig. Sec.,
W.R. Fd Coy, R.E.
3 Br. Subdivns.

RIVER CLYDE.

F.S. Nº6 Nº5

2/R.F.
(less 2 Cos.& M.G.Sec.)
N.& M. Beach Pl.

Land in 4 tows
(2nd trip on Beach X)

H.Q.86th Bde.& Sec.Sig.Dn
2/Ldn. Fd. Coy. R.E.
(less Detnt.)
(Tent Subdivn.89thFd.Amb.)
H.Q.& 3 Pltns.Anson Bn.
N.& M. Beach Pl.

F.S. Nº4 Nº3

Land in 4 tows
(2nd trip on
Beach W)

3 Pltns. R.N.D.
N.& M. Beach Pl.

F.S. Nº2

Land in 2 tows
2nd trip on
Beach V)

B 3   **B 2**   **B 1**

N.& M. Beach Pl.= { Naval & Military Beach Personnel.

Issued with the Operation Orders for the Landing.

Ordnance Survey, 1928.

X BEACH

One of the most outstanding features of the landing at X Beach has to be the actions of HMS *Implacable* and its Captain Hughes Lockyer. All the ships that had been ordered to give covering fire had been told to stand offshore and use indirect fire to engage the Turkish positions. This, however, was not good enough for Captain Lockyer who manoeuvred the *Implacable* to within 500 yards of the beach to engage the few Turkish positions here at almost point-blank range. The results against the dozen or so Turkish defenders was pure terror which led them to flee for their lives. A measure of just how close the ship was to the shore can be gauged by one of the few casualties of the landings at X Beach that of a fleet surgeon who was killed by a sniper whilst watching the proceedings from the deck.

Contemporary (but post-landing) shot of the objective of the 2nd Battalion of the Royal Fusiliers: X Beach.

Above left and right: Incredible photographs showing HMS *Implacable* in action giving support to the men of the 2nd Battalion, Royal Fusiliers, who landed on X Beach on April 25, 1915. This picture shows *Implacable* (the ship on the right) firing her main armament at Turkish shore positions. Tiny, ant-like landing boats are visible between the two larger ships with others away to the right of the photo. The second picture almost looks like some peace-time training exercise, but the background terrain gives the game away. Both photographs were taken at dawn on the 25th.

By 0730 hours, four companies of the Royal Fusiliers and most of their supplies had been landed without a casualty and by 1100, Hill 114 and approximately 800 yards of ground to the left had been taken. But it was here that once again a lack of maps, good staff planning and the knowledge of what else was going on, led to yet another missed opportunity. Having conquered the high ground, the Royal Fusiliers now had an almost unspoilt view

Left: The view today from X Beach looking across to S Beach. When one stands on the spot it is hard to imagine why the troops at these two locations were not ordered to link up and attack the Turks who were still offering stiff resistance at V Beach and help the remnants of the Lancashire Fusiliers who were pinned down on the bloody shambles of W Beach just a short distance away. Had this been done quickly on the first morning, and a push up the peninsula towards the Anzac positions been possible, the campaign may well have developed very differently.

Left: Having come ashore virtually unopposed, and eventually linking up with the Lancashire Fusiliers at W Beach, it became impossible for the Royal Fusiliers to take further ground without reinforcements. Here men from the 2nd Battalion dig a reserve line at the top of X Beach soon after landing on the first day.

Right: The top of the cliffs today. Whilst X Beach remains virtually unchanged, it receives few visitors and is unmarked by either memorials or monuments. The West Krithia Road on the right leads on towards Gully Beach, Pink Farm and eventually to Krithia, which has now reverted to its original Turkish name of Alcitepe.

across the peninsula towards S Beach where the South Wales Borderers had also landed virtually unopposed. If either regiment's officers had been properly briefed and known the other was there, and communications could have been established quickly, it is possible that they could have linked up and surrounded the defenders of V and W Beaches. Alas, having taken so much ground, the Royal Fusiliers front was already overstretched yet they had still not met any of the forces that were supposed to be pushing up from the south.

Gaps were starting to appear in the front line and reinforcements were not forthcoming. Once again, due to a critical lack of understanding on the part of the planners, too few troops had been landed at a place that held a vital strategic importance, as well as only being lightly defended by the Turks. As with Y and S Beaches, X Beach was, through no fault of the troops who came ashore there, destined to become another missed opportunity.

A Lee Enfield rifle oil bottle and cartridges found at Helles.

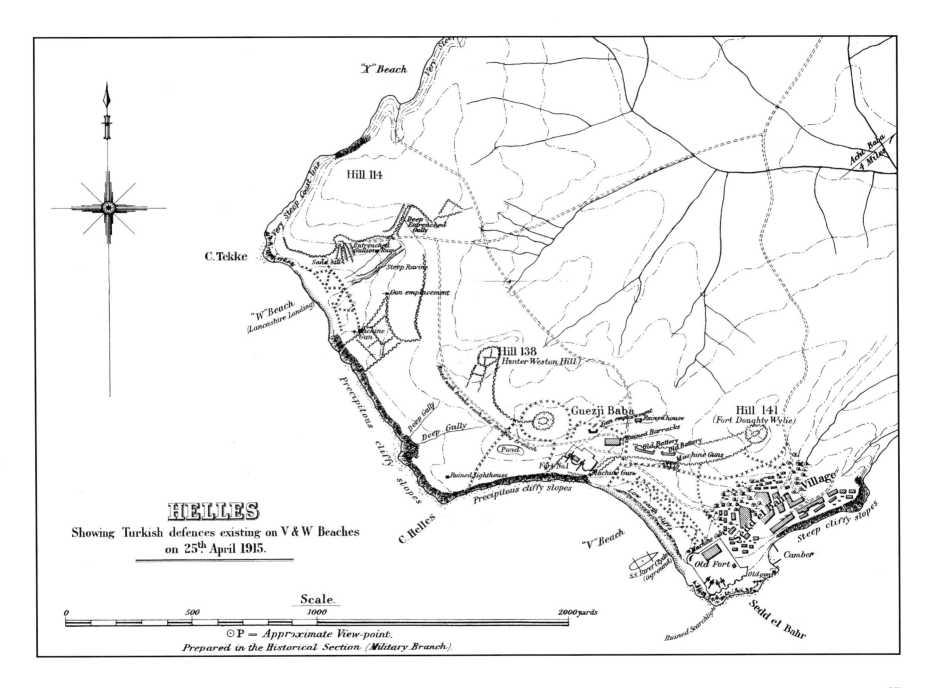

"X" Beach

Very Steep

Very Steep Coast Line

Hill 114

Deep Entrenched Gully

Entrenched Gullies & Ruins

C. Tekke

Sand hill

Steep Ravine

Gun emplacement

"W" Beach
(Lancashire Landing)

Machine Gun

Precipitous cliffy slopes

Hill 138
(Hunter Weston Hill)

Road with bank each side forming trench

Deep Gully

Deep Gully

Guezji Baba

Gun emplacement   Ruined house

Ruined Barracks

Pond

Old Battery   Old Battery

Machine Guns

Hill 141
(Fort Doughty Wylie)

Ruined Lighthouse

Fort No.1

Machine Gun

Precipitous cliffy slopes

C. Helles

Low earth cliff

Village

Sedd el Bahr

Steep cliffy slopes

HELLES
Showing Turkish defences existing on V & W Beaches
on 25th April 1915.

"V" Beach

Machine Gun

Old Fort

Camber

S.S. River Clyde
(aground)

Old gun

Sedd el Bahr

Ruined Searchlight

Scale.

0   500   1000   2000 yards

⊙P = Approximate View-point.

Prepared in the Historical Section (Military Branch).

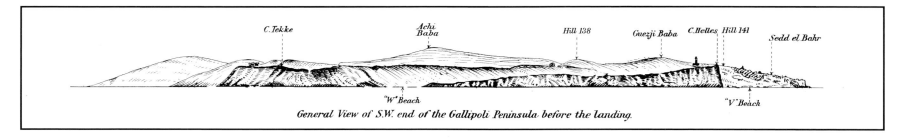

General View of S.W. end of the Gallipoli Peninsula before the landing.

W BEACH

About a mile further round Cape Helles lay W Beach or Lancashire Landing as it is probably better known. The coastline here lends itself to the defender in every respect and when this aspect is added to a carefully prepared defence line, it is easy to see why the German advisors thought this position impregnable to men attacking from open boats. The defences included redoubts that could only be approached without the attacker being able to take cover; lines of barbed wire that were also hidden in the shallows; mines and overlapping fields of fire from strategically placed machine guns.

Everything was in place for a complete disaster which, in casualty terms, it was destined to become, yet the bravery and resilience shown on W Beach was to become legendary throughout the armies of the empire.

As can be guessed from the name 'Lancashire Landing' the men who were to land here were Lancashire Fusiliers who, having slipped the tow ropes some 50 yards out, were being rowed

Left: Dugouts were carved out in the cliffs throughout the peninsula, many being given nicknames of which 'Sea Terrace' and 'Beach Terrace' appear to be the most common. This view, looking south from X Beach towards Bakery Beach (and W Beach), shows just how exposed the landing sites were to Turkish fire from above. Right: The difficulty now in trying to walk the old coast road is evident today as erosion is constantly reshaping this part of the coastline.

ashore by young bluejackets. Just before the open boats were about to ground on the silent beach, the Turks opened fire with everything they had causing terrible casualties. The only escape was to go over the side and into the water. Many men drowned under the weight of their packs whilst others became hopelessly entangled in the thickly-laid underwater barbed wire. However, some men managed to reach the shore by pulling at the wire with their bare hands in a desperate struggle to escape the firestorm.

Above: Men of the 1st Battalion, Essex Regiment, landing at W Beach on the morning of the first day. In the background, lying where they fell, are men of the Lancashire Fusiliers. Right: The distinctive Cape Tekke headland makes this photograph one of the easier to match up. Today the deserted W Beach holds few clues as to its evocative past and the casual visitor could be excused for not realising the heroism, sacrifice and suffering that unfolded here in the calm water.

Following a mêlée that has few rivals in ferocity, the Turkish trenches in the centre of the beach were slowly overcome with the bayonet by isolated groups of Fusiliers. Brigadier-General Steuart Hare, commanding the 86th Brigade, who had witnessed the slaughter from the second wave of boats, ordered the oarsmen of his craft to make for a group of rocks on the northern side of the beach. Here the sea was calm enough for the men to disembark and was apparently sheltered from the fire that was causing so many casualties in the centre. After a relatively unopposed landing, this force found itself only a few yards from the Turkish northern flank, and one of these men, Captain Thomas Frankland (see page 221), shot a number of the defenders with a borrowed rifle and soon after the Turkish fire started to diminish.

However, once again, the lack of communication and availability of accurate maps was about to cost the Allied campaign dear. On the right, men of A Company had just taken the low cliffs, when a large naval shell exploded killing a number of the men who had already survived the horrors of the initial landing. Further to the right, two separate units of Lancashire Fusiliers were both assaulting heavily defended redoubts around Hill 138. Both believed the position they were attacking was the one mentioned in their orders. However, having suffered such hideous casualties in the landing, and both being unaware of the others' existence, it is not surprising that neither could make any headway.

To the left, things had gone slightly better and Captain Richard Willis and Major George Adams's troops had finally linked up on top of Hill 114 with the advancing Royal Fusiliers from X Beach. It was quickly decided to reinforce the Fusiliers with the men of the Anson Battalion and the Essex Regiment (who had been diverted from the carnage of V Beach) but, due to the boats being used for the evacuation of the large number of wounded, neither unit could get ashore until much later in the day by which time the chance of continuing with the advance had gone.

Later, the action on W Beach was to become perhaps more famously known as the 'six before breakfast', a reference to the six Victoria Crosses that the 1st Battalion Lancashire Fusiliers won on this day. (Captain (later Major) Cuthbert Bromley, Corporal John Grimshaw, Private William Keneally, Sergeant Alfred Richards, Sergeant Frank Stubbs and Captain Richard Willis).

The British cemetery at Lancashire Landing shortly before the evacuation. This is now one of over 30 beautifully maintained CWGC cemeteries on the peninsula. Gunner Joynson's grave is in the foreground — just as it was in the 1915 photo. It became quite an honour to be buried at Lancashire Landing and when some men were re-interred from the nearby Greek islands it was to this cemetery that they were brought.

V BEACH

If the landings at W Beach had been predictably horrific, then much the same can be said of those on V Beach where a cove again gave a natural advantage to the defenders. The British planners, who had vastly overestimated the size of the Turkish forces defending both V and W Beaches had, at the same time, severely underestimated the strength and ingenuity of the defences and the grit and determination of the defenders.

The plan at V Beach was to land as many men as quickly as possible before overrunning the Turkish defences and capturing the village of Sedd-el-Bahr and then pushing up the peninsula to link up with the men who had landed further up the coast. However, much of the entire landing plan was dependant on things going well at V Beach but, as things went from bad to worse, they seem to have had an almost hypnotic effect on Major-General Hunter-Weston and his staff. For some inexplicable reason, no one seemed able to turn their attention to any of the less well-defended beaches, and the possibility of saving the first day's landings by encircling the defenders of Sedd-el-Bahr and V Beach was lost.

As at all the beaches the plan was for men to be towed ashore following the bombardment and to secure the beach-head. They would be followed by the main force who were supposed to push inland shortly after being disembarked. The only difference on V Beach was that a converted collier, the SS *River Clyde*, was to quickly land large numbers of men from the Royal Dublin Fusiliers, the Royal Munster Fusiliers and the Hampshire Regiment. The idea of using the ship as a form of modern day Trojan Horse was that of the resourceful Commander Edward Unwin who would also be its captain for the landing.

Left: The view from Fort No. 1 at Cape Helles — a photograph taken after the landings. It was vital to deceive the Turkish defenders of this position into withholding their fire for as long as possible to permit as many British troops to get ashore in the shortest possible time. Thus the idea of using the *River Clyde* as a maritime Trojan horse was born. In the background can be seen the camps and stores of V Beach and Sedd-el-Bahr, while behind them is the entrance to the Dardanelles with the Asiatic coastline in the far background. Right: Today at weekends this area overlooking V Beach is often bustling with Turkish tourists visiting the new memorials which have recently been erected here. However, if viewed on a quieter day, the outlook of the fort has changed little in over 85 years . . . with the exception that is of more weeds and less horses!

This remarkable picture recording the scene on V Beach on the morning of April 25. Taken from the bridge of the *River Clyde*, it clearly shows scores of men lying dead on the foredeck as well as the remnants of the floating pier on the left which is now just drifting aimlessly. On the beach, huddled behind the sand-banks, can be seen the men who survived the withering Turkish fire and managed to get ashore. Ahead of them lies the open and exposed ground criss-crossed with barbed wire and beyond this the lighter coloured earth that marks the dug-in Turkish positions.

Due to the confusion which reigned during the next few hours, most of the accounts covering the early period are somewhat confused and slightly contradictory but, in view of the conditions, this is only to be expected. What is known, though, is that the men of the Royal Dublin Fusiliers who were being rowed ashore were only able to make slow progress due to strong tidal currents. The *River Clyde*, meanwhile, was starting to catch them up and was forced to either slow down or arrive early. This, meant that she did not ground as near to the shore as her captain would have liked. By now, the men in the towed boats were preparing to disembark while the Turks, showing superb discipline, held their fire until the last moment. The latest Gallipoli tragedy was under way. Most of those in the small boats perished before even seeing the defenders as a torrent of machine-gun and rifle fire swept the beach from three sides. Only those who were landed directly under the walls of the fort, or those lucky enough to scramble up to a small bank that ran almost the length of the beach, stood any chance of survival.

Commander Unwin, on seeing the massacre that was taking place, knew he had to disembark the 2,000 men on board the *River Clyde* quickly as failure to do so would mean annihilation for the beleaguered remnants of the covering force. Unfortunately, at this crucial moment, the barges that were supposed to swing round and make a floating jetty from which the men were to disembark, failed and were of no use. Unwin reacted quickly and bravely to the situation. Leaping over the side and into the water, followed

Today, an initial impression of the scene is of timelessness . . . though without the extra height of the bridge of a large freighter, an exact match is not possible. However, by working his way back across the old pier that once led to the *River Clyde* (across some exceedingly slippery rocks), the author was able to take this photograph which gives a good idea of the view that faced the men who charged ashore that bloody April morning. It is interesting to see how much of the sand-bank that saved so many lives 80 years ago has now almost completely eroded away.

by one of his ratings named William Williams, they quickly started to tie lighters and cutters together to form a makeshift pier that the troops could use to get ashore. While he and Williams were still physically holding this ramshackle arrangement together in the bullet-swept and bloodstained water, Commander Unwin called for the disembarkation to begin.

From the sally ports that had been cut in the side of the collier poured the Irishmen. Captain Guy Geddes exited on the port side but the following 48 men got no further than the gangplanks leading down to the makeshift pier. Seven out of ten men trying to make the shore became casualties before reaching dry land. Others were drowned under the weight of their packs as they strove to join the few survivors on the beach. The men disembarking next were hin-

dered because of the exits being blocked by the dead and dying but still they charged in a death-defying feat of bravery that has rarely been equalled and probably never surpassed.

Meanwhile, Captain Geddes, who had somehow defied the odds and got ashore, became quickly aware of the situation. The wire on the beach above the small embankment remained intact and any man brave enough to attempt to cut it was mown down in seconds as the bodies lying all around the wire bore testament. He also saw that if the Turks pushed out of the fort they could enfilade the small embankment and slaughter those sheltering behind it. It was then that he asked for volunteers to run the gauntlet across a small piece of open ground towards the fort to try and enter it to relieve the pressure being exerted on the beach. Every

man in the vicinity volunteered and of the five men who sprinted across with him, two were killed in the attempt while Captain Geddes and another were wounded. Slowly, more men trickled towards this isolated group. Realising that the Turks could not now attack their flank but he, too, could make no progress, Captain Geddes signalled this back to the *River Clyde*. By now, the 'pier' was becoming a little more stable as a third cutter had now been tied to the others, although Williams had been killed by a shell from the Asiatic side and Unwin had to be replaced in the water due to the effects of the cold. Both later received VCs for their actions (as did four others in the assisting of the landings at V Beach: Midshipman George Drewry, Midshipman Wilfred Malleson, Seaman George Samson, and Sub-Lieutenant Arthur Tisdall).

One final daylight charge was made from the *River Clyde* but once again the casualties were terrible and those who had just got ashore urged that no further men should be landed until nightfall. Lieutenant-Colonel Herbert Carrington-Smith (2nd Hampshire Regiment, killed later that day by a sniper whilst on the bridge of the *River Clyde*) agreed that it was futile to try and land any further troops. So the 1,000-odd men still left on board were spared the certain death of trying to make for the shore in daylight.

The rest of the day at V Beach was spent with exchanges of rifle fire and sniping, whilst a deep gloom and sense of shock spread amongst the survivors, both ashore and still in the darkened hull of the *River Clyde*. These men were not to know that only a short distance away other British troops had got ashore unopposed and were awaiting orders. However, their commanders, watching from the safety of passing battleships, had not seen the advantages in ordering an advance to help those stranded on V Beach.

The idea of using the *River Clyde* as a Trojan horse was the brainchild of Commander Edward Unwin. Large holes were cut in the sides, level with the decks, and sloping gangways (suspended by wire hawsers) were run out so that the troops could pour down them as soon as the ship grounded. Sandbagged machine gun positions protected with steel plating were erected on the bridge and bows to shield the men. Unwin (right) is seen here receiving congratulations at being awarded the Victoria Cross on August 16 (see page 205). After the war Unwin resigned his commission to become a famous yachtsman. He died in 1950.

> *They cut a hole in it and made a little pier so we were able to walk straight off and on to the beach . . . The first thing we saw were wrecked Turkish guns, the second a big marquee. I remember how we rushed it (thinking of village fetes). We unlaced it and rushed in. It was full of corpses. Dead Englishmen, lines and lines of them, with their eyes wide open . . . It was our first fear.*
>
> ANONYMOUS SURVIVOR OF THE *RIVER CLYDE* LANDING

The brave *River Clyde* was abandoned and left behind after the evacuation, beached firmly at Sedd-el-Bahr. The photos above and below show her battered hull as found by the Turks — later reproduced as souvenir postcards. When the war was over, she was refloated and towed to Valletta Harbour in Malta (above right) where she underwent a programme of repairs and refitting (below right). Curiously, even after this work was completed, she still sported the sallyports, cut into the sides. Re-named *Angela*,

the Merchant Services Guild presented the ship with a commemorative plaque (inset) recording her illustrious past. Under Spanish ownership she was renamed again, becoming the *Muruja y Aurora*, and she plied the Mediterranean freight routes for many years until being retired in 1966. Before selling her to the scrapman, her Spanish owners offered her to the British Ministry of Defence but, with little official interest, this gallant survivor of V Beach ignominiously ended her days in the melting pot.

No. 74. Durch unsere Kanonenschüsse demoliertes und als Landungsbrücke des Feindes dienendes Schiff vor Seddul-Bahr

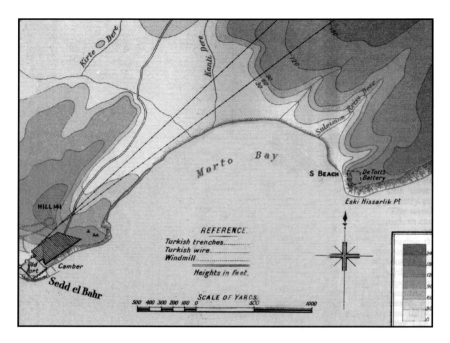

The Morto Bay section of the Turkish Defences Situation Map of April 25, 1915 reproduced from the British official history.

This view taken in 1999 from above S Beach looks towards Morto Bay and the location of the main Allied landings. To the left can be seen the village of Sedd-el-Bahr and the slope of Hill 141, while further along the Helles memorial stands out before the land becomes broken by the spurs and 'deres' that played such a key role in the fighting.

S BEACH

The situation at S Beach was in reality very similar to that of Y Beach. The Turks had not expected anyone to attack at this spot and hence they had only left a platoon to defend it. The plan was to capture an old disused works at the top of the cliffs called De Totts Battery and then await the expected break-out from V and W Beaches. Then, as with the other beaches, the intention was to link up and push on for Achi Baba and Krithia and eventually join up with the Anzacs near Maidos. As with so many things about the entire campaign, this looked great on paper but, in reality, it was too ambitious with no contingency plans.

The early stages on S Beach did not go well. The trawlers made little headway against the current leading to the whole attack running behind schedule. The troops that were put ashore here were three companies of the South Wales Borderers under Lieutenant-Colonel Hugh Casson. It was on his orders that one

company were in shirt sleeves and minus their heavy packs allowing them to go straight into battle and storm to the top of the high ground and capture de Totts Battery as quickly as possible. The plan was a complete success with the first company capturing the high ground, leaving the following boats less vulnerable than they otherwise might have been. One small Turkish outpost halfway down the cliff did cause a few casualties amongst the heavily-laden open boats but soon after 0800 hours the entire position was in British hands and all was quiet.

Colonel Casson was in no doubt that the landings on V Beach were in trouble but his orders gave him no clue as to what he should do in this circumstance. This is an instance where a more dynamic commander than Hunter-Weston — and a more forceful C-in-C than Sir Ian Hamilton — could have saved the day. Hunter-Weston, realising the terrible trouble V Beach was in, should surely have ordered the South Wales Borderers on S Beach to attack the rear of the Turkish defences at Sedd-el-Bahr. Hamilton, meanwhile, on seeing that things were going wrong, should have become more involved and stopped making suggestions and started issuing orders. However neither took place and Colonel Casson did not have the authority to march his men to the south to try and help. Had he got there just as a break-out was achieved, he would have had to back-track some two miles to regain his starting position, thus delaying the whole operation. Doubtlessly Casson was under the misguided impression that if V Beach was seriously held up he would receive orders to help but no orders came. Whilst hundreds were being slaughtered nearby, nothing stirred at S Beach.

The end result was that whereas the Turks, already stretched to the limit, could not possibly hope to even delay any concerted advance from here, the Welshmen merely dug in. So more opportunities for a quick victory slipped away. It is ironic to note that Sir Ian Hamilton states in his war diary that he feared the troops at S and Y Beaches were not strong enough to link up and attack the defenders of Sedd-el-Bahr. In fact, the units of just these two beach-heads were stronger in numbers than the entire Turkish forces south of Achi Baba.

After the French completed their diversions on the Asiatic shore (which considering the light resistance originally met could possibly have been exploited further), they were then re-landed at S Beach which then became part of their sector and it would be these same French forces that would eventually link up with V Beach on the morning of April 27.

Left: Looking from the northern slopes of Hill 141 towards Morto Bay, S Beach, Eski Hissarlik Point and De Totts Battery, shortly after the link-up of S and V Beaches. Right: After an extensive search (which included a run-in with a very unhappy looking snake!), the exact location was pinpointed. The same tree, although gnarled and aged, still stands amid fresh growth whilst S Beach remains clearly visible as does the area of the old De Totts Battery near the new Turkish memorial.

APRIL TO AUGUST

SLAUGHTER AND STALEMATE AT ANZAC
THE THREE BATTLES OF KRITHIA AT HELLES

APRIL 26

April 26 was, as to be expected after a day of such trauma, a period of consolidation both at Anzac and at Helles. After Sir Ian Hamilton's message, work at Anzac had been feverish as all talk of evacuation faded and the task in hand was tackled in earnest.

Throughout the front line areas, jockeying for position had been the order of the day as localised fighting erupted and then quickly faded. At one stage, after a Turkish attack, a group of Australians decided to take advantage of the situation and they counter-attacked. Many others, believing that a general advance had been ordered, followed but they quickly discovered that instead of moving forward they were marching along no man's land, parallel to the front lines. They suffered heavy casualties as they did so. This localised 'attack' was the only major event to take place as both the Turks and Anzacs rebuilt their strength and awaited the next round.

Following the initial landings, even before the beach was completely safe from sniper fire, men and supplies were quickly landed at Anzac Cove — seen here packed with troops on April 26, 1915.

The line of the new road as well as the changing shape of the beach are well illustrated in this comparison photograph taken over 80 years later. It is also interesting to note that whilst in 1915 the cove appears to be glorious sand, today it is far stonier.

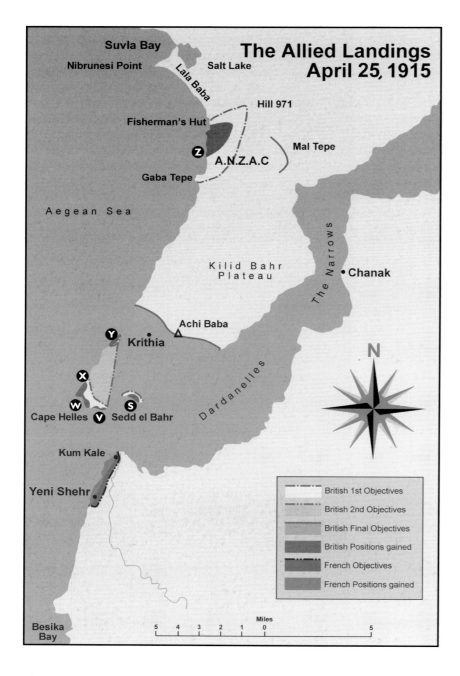

The Allied Landings April 25, 1915

Suvla Bay
Nibrunesi Point
Salt Lake
Lala Baba
Hill 971
Fisherman's Hut
Z
Mal Tepe
A.N.Z.A.C
Gaba Tepe
Aegean Sea
The Narrows
Kilid Bahr Plateau
• Chanak
Achi Baba
Y
Krithia
X
Dardanelles
W
S
Cape Helles **V** Sedd el Bahr
Kum Kale
Yeni Shehr

N

	British 1st Objectives
	British 2nd Objectives
	British Final Objectives
	British Positions gained
	French Objectives
	French Positions gained

Besika Bay

Miles
5   4   3   2   1   0   5

To the south, the main hold up, which in turn was delaying all the other landing points, was the body-strewn V Beach. Throughout the night men had been making local reconnaissances and they had even managed to cut a narrow gap in the wire. Shortly after dawn the big naval guns started shelling Sedd-el-Bahr as a prelude to an assault on both the fort and the village but, once again, a lack of communication led to problems. The Navy began firing at the village whilst the army wanted the fort, through which it would have to pass to reach the village, targeted instead. After a stop-start barrage, as signallers desperately tried to correct the aim of the ships, the attack against the fort commenced. Some men went forward through the gap in the wire while others attacked from the beach through the holes that had been blasted in the walls from earlier bombardments. The fort was quickly cleared but as the men tried to leave through a small gate that led into the village, they were met by accurate fire that halted all progress.

It was at this point that three staff officers, who were still on board the *River Clyde*, took stock of the situation and realised that the momentum had to be maintained if they were ever to get off of V Beach. The three officers, Colonel Charles Doughty-Wylie, Colonel Weir de Lancey Williams and Captain Garth Walford, quickly got into the fray, with Doughty-Wylie and Walford assisted by Captain Alfred Addison of the Hampshire Regiment on the right and Williams to the left. Walford led his men through the gate and into the village and commenced the house to house fighting in which both he and Addison were killed, Walford later being awarded a posthumous Victoria Cross for this action.

By now, the main feature that had to be taken at V Beach was Hill 141. This overlooked the beach to the north of the fort and it was here that Colonel Doughty-Wylie made his mark. Earlier attempts by exhausted members of the original landing force had all ended in failure but Doughty-Wylie seems to have somehow managed to motivate his men who were already far beyond the normal course of human endurance. He led them up the hill towards the entrenchments wielding only a cane (he had previously worked with the Red Cross in Turkey, making many friends there and was not apparently keen to kill Turks personally). This time the troops following him succeeded in taking the fortifications at bayonet point but the Colonel was killed on reaching the

Above left and right: The old fort at Sedd-el-Bahr was a regular target for the naval guns right from the first shelling of the Gallipoli peninsula in 1914. Here it is seen after the naval bombardment which targeted it before its capture on April 26.

Today the castle is little more than a shell in which one can find cattle grazing! One of the only remaining identifiable part is the wall that runs alongside V Beach which can be seen in the picture (below left) taken looking towards the village of Sedd-el-Bahr.

top of the summit where he was buried. (An interesting footnote to this story, witnessed by many British and French troops on November 17, was when a woman came ashore from a transport ship, laid a wreath on his grave and then left, speaking to no one. Lilian Doughty-Wylie, who was working as a nurse for the French, had managed to secure their permission to visit the grave. She placed her wreath on the cross which had been built by the ship's carpenter from *River Clyde*. Another account claims that the

visitor was his old friend Gertrude Bell to whom he wrote on the eve of the landings, and who certainly did visit his grave in 1919. Colonel Doughty-Wylie also received the Victoria Cross for this action — see page 207.)

The remainder of the Turkish troops fled towards Krithia, many falling as casualties to the machine guns of the Hampshire Regiment that were rushed to the summit of Hill 141. So it was that at approximately 1500 hours the beach was finally made

The grave of Lieutenant-Colonel Charles Doughty-Wylie. The wreath was laid by his wife, Lady Lillian Doughty-Wylie, believed to be the only woman to step foot on the peninsula during the conflict. A veteran of the Hazara Expedition in 1891; the Battle of Omduran in 1898 (where he was Mentioned in Despatches); the Boer War (severely wounded at Wittebergen in 1900), and the Somaliland Field Force in 1903-04, Doughty-Wylie was Acting Vice-Consul, Mersina and Konia (where he managed to keep some order and save many lives during the Turkish massacre of Armenians at Adana). He then became Consul at Addis Ababa, Abyssinia (now Ethiopia). It was during a leave period from this posting in 1912 that he worked as Director-in-Chief of Red Cross units working in Turkey during the Balkan War, leaving Constan-

tinople in 1913 when the Sultan presented him with the Order of Medjidjie. This work must have made his subsequent posting to the Dardanelles invasion force a somewhat sombre event — his undoubted usefulness through his knowledge of the character of the enemy being tempered by now having to do battle with former colleagues. Nevertheless, his heroic end solidly underlines the professionalism of his generation with regard to the pursuance of duty above all else. Today Doughty-Wylie is the only Commonwealth soldier not to be buried in one of the immaculate CWGC cemeteries that cover the peninsula. Instead he still lies where he fell on the summit of Hill 141 where he fought the action which won him the Victoria Cross but cost him his life. Left: The grave in 1915 and in 1999 (right).

relatively secure. The defensive perimeter around the beach was dug around the extreme eastern edge of the village and thus failed to link up with the South Wales Borderers on S Beach. However sniping continued from the village for the next few days until the last die-hards were eventually rounded up. The main beach and main hope for a quick advance to Constantinople had finally dragged itself from the bloodstained water some 34 hours after landing. During this time, the Turks were rushing reinforcements to the area assuring that there would now be no great break-out or quick advance in the campaign.

The order went out that no general advance was to be made until reinforcements were landed the next day. Throughout the night of April 26, French troops started to come ashore on V Beach but, due to a lack of small boats, by morning only two battalions had been landed. Meanwhile the Turks continued to dig in, awaiting a fresh assault by the British who, unbeknown to them, were too disorganised and fatigued to attempt anything so soon. The British had vastly overestimated the strength of the Turkish forces and their rate of reinforcement and so dug in, expecting a fierce counter-attack that the Turks were in no position to deliver.

The men round about were full of admiration and sorrow [for Lieutenant-Colonel Doughty-Wylie]. They told me he was first the whole way up the slope and it was only in the last few yards that some four or five men had got up to and passed him actually over the Castle walls; personally I noticed him on two or three occasions always in front and cheering his men on.

As soon as I came up and realized that he was dead I took his watch, money and a few things I could find and had him buried where he fell. I had this done at once having seen such disgusting sights of unburied dead in the village that I could not bear to leave him lying there.

This was all done hurriedly as I had to reorganize the line and think of further advances or digging in; we just buried him as he lay and I said 'The Lord's Prayer' over his grave and bade him goodbye.

That night when things had quieted down I asked Unwin to have a temporary cross put up to mark his grave. I left next day and was unable to go back to visit the place until about a week ago. I then found the cross had been put up; but the grave wants building up a little. I am firmly of the opinion that poor Doughty-Wylie realized he would be killed in this war; he was rather a fatalist: I am also convinced he went singing cheerily to his end.

COLONEL W. De L. WILLIAMS

The grave [of Lieutenant-Colonel Doughty-Wylie] was located on a small knoll just outside of the village. I was requested by the Imperial War Graves Commission to make the site more permanent as his widow had in view building a monument over it. We went to the spot and I instructed my men to make a trench down to solid ground around it, then to pour concrete in it and to cap the whole grave with a 6-inch slab of concrete. We got started first by removing the tangle of barbed wire over it and then carefully to remove the top soil.

Within a few inches his body became visible — enveloped in a ragged uniform with belt huddled in a crouched position. I marked off the location of the foundation I wanted. I then mounted Harry to visit the other cemeteries on my morning round.

I got back as soon as I could and looked. I did not know whether to laugh or cry.

What had obviously happened is that the trench in the soft soil had collapsed so that my men removed the body from the grave and finished the excavations.

Then they had placed his skull at the top of the grave and made a geometric pattern of his bones — even to his finger bones!

I hurried to get the foundations around the bones and waited to put the concrete slab over him. I hope he now rests in peace.

A. E. COOKE
ENGINEER, SIR JOHN PAYNE GALLWAY LTD
(who supervised the Imperial War Graves Commission cemetery construction from April 1923)

APRIL 27-30 — ANZAC SECTOR

From this early stage, the Anzac sector was not destined to increase much in size until the end of the campaign. However, despite only occupying a restricted area covering a total length of a mile and a half which at no point was deeper than 1,000 yards from the shoreline; it was a real achievement that they were not pushed back towards the sea and annihilated. A lot of credit for this must go to the Australian 2nd Battalion under Lieutenant-Colonel Alfred Braund whose troops somehow managed to cling onto positions around Russell's Top for 72 hours. These precious hours were used in reorganising disjointed units and giving the Anzacs time to start sorting out the chaos of stores that lay on the beach. To the left of Walker's Ridge were the New Zealanders, fighting in the tumbling landscape that led down towards Fisherman's Hut. The Kiwis started operating patrols from here and they proved to be excellent at it. However, it was not long before the Turks realised this and so did not position too many men here. The New Zealanders now dominated not only the ground that fell away from below them but also the distant Suvla plain as well.

The heavy counter-attack that had been feared by all at Anzac started on April 27 but the same heavy terrain that had so hindered the Anzacs now worked in their favour. Fresh Turkish troops from Bulair had arrived tired and thirsty with little idea of their objectives and, due to the terrain, were getting lost and arriving at their starting points late or, in some instances, not at all. The attack quickly broke down as isolated Turkish units became victims of the relentless fire from the now dug-in Anzacs.

Throughout April 28-29, four battalions of the Royal Naval Division were landed to help prop up the fatigued and pressured Anzacs. Initially, the Anzacs viewed these troops as somewhat puny and inexperienced but, after their machine guns helped save the day at the all-important Courtney's Post, they became part of the fellowship of Anzac.

Top right: Anzac Cove looking south, believed taken on April 25 with troops already ashore and the stacks of crated supplies building up. Right: Today instead of Australians landing on the beach they are now sunbathing! The construction of a new coast road has since resulted in the removal of the chunk of hillside from Hell Spit.

Left: In spite of the capture of some ground inland, the Anzacs had to suffer relentless sniping as Turkish riflemen, some ingeniously camouflaged, continued their deadly work for some considerable time. Here Australians seek out snipers shortly after the landing on April 25. Right: With no danger of snipers today, a little more time could be spent by the author in locating and photographing this spot which, as can be seen by the foreground, is just off the metalled road.

Above left: Taken from the seaward side of the Sphinx at the beginning of North Beach, this photograph was taken shortly after the landings. At the time the area was still exposed to sniping — hence the digging of trenches and saps. Above right: To obtain a comparison, once again thick scrub was a problem but in this instance it proved to be less of an obstacle than that caused by the large trench that still runs right across this area. The earthwork is almost invisible because of the large amount of scrub that now grows within it and, once it is reached, it proves virtually impossible to cross. However, the view from here has changed little with only the new road and Ari Burnu Cemetery — marked by the cluster of bushes — to depict the passage of time.

The clutter of stores at Anzac Cove on April 28, 1915 — an interesting photo to compare with the picture on page 54. The speedy increase in crates is striking. Right: The present day comparison shows quite clearly the changes at Anzac Cove since 1915, the main alteration being the new road that now runs along the coast. The beautiful Beach Cemetery is situated just to the right.

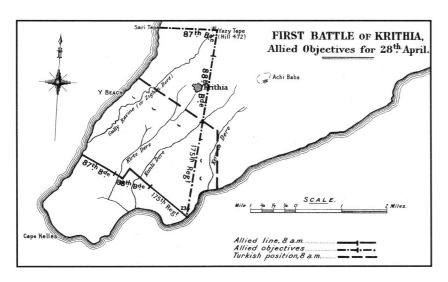

FIRST BATTLE OF KRITHIA,
Allied Objectives for 28th April.

APRIL 27-30 — HELLES AND THE FIRST BATTLE OF KRITHIA.

Whilst organising the details for the renewed offensive of April 28, Lieutenant-General Hunter-Weston could not overlook certain crucial factors, the main one being that of the number of casualties already sustained. Of the three Brigade-Majors landed, only one was now alive, and of the 12 Battalion Commanders, only three remained unwounded and at their posts. Casualties amongst the ranks varied from about 10, to somewhere near 50 per cent. Added to this, most of the remaining troops had been constantly digging or fighting and had gone without sleep for some 96 hours. This was certainly not the way to start an attack that involved the difficult military manoeuvre of pivoting, whilst in contact with the enemy, to gain a specified objective.

The plan had been somewhat modified and the idea of capturing Achi Baba had been scrapped in favour of pushing forward on the left and in the centre, capturing in the process Hill 472 and Sari Tepe to the north and the village of Krithia, approximately a mile and a half to the south. The French on the extreme right were to remain static on Hill 236, whilst their left flank was to pivot around with the 29th Division, with whom they were to remain in contact. The 87th Brigade was to seize Gully Ravine, Sari Tepe and Hill 472. The 88th on its right were to take Krithia and the immediate surrounding area whilst the 86th were to be held in reserve. Divi-

Shells from British warships exploding near Nagara on April 27, 1915. The guns were firing right over the peninsula from off Anzac, trying to disrupt Turkish reserves and supply shipping. They did indeed have some success and one remarkable shot hit a Turkish transporter in the narrows.

sional orders were issued in accordance with this plan although they did not give any idea of expected enemy strength or available artillery support.

Perhaps the biggest problem of all was that at the starting point the Allied front line was two and a half miles long and held by weakened units. If all the objectives were taken, these units would inevitably suffer further casualties and then have to hold a front line that would be nearly five and a half miles long.

As the time neared for the attack to begin, the orders were hurriedly explained to the officers who were to lead their men. Most, however, were too exhausted to pay much attention and, with the poor maps they were issued, it is probable that the majority only had a vague idea of what was expected of them. To counter this deficiency, Brigadier-General William Marshall (General Officer Commanding 87th Brigade) had been appointed by Lieutenant-General Hunter-Weston to operate in a roving role to oversee the advance. However, with no headquarters or means of communication this was doomed to be a thankless task.

At 0800 hours, the troops pulled themselves up and started off. On the left were the men of the Border Regiment and the

Before their destruction by Turkish shells, five distinctive towers at Helles were a landmark familiar to everyone in the early days of the campaign. They were believed to be part of a Roman or Byzantine aqueduct system that ran towards Morto Bay and S Beach from the vicinity of Sedd-el-Bahr. Above: In this photo taken from the extreme northern slopes behind Hill 141, Turkish shells can be seen exploding around the junction of the Krithia road and the fork that leads towards S Beach and Morto Bay.

Although the author has been told on a number of occasions that it is still possible to find the bases of at least one of these towers, they remain undetected, either because of the undergrowth or possibly because the last of the bricks have been removed. Opposite page, centre left: Apart from this, the scene has remained largely unchanged with Achi Baba in the distance. The track in the foreground that curves away to the left now takes a slightly different line and is not visible through the bushes.

Inniskilling Fusiliers with some attached from the Anson Battalion. In the centre were the Essex, the Hampshire and Worcestershire Regiments, whilst on the extreme right were three battalions of the French 175th Regiment. For the first hour all went well and the capture of Krithia seemed like a formality as the few scattered Turkish defenders bolted, in some cases without firing a shot.

As they marched through the scrubby terrain, the difficulties of the operation became quickly obvious. The troops in the centre were in front of those to their left when they should have been behind, while the troops to their right could not keep pace. To top it all, the French, with difficulties of their own, had not even started the advance. This left the men of the Hampshire and Essex Regiments with both flanks exposed. Meanwhile, as the advance continued, Turkish resistance started to stiffen and by 1130 hours the 88th Brigade, which had advanced furthest, was short of ammunition and water and was forced to a standstill. Suffering the combined effects of Turkish fire, thirst, low ammunition, morale started to sag and the left side of the front had become static. Brigadier-General Marshall, who arrived at the front about this time, decided to throw his reserves into the fight. The 86th Brigade were ordered up to help the 88th, as well as to resupply them with ammunition which was now at a critically low level. On the extreme right, the gaily coloured uniforms of the French were attracting Turkish artillery, causing them to fall back and taking with them the flank of the 88th Brigade.

This photo was taken by a member of the Ceylon Planters (i.e. the Ceylon Rifles) looking from the old front line near Pink Farm towards Achi Baba.

It is hard to find any traces of the trenches that once crisscrossed this area, most having been ploughed out years ago. However, where the old earthworks pass through wooded areas, it is often possible to follow the line of a washed-out trench for a few yards or more.

Above: This panoramic view shows No. 17 Field Hospital which lay between V Beach and the west coast of the Gallipoli peninsula. Below: With Achi Baba in the distance, the view 80-odd years later is little changed, apart from the new road which appears to follow the old watercourse. The open aspect, the result of the arable farming when the fields are ploughed, stops the growth of trees and scrub and helps the search for traces of wartime features.

Brigadier-General Marshall was also ignorant of the fact that the reserves consisted of only about half the strength he was expecting. This was due to an urgent plea for more men on the extreme right of the attack which left only two battalions to reinforce the assault on Krithia. These troops were as poorly informed and as equally tired as those already in the attack; nevertheless, some members of the Lancashire Fusiliers and the Royal Fusiliers succeeded in reaching and taking the feature known as Fir Tree Wood with very few casualties. From here, they pushed on towards Krithia and actually got to within half a mile of the village. The Turks were now in a full retreat towards Achi Baba. Once again, though, defeat was about to be snatched from the jaws of victory. The troops now arriving at Fir Tree Wood were unaware of the small party up ahead and the senior officer, fearing the position untenable, ordered a retirement. Consequently the Turks, now slowly sensing the disorganisation of the attack, started to move forwards again. This forced the advance party of fusiliers to retreat and with them went the possibility of British troops occupying Krithia on this day.

Meanwhile the situation on the left had become critical. After suffering terrible casualties against the recently reinforced Turks in this area, the British were now in full flight and being pursued by a number of Turkish soldiers, led by an officer brandishing a sword, but one shrapnel shell that held over 20,000 shrapnel balls from the *Queen Elizabeth*'s 15-inch guns, put an end to this counter-attack. Other than the consolidation of the useful landing area of Gully Beach, little else was achieved and no further territorial gains or losses were made.

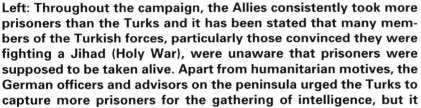

Left: Throughout the campaign, the Allies consistently took more prisoners than the Turks and it has been stated that many members of the Turkish forces, particularly those convinced they were fighting a Jihad (Holy War), were unaware that prisoners were supposed to be taken alive. Apart from humanitarian motives, the German officers and advisors on the peninsula urged the Turks to capture more prisoners for the gathering of intelligence, but it

seems that this rarely happened. Most Allied soldiers were fully aware of the short shrift that they could expect if wounded and left on the wrong side of the line. Here Turkish prisoners are marched back to their compound. Sedd-el-Bahr and the French camps lie in the background. Right: Now the undergrowth has completely blocked the view of the town and it is hard to believe that this quiet road was once a hubbub of noise and activity.

The French, after initial set backs, had managed to move forward a little on the right but strong counter-attacks by fresh Turkish forces, recently arrived from Bulair, checked the advance and then started pushing the French back. This in turn led to the 88th Brigade becoming enfiladed and forced them to retreat to their starting position.

The First Battle of Krithia drew to a close with all units being hopelessly intermixed and back within their original trenches and on this one day alone the Allies suffered nearly 2,000 casualties. Just as the men who had survived the past few days thought it could not get any worse, it began raining and, as can probably be guessed, greatcoats had not been considered as necessary kit.

The Turks now strove to gain the upper hand and began preparing a counter-attack to try to drive the British and French into the sea. However, von Sanders realised that any attempt by day was tantamount to suicide, as the British naval guns dominated the ground around Helles and could inflict massive casualties on any Turkish formation they spotted, so this only left him one course of action, that of the night attack. As darkness fell on May 1 all was quiet but, after a short bombardment, cries of 'Allah!' came from the Turkish lines heralding the start of their offensive. The initial force of the attack was felt by the Dublin and Munster Fusiliers near Pink Farm. (Due to both units suffering terrible losses they had been temporarily amalgamated and nick-

Left: The old Turkish cemetery just outside Sedd-el-Bahr looking towards Achi Baba. The civilian cemeteries were wired off and made out of bounds to troops to guard against any kind of grave robbing or vandalism. The Allies went to great lengths to ensure that historical and cultural sites were not ruined and, on one part of the French line, where many Roman relics were being uncovered during the digging of trenches, officers were appointed to record the finds. It is therefore somewhat ironic that many of these officers were killed by shells fired from the historic Plains of Troy. **Right: The road and location of Achi Baba made this comparison one of the easier to find added to which a local resident, curious about what the author was doing, assured him that this was once the site of an old Turkish cemetery. A bus thunders down the hill ahead.**

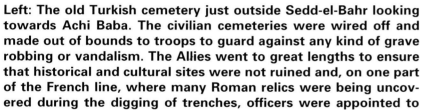

named the 'Dubsters'.) These positions were quickly overrun and soon the Turks were pouring through the beach. Fortunately for the British, men of the Royal Fusiliers and the Royal Scots first held the attack at bay and then managed to recapture the lost trench. This, in turn, cut off any surviving Turks who had earlier breached the line. On other parts of the British front, the Turks were meeting even fiercer fire as the professional rifleman of the 29th Division cut swathes in the ranks of the attacking infantry.

The main thrust of the attack was against the French to the right of the British positions. Not for the first time (or indeed the last) the men of the Senegalese units fought until their European officers became casualties at which point they lost all cohesion and ran. As the situation neared critical, the quick actions of some men from the Royal Horse Artillery, who were joined by a platoon from the Worcestershire Regiment, saved the front line from complete collapse. As daylight started to creep in from the east, the view in front of the British and French trenches was horrific with hundreds of Turkish dead strewn across no man's land. The British and French now took this opportunity to counter-attack. The British on the left captured over 100 prisoners and advanced 500 yards near Gully Ravine, whilst the French on the extreme right gained a little ground before becoming held up. Some gains were made in the centre but these were later lost as the positions became impossible to hold due to the enfilading fire the Turks could now bring to bear.

Following the interrogation of prisoners captured during this action, it was realised that enemy reinforcements were now arriving on the peninsula in large numbers. It was realised that if any kind of attacking momentum was to be built up, it would need to be soon. Plans were therefore quickly laid for what would become known as the Second Battle of Krithia.

The landing of the stores at Anzac was always a problem, eased only as more piers and jetties were constructed. However, the Turks had the ranges of many of these landing areas down to a few yards and repairs had to be constantly carried out to keep supplies moving. Here a pile driver is in operation helping in the construction of one such pier on North Beach, Anzac. Right: Today little remains above water but a snorkelling trip in the clear sea helped pinpoint their former locations. In the background can be seen the site of No. 2 Outpost while in the far distance lie the lower slopes of Kiretch Tepe.

MAY 2 — THE ANZAC ATTACK

Since the opening two days, enemy activity around the Anzac sector had decreased significantly. This had led the commanders there to believe that they were only being contained by a small force and that every spare Turkish soldier had been withdrawn to help reinforce the defences to the south around Krithia. Thus it was decided to seize the opportunity to try and capture Baby 700, the name given to the high ground that overlooked the Anzac positions in Monash and Shrapnel Gullies.

The plan was a complex one in which Australians of the 4th Brigade were to attack via the eastern fork of Monash Gully, whilst the New Zealanders of the Otago Battalion would come in from the western side. On reaching their objectives, these troops were to be supported by more New Zealanders from the Canterbury Battalion, with the Nelson Battalion of the Royal Naval Division and the Portsmouth and Chatham Battalions of the Royal Marine Light Infantry in reserve.

The attack did not start off well as the Otago Battalion reached their starting point an hour and a half late. The Australians on the right initially made good progress but were held up by heavy fire as they reached the Second Ridge. Even after some desperate fighting, the Otago Battalion only held a line just north of Pope's Hill and had still not made contact with the Australians to their right. However, believing the attack to be going well after the initial forward movement of the Australians, the Canterbury Battalion was thrown into the fray. They tried to push straight through via the Nek but due to the heavy defences here this proved to be impossible. So they, too, were forced to move across to Monash Gully and attack from the western fork but very few of the men found their way through the difficult terrain. Those who did, joined by men of the Australian 15th Battalion, plugged the gap between the Australians and the New Zealanders of the Otago Battalion.

By 0200 hours, things were still awfully confused but HQ and Major-General Sir Alexander Godley, (New Zealand and Australian Division) believing that things were still going well, sent the Royal Marines of the Portsmouth and Chatham Battalions up to the front. Unfortunately both these units were bivouacked some way down Shrapnel Gully and, fighting against the tide of wounded, it was daybreak before they reached Pope's Hill. After further delays, they eventually commenced climbing the hill just in time to be caught by a number of rounds of Allied artillery that were falling short of the crest they were aimed at.

It was about now that men started falling back to their starting positions and the young marines were swept along with this confused tide of humanity. Shortly after lunchtime, not one man remained in any position further forward than that occupied 24 hours earlier. Baby 700 remained firmly in Turkish hands at a cost of over 600 Allied casualties, the only fact saving the Allies from a complete disaster was that the Turks had suffered nearly 14,000 casualties since the first landing at Anzac. They were therefore hardly in a position to capitalise on the opportunity that a counter-attack would have brought them.

MAY 6-8 — HELLES: THE SECOND BATTLE OF KRITHIA

In spite of the heavy losses that the French had recently experienced, and with their own commanders reluctant to use the Senegalese for anything other than reserve duties, it was decided to go ahead with another attack at Helles. According to British reconnaissances, there was still no strong defences in front of Achi Baba. Also casualty estimates showed that the Turks had suffered even worse than the French, whose forces were now bolstered by troops of the Hood and Howe Battalions of the Royal Naval Division. It was obvious that any further delay was going to be more beneficial to the Turks than to the Allies so the planning for the Second Battle of Krithia continued.

The first priority was to reinforce the understrength units still holding the front line. This was done with four more battalions of the Lancashire Fusiliers (125th Brigade) who had just arrived from Egypt and an Indian Brigade (not at full strength for fear that the Muslims amongst the troops might not fight the Turks). Also, brought down from the Anzac sector the day before the offensive was to begin, was an Australian Brigade and a New Zealand Brigade.

The plan this time was for the French sector of the line to advance in concert with the British right flank towards Achi Baba. On the extreme left of the front, the British forces were to once again advance towards Sari Tepe and Hill 472. However the planning failed to recognise the difficult geography of the area which was scarred by four deep water courses, from left to right, Gully Ravine, Krithia Nullah, (Kirte Dere) Achi Baba nullah (Kanli Dere) and, the most significant, Kereves Dere. These four watercourses divide the country into four spurs, or fingers of land, which were known as Gully Spur, Fir Tree Spur, Krithia Spur and Kereves Spur. Sir Ian Hamilton was keen to start the attack before first light to try and get in amongst the Turkish positions before daylight but Lieutenant-General Hunter-Weston felt that after the loss of so many competent officers, any night attack was doomed to failure. Sir Ian once again relented to his subordinate and the attack was set to commence at 1000 hours.

Due to a lack of ammunition and no real knowledge of Turkish positions, the opening barrage was of little use. In the centre, in the area around Fir Tree Spur, the 88th Brigade initially made good progress with the scouts out in front meeting only light

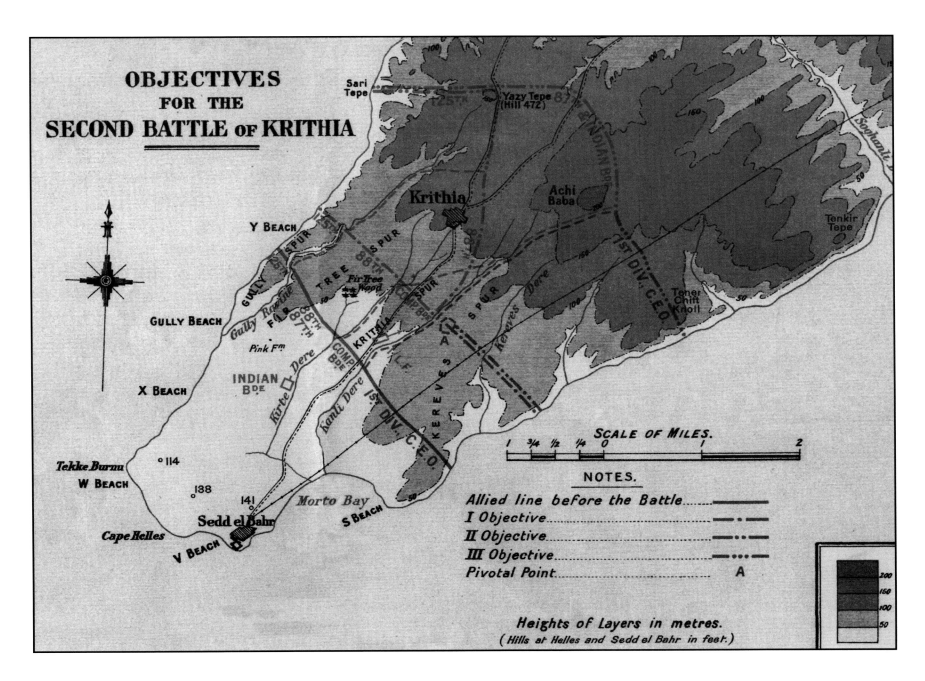

OBJECTIVES
FOR THE
SECOND BATTLE of KRITHIA

Sari Tepe
Yazy Tepe (Hill 472)
Krithia
Achi Baba
Tenkir Tepe
Y BEACH
GULLY BEACH
FIR TREE SPUR
Fir Tree Wood
Tener Chift Knoll
GULLY RAVINE
Pink Fm
KRITHIA
X BEACH
INDIAN Bde
KEREVES SPUR
Kereves Dere
Kirte Dere
Kanli Dere
114
Tekke Burnu
W BEACH
138
141
Morto Bay
S BEACH
Sedd el Bahr
Cape Helles
V BEACH

SCALE OF MILES.

1   ¾   ½   ¼   0   1   2

NOTES.

Allied line before the Battle
I Objective
II Objective
III Objective
Pivotal Point.................................. A

Heights of Layers in metres.
(Hills at Helles and Sedd el Bahr in feet.)

200
150
100
50

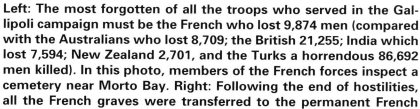

Left: The most forgotten of all the troops who served in the Gallipoli campaign must be the French who lost 9,874 men (compared with the Australians who lost 8,709; the British 21,255; India which lost 7,594; New Zealand 2,701, and the Turks a horrendous 86,692 men killed). In this photo, members of the French forces inspect a cemetery near Morto Bay. Right: Following the end of hostilities, all the French graves were transferred to the permanent French

Cemetery which is off to the left and out of view in this picture. However, whilst walking across the site of the old burial ground, bones were still in evidence, underlining what a difficult undertaking it must have been to relocate thousands of dead after the campaign was over. The large monument to the left is the Turkish memorial and cemetery overlooking S Beach while the land mass further away is the Asiatic side of the Dardanelles.

resistance. However, as the attack progressed, it became clear that with the French and the 125th Brigade making little headway, both their flanks were becoming perilously exposed. The 88th Brigade continued to make small advances around Fir Tree Wood but was unable to take the woods as two machine guns covered its approaches. As it became obvious that other units were being held up, the 88th Brigade were ordered to dig in, having gained about 400 yards and having suffered no more than about 50 casualties per battalion.

To their left, the men of 125th Brigade were having a hard time. They were attacking towards Y Beach which had been abandoned under such unfortunate circumstances on April 25. Now Y Beach was heavily defended and all attempts to force the machine-gun nests here were meeting with heavy casualties. The

destroyer that was monitoring the advance of the 125th Brigade was unable to shell the guns; consequently this newly-landed unit suffered over 350 casualties for the gain of very little ground.

The French on the right of the attack were equally having little success. They started their attack about an hour and a half late and, while the extreme right had captured some important ground overlooking Kereves Dere, they had now been checked. The troops on their left were unable to make any progress against a well-organised trench system that was later known after its capture as 'La Redoute Bouchet'.

It was about now that a large gap appeared between the French flank and Kanli Dere. This was spotted by Commodore Oliver Backhouse (General Officer Commanding 2nd Naval Brigade), who ordered elements of the Royal Naval Division into action. These units fought admirably and at one stage were making significant progress towards the French objectives. Yet, as was to happen so many times throughout the Gallipoli campaign, there was no cover on the flank and these units were forced to withdraw, having gained nothing more than casualties.

As the day ended, Krithia and all the other objectives were as far away as ever. The main Turkish force had not even been engaged and it was the small outposts that had halted the whole advance across the front. Despite the confusion, casualties had been relatively light so Sir Ian ordered the offensive to be resumed at 1000 hours the following day. To be included this time were the 127th Brigade of the 42nd (East Lancashire) Division which had just arrived on the peninsula.

The orders for the next day's attack were not issued until after 2200 hours, the only change from the vague orders of the previous day being more rhetoric to try to spur the men on. What was really needed however, was for more high explosive shells and someone to come up with a better plan as opposed to yet another full frontal advance in broad daylight after a derisory barrage.

On the left flank, HMS *Swiftsure* and *Talbot* shelled the still-hidden Turkish machine-gun post near Y Beach. However, as soon as the attack started, the gun opened up again causing heavy casualties amongst the Lancashire Fusiliers. The King's Own Scottish Borderers and the Inniskilling Fusiliers were sent to help the territorials push forward but, even after a barrage from the *Queen Elizabeth*, the machine gun nest remained in action and the situation around Gully Spur unchanged.

With the hold up of the 125th Brigade on the left, the plight of the 88th Brigade was predictable. Their flank was quickly exposed and, although both the Essex Regiment and the Worcestershire Regiment pushed on to Fir Tree Wood and some advanced units even slightly beyond, without any support on their left flank they were soon forced to retire.

Although an advance of some 300 yards had been made at some points, by early afternoon most of the units were back in their starting positions and the Brigade Commander sent word back that no further advance was possible until they could be supported on the left. Lieutenant-General Hunter-Weston, seeing that the attack was going the same way as the one the previous day, took action to try and correct the situation before nightfall. The

Steve Newman: 'Looking towards Achi Baba — almost invisible in the haze — from the location of the old observation post in the French sector, I could find no traces of the old Turkish cemetery or the original tree . . .

. . . but a post-war replacement serves admirably for the comparison I took in May 1999.'

Turkish soldiers manning a trench at Gallipoli. It is worth noting the Arab-like headwear of the soldier nearest the camera. For many of these troops, the conflict was seen as a holy war against Christendom in which the Allied soldiers were perceived to be trying to take away the traditional Moslem way of life.

New Zealanders were ordered up to the vicinity of Pink Farm whilst the 87th Brigade were brought up to help the 88th Brigade advance along Fir Tree Spur. The bombardment was set for 1630 hours signalling the renewal of the attack.

The shelling commenced on time but the attack quickly petered out whereupon the advance ground to a halt. On the right, the French, who had made no inroads at all, were now of the opinion that it was impossible to make any headway against the strong defences of Kereves Dere until the British units on their left had moved forward. However, the British had already advanced and were constantly being cut off by the hold up on the extreme left around Y Beach and Gully Spur. So, with virtually nothing gained other than some 800 more casualties, the second day of the battle drew to a close.

With nothing to show for the daylight attacks for two days running, apart from giving the Turks more time to improve their defences, one might have thought that a change of tactic was now called for. Unfortunately it was not to be and the orders issued shortly before 2300 hours called for a resumption of the attack at 1030 next morning. The plan, or rather lack of it, had been only slightly modified from the two previous days and the only part the French were to play was to hold a position that GHQ thought they had already captured. In reality, however, this strong point was still held by the Turks and was in fact being reinforced.

The New Zealand Brigade was ordered to advance through the positions of the severely understrength 88th Brigade and then push on towards Krithia. Three battalions of New Zealanders were to be initially involved in the advance with the Wellington Battalion on the left; the Auckland Battalion in the centre and the Canterbury Battalion on the right. The Otago Battalion, which as we have already seen, had suffered so heavily in the attack on Baby 700 a few days earlier, was to be held in reserve.

To protect the flank of the New Zealanders in their advance along Fir Tree Spur, men of the South Wales Borderers and the Inniskilling Fusiliers were to send small parties of men to locate the elusive machine-gun post that had held up proceedings for the last two days. On finding it, they were not to attack it but to report back and advise on the best way of dealing with it. So, instead of a general advance all across the line, the attack was to be spearheaded by an understrength New Zealand Brigade. They would be

This is how the old trench lines at Helles look today. The pictures were taken near the site of the old Fir Tree Wood from where the New Zealanders made their almost suicidal charge across the 'Daisy Patch' during the Second Battle of Krithia in May.

attacking Turkish positions that had not been accurately reconnoitred and were now held by some nine battalions of infantry. Just to confuse matters more, most of these orders were not received by the men due to carry them out until, in some cases, only minutes before the assault was due to take place.

At 1015 hours the bombardment commenced but by this stage all artillery was limited by the amount of ammunition they actually possessed. The front line was now some ten and a half miles long and no one really knew the exact positions of Turkish emplacements which made the entire barrage of very limited use.

On Gully Spur, some members of the South Wales Borderers and the Inniskillings made a little progress but they were still unable to locate the Turkish machine gun that cut down anyone venturing onto the high ground. This failure again to secure the flank meant that the Wellington Battalion on the left suffered heavy casualties and was forced to relinquish what little ground they had gained. In the centre, the Auckland Battalion reached the far side of Fir Tree Wood but they also could not hold the ground.

The Canterbury Battalion made some 300 yards before being checked and forced to dig in. By lunchtime all was static and by 1530 hours, after futile efforts to relaunch the attack, all was quiet.

On hearing that Lieutenant-General Hunter-Weston was going to try and restart the assault, Sir Ian Hamilton took it one step further, ordering the whole Allied line to advance on Krithia at 1730

The poignant scene after the gallant attack by the 2nd Infantry Battalion, AIF, at Helles. This photo was taken the following morning looking back across the ground over which they had charged . . . littered with packs . . . rifles . . . and, near Redoubt Cemetery, the bodies of the slain.

Today the silent, summer scene could not be more of a contrast.

hours precisely, following a 15-minute barrage. For this new attack, the 87th Brigade were given the unenviable task of charging the hidden machine guns at Y Beach. The New Zealanders, supported by the 88th Brigade, were to attack along Fir Tree Spur across an area known as the 'Daisy Patch' which was about to become one of Gallipoli's most infamous killing grounds. The Australians, who up until now had been held in reserve, were given the order less than half an hour before the advance was set to begin, that they were to advance along the exposed Krithia Spur.

Every big gun that had any supply of ammunition was ordered to fire and, to those now waiting to advance, it seemed as if nothing could survive the heaviest bombardment of the campaign so far. However, the Turks were now getting used to the routine of a 15-minute barrage and they just remained sheltering in their positions to await the attack. Amongst the first casualties were members of the Australian Brigade who, as they hurried along exposed areas in a bid to reach the front line on time, came under heavy Turkish counter-fire.

On the left, the men of the South Wales Borderers were among the first to advance. They were to be mown down in rows as they desperately tried to attack the machine guns that had still not been located. Not a single yard was gained yet still they tried to press on. To the right of these men were the New Zealanders who in their charge across the Daisy Patch were literally being ordered to commit suicide. This they did in their hundreds, along with their British comrades of the 88th Brigade. In a few places a little ground was gained but nowhere could it be held. Most of the troops who had survived the charge forward were then forced to run the gauntlet again as they tried to find cover back to their starting positions.

Whilst the New Zealand attack was grinding to a bloody standstill, the Australians had now reached the British front line and commenced their charge. All who witnessed this advance would never forget it for as long as they lived. Even as the casualties mounted, the Australians still pushed on, eventually succeeding in gaining some 700 yards and, for the first time, the main Turkish entrenchments could be seen. But at what a price! In the 25 or so minutes that it lasted, this attack cost the lives of over 1,000 men out of the nearly 3,000 involved. This was nearly four times the number of men — out of a force approximately three times the size — than in the charge of the Light Brigade (which in 20 minutes cost the lives of 247 out of a force of 673); indeed the British official history called it an 'unrecognised Balaclava'.

To the right of this action the French attack had begun, all seemingly going well as they advanced in their bright uniforms with drums and bugles sounding but, as they neared the crest they were supposed to capture, accurate and intense Turkish artillery forced them to retire. Yet, during a bold counter-attack shortly afterwards they succeeded in taking 'Redoubte Bouchet', an important position that would remain in their hands until the evacuation some eight months later. Sir Ian was watching proceedings from Hill 141 and his last view of the battlefield before nightfall was that of the French retreating prior to their successful counter-attack.

While the Australian and New Zealand flanks were now linked, the right of the Australian line was unprotected so men of the Lancashire Fusiliers and the Drake Battalion were sent to plug the gap. This meant crossing the same stretch of land that had just cost the Australians nearly 1,100 casualties. As night fell, these men linked up with the Australians, having suffered not a single casualty, which inevitably leads to the unanswerable question: 'what if the attack had taken place at night?'

All remained quiet that night save for the cries of the wounded which persisted for hours. The Second Battle of Krithia was over as was the Allied attempt to force the straits cheaply with a small force. For the loss of some 6,500 men — over 30 per cent of those engaged — all that had been achieved was, at best, the possession of about 1,000 yards of Turkish scrubland.

Left: A famous picture — though it looks somewhat posed — of an Australian giving a wounded Turk a drink. Water was a huge problem for the Allies throughout the campaign and for the wounded, who often had to lie for hours out in no man's land waiting for darkness before they could crawl back to their own lines, it must have been a living hell. Right: With Achi Baba again looking on in the distance, one can only wonder what unrecorded and unremembered events occurred in these blood-soaked fields. This particular photo was taken on Fir Tree Spur near the trench that was once known as 2 Australian Line.

MAY AT ANZAC — REINFORCEMENTS AND COUNTER-ATTACKS

Following the failure of the attacks on Krithia, and with an unstable political situation at home following further disasters in France, there was little to do now but try to hold the ground that had already been gained. Meanwhile, a decision regarding the four divisions Sir Ian thought would see them through was due anytime and, until these reserves were despatched, further serious offensives were out of the question.

Left: The grave of Major Hugh Quinn of the 15th Battalion Australian Infantry, killed on May 29 and after whom the most dangerous position on Anzac (Quinn's Post) was named. Above: As in 1915, so today the headstone in Shrapnel Valley Cemetery is still overlooked by the place which bears his name. The ridge in the distance marks the old Anzac line and the Turkish memorial, barely visible on the skyline, is only yards away from the cemetery at Quinn's Post.

In the Anzac sector the situation was more unpleasant than anywhere else. Turkish snipers had been claiming victims from Dead Man's Ridge and in turn the Anzacs had been sniping from Pope's Hill to try and counter this menace.

It was about this time that a position in the centre of the line started to gain the reputation as the most dangerous spot on the entire peninsula. This was named Quinn's Post, after Major Hugh Quinn of the 15th Battalion Australian Infantry who was killed here on May 29. It was said that the men who were lower down the valley would look up at Quinn's Post 'the same way that a man would look at a haunted house'. The reason, other than its fearful reputation, was that everybody knew a Turkish breakthrough here would mean disaster for the entire Anzac sector. The Turks would be able to charge down Monash and Shrapnel Gullies (the latter also sometimes referred to as Shrapnel Valley) and straight to the main landing point of Anzac Cove, thus obviating any chance of an evacuation. To show one's head over the parapet here meant certain death as the Turks had a clear shot from three sides. The trenches were constantly crowded with men to counter any Turkish surprise attack rushing the trenches and hand-grenades caused a lot of casualties. The only defence for the Anzacs was to try to throw them back before they exploded.

Little by little, through countless acts of gallantry and pure hard work, the Anzacs improved the position. They dug a number

Top left: Shrapnel Valley Cemetery looking towards the lower slopes of Plugge's Plateau, believed to have been photographed in the late summer of 1915. Above: While the slopes behind have barely changed, the order and peacefulness of today's cemetery makes quite a contrast to how it looked over 80 years ago. From just behind the cemetery it is possible to follow a path that leads up onto Plugge's Plateau. Although very steep, the views obtained from the top make it well worth the climb. The SMLE rifle bayonet, (below) was found in the valley when taking this picture.

of saps forward and then linked them together thus moving the front line ever closer to the Turkish positions which in places were only a few yards apart.

After hearing that the Turks were mining around Quinn's, orders were given to start trench raids to seize prisoners. The first of these took place on May 9, and was carried out by troops of the 15th Battalion who entered the enemy trenches at three points. The attack started well and the Turks were caught completely by

Above left: The view from Shrapnel Valley towards the ridge that was once the front line. The section here is surmounted by the Turkish memorial that stands in the cemetery to the 57th Regiment, near Quinn's Post. It is easy to see from this view how vital it was to the Anzacs to hold this position for less than 100 yards behind lies the sea. If the Turks had taken Quinn's Post, they would have been able to fire down almost the entire length of the Anzac lines, thus making the entire position untenable. **Above right:** This picture, taken from Quinn's Post looking back down towards the sea, shows the view that the Turks would have had if they had captured Quinn's. In the distance can be seen the cemetery that stands at the mouth of Shrapnel Valley.

surprise. The Anzac troops, so desperate to break-out from the trench warfare to which the battle was deteriorating, almost as one decided to push on. Alas in the darkness and confusion the three separate groups of attackers failed to link up. The Turks quickly reinforced the position and under a heavy counter-attack, spearheaded by showers of hand-grenades (of which the Anzacs were desperately short), the Anzacs were forced to retire having suffered some 200 casualties.

It was on May 12, that the Australian Light Horse and the New Zealand Mounted Brigade both arrived from Egypt for dismounted service. Although inexperienced these men were to prove fine soldiers in the battles ahead.

The 2nd Light Horse, who had been holding the position at Quinn's since shortly after their landing, were suffering unsustainable casualties from abandoned trenches that had been dug by earlier occupants. These trenches, out in front of the Australian

Anzac water bottle and mess tin found near Quinn's Post.

positions in no man's land, were now affording cover to the Turks. After viewing the situation, and having the periscope he was using shot out by a Turkish sniper, General Birdwood and General Godley, decided that another attempt should be launched to cover the back-filling of this trench. Just before 0200 hours on May 14, the raid began but, within 20 minutes, 46 of the 65 men involved were either dead, wounded or missing, including Major Dugald Graham who was leading the attack.

Following this disaster, the emphasis at Anzac was now focused on tunnelling and mining instead of attacking across the open. Engineers were also given the task of using whatever materials they could secure to try and provide some form of roofing that would give protection from the Turkish grenades.

On May 18, aerial reconnaissance showed that Turkish forces were building up in the Anzac region and that a heavy attack could be expected at any time. On the same day, the 2nd Brigade arrived back from Helles; it was to prove not a moment too soon.

Throughout the night, the 12,000 or so Anzacs available for defence slept only fitfully. It was far too quiet and all were by now fully aware that a fierce Turkish attack could be expected in the early hours. Anticipation hung in the air. At 0300 hours, the Anzacs stood to, peering into the gloom as first light approached. Some 20 minutes later, at first near Wire Gully but then all across the front, the Anzacs could see thousands of Turkish troops advancing slowly towards them. In most places the Turks had to cross nearly 200 yards of exposed ground. After holding fire until well within range, the Anzacs let rip with anything that could fire. For the next two hours or so the Turks desperately tried to breakthrough the Anzac lines and suffered enormous casualties in the process.

It is testament to their bravery and fighting spirit that at some points of the front men were trying to buy a place in the firing line, using any luxury they may have saved to barter for a good position. Only at Courtney's Post did the Turks break the line when, following a bombing attack from behind some sheltered ground, seven Turks succeeded in taking one corner of Courtney's. However, due to the bravery of Lance Corporal Albert Jacka who was the only survivor of the bombing attack, the gain could not be consolidated. Jacka, having worked his way round behind the Turks, was seen to bayonet five of them before shooting the other two.

(For his actions, he would achieve the honour of receiving the first Victoria Cross of the war to be awarded to an Australian.)

By 0500 hours the Turks were licking their wounds and by 1100, following some local skirmishes, the attack was dead. Despite the knowledge that the assault was imminent, no orders for any sort of counter-attack had been issued and so the chance to seize the high ground, that for a while was only held by confused and traumatised survivors, slipped away. It was only some three hours later that orders were issued to the New Zealand Mounted Brigade for a limited assault. By this stage though, the Turkish officers on the spot had reorganised their men and, after the first wave were quickly mown down, the senior New Zealand officer wisely cancelled any further attempts.

The road that runs up the heights towards Chunuk Bair passes many cemeteries and memorials en route. In the foreground to the left can be seen Quinn's Post Cemetery, while the Turkish cemetery to the 57th Regiment lies on the opposite side of the road. Here it runs right along through the former no man's land and during the campaign the front line trenches were often little more than 10-15 yards apart.

Above: The Turkish envoy who arrived with a request for an armistice to bury the dead on May 22 was carried by two men on a stretcher over the trip wires in the water. The officer had been blindfolded before approaching the Anzac lines so that he could not report back about the state of the defences.

The disastrous Turkish offensive of May 19 cost them some 10,000 casualties of whom 3,000 were killed, the Anzacs having suffered about 100 killed and some 500 wounded. Many of these men had been hit whilst standing on the parapet to take a better aim at the massed ranks that were advancing towards them.

Below: Whilst no trace remains today of the trees on the beach, the Gaba Tepe headland makes for an easy comparison. It would be difficult to imagine a greater contrast between the British warship and a tiny Turkish fishing boat in almost identical positions.

Strategically, the most important gain was the acquisition of a number of accurate maps from dead Turkish officers which complemented similar documents captured after the Second Battle of Krithia. The Allies wasted no time in copying these maps and issuing them to their own officers.

On May 24th there was an armistice. I was involved in that as an observer, nothing else. I wasn't among the burial parties. My job was to look out for Otago bodies. Actually I only found one. The rest were either buried before I got there or on the Turk side of the line. They put a line of pegs halfway between the two lines, each peg with a little strip of white calico. We buried all the men on our side of the armistice line and they buried all the men on their side.

But that wasn't the first idea. The first idea was that we would pick up Turks on our side of the line and carry them over the centre line. The Turks were to do the same with our fellows on their side. This turned out to be impossible. You couldn't move the bodies. After three weeks or more in the heat and sun they were just falling to pieces. The one Otago body I sighted had a chest wound. He had blown up like a balloon. Other bodies had blown up and burst. I couldn't stand the stench. The burial parties just dug holes beside the bodies and rolled them in.

But in front of Quinn's Post there were heaps of bodies. There were just eleven yards between the Turk line and the Anzac line and these heaps of bodies. They were lying in all sorts of positions, a lot of them swollen. It's amazing to think that they were all buried in that little patch of ground between the two lines. Just a space of eleven yards. They spread lime over the top of the bodies. That didn't do much good. It didn't do me much good either. The stench was the start of my dysentery. I was running to the latrines all the time afterwards. Eventually I passed nothing but blood.

GEORGE SKERRET
NEW ZEALAND MEDICAL CORPS

The good weather was now to cause an unpleasant problem. With the presence of thousands of unburied bodies in close proximity to the Allied lines, the soaring temperature was soon to cause a massive risk to health. The idea of a cease-fire to bury the dead was not greeted too well at GHQ but they realised its necessity and agreed that if the Turks were to ask, permission would be granted. However, things had already developed unofficially at the front where the cries of the wounded and the smell of putrefying flesh were unbearable. Colonel Robert Owen of the 2nd

Above: With the threat of an epidemic a real possibility, something had to be done about the rotting corpses lying out in the sun in no man's land. Following the agreed armistice, men from both sides can be seen burying the dead near The Nek on May 24. However, when the shelling resumed, many of these bodies were blown back out of their shallow graves, and veterans of both sides agreed it could be more hellish interring the dead than fighting the living.

One of the most famous and brave men at Anzac must be John Simpson Kirkpatrick, probably better known as 'the man with the donkey'. Kirkpatrick, who had enlisted as John Simpson, was born in England but had moved to Australia before the outbreak of hostilities. He joined up and served with the 3rd Australian Field Ambulance, landing with them on April 25 near Ari Burnu. Seeing how inadequate the medical facilities were for bringing down the wounded from the front, he commandeered a donkey on which to carry the wounded. There are several different stories as to its name which is variably given as 'Duffy', 'Murphy' or 'Scottie', but it seems probable that he lost a number of animals to enemy action and therefore all three are correct. Simpson and his donkey became a familiar sight to those at Anzac as they slowly made their way up and down Monash and Shrapnel Valleys with the wounded. The donkey wore Simpson's Red Cross arm band around its head and some tell of Simpson removing this once he reached the beach, pulling out his revolver, and fighting his way back up the valley to the front line. Simpson's almost blasé attitude to the risks he was running became legendary but alas his luck finally ran out on May 19 when he was struck in the chest by a bullet near Steele's Post.

Australian Brigade had hoisted a Red Cross flag as a preliminary move to clear the way for stretcher bearers from both sides to bring in the wounded. Unfortunately the flag was immediately shot to pieces but the Turks quickly sent a messenger across with a verbal apology. Owen then explained what he wanted whereupon the Turks hoisted their own Red Crescent flag and stretcher bearers immediately appeared from both sides. Many of the wounded who had lain without water under the burning sun were removed and some burying of the numerous dead was also achieved. Brigadier-General Harold Walker, (General Officer Commanding New Zealand Brigade and 1st Australian Brigade) who just happened upon the scene, spoke with some Turkish officers in no man's land and they agreed to speak to their superiors about a formal cease-fire. However, believing the Turks had initiated the whole event, HQ sent the following message back: 'If you want a truce to bury your dead, send a staff officer, under a flag of truce, to our headquarters via the Gaba Tepe road between 10 a.m. and 12 noon tomorrow, 21st May.' Thus, pride on both sides was

Simpson and four-legged helper once walked here in Shrapnel Gully (or Valley — both words are used) — a peaceful place today.

stealing weapons, the Turks venturing too close to Anzac lines, etc — were solved by 'referees' but on the whole very few problems were encountered.

The stalemate at Anzac was now complete. The Turks realised that the Anzacs stood little chance of storming their higher positions in any massed attack, whilst equally the Anzacs realised that they could hold off even the most determined of Turkish attacks.

His body was borne back to the beach where he was buried. Simpson was known to all at Anzac and he was recommended for both the Victoria Cross and the Distinguished Conduct Medal. However, despite any number of individual stories of his daring and courage, no one act of bravery could be singled out from eyewitness accounts of his many exploits. Thus this very brave man received no official recognition other than a Mention in Despatches.

saved: the Turks could point to the Australians having initiated proceedings whilst GHQ were under the correct belief that they had not originally offered any truce.

For those men in the front line, the question of who asked who was quite irrelevant: the cease-fire was merely seen as a chance to make their horrendous conditions slightly more tolerable and it was set for May 24. It began at 0730 hours and lasted until 1630. The ground was covered with thousands of dead, a horror that none of those who witnessed it were ever likely to forget. After the initial tension, as both sides realised the other had not planned some treacherous deed, the troops started to swap badges and souvenirs. A few minor problems — the Australians

Today he still lies in the beautiful Beach Cemetery, his final resting place probably the most visited on the entire peninsula.

The bakery at Helles started producing bread at the end of May 1915 — it was one of the only sources of fresh food available on the peninsula. The location, quickly named Bakery Beach, lay between W Beach and X Beach.

MAY-JUNE — CONSOLIDATION AND PREPARATIONS FOR THE NEXT ADVANCE ON KRITHIA

Following the failure of the Krithia offensive, Lieutenant-General Hunter-Weston had little choice but to rest the men of the 29th Division. Since they had landed so bloodily, they had been involved in both battles for Krithia and had spent some 17 consecutive days in the front line. They were replaced by the recently arrived 3rd Brigade of the 42nd Division, as well as by men of the Royal Naval Division who had been released from their earlier duties in the Anzac sector. With the enforced stalemate upon him, Lieutenant-General Hunter-Weston issued orders for local commanders to try and map the areas they were facing and to submit any ideas for local advances.

Acting on these orders, Major-General Vaughan Cox of the 29th Indian Brigade, suggested that a small party of his men could capture, at night, the previously undetectable machine gun emplacement that was housed somewhere on the ridge above their positions. This was the very same one that had thwarted the attempt to seize the initiative during the Second Battle of Krithia.

Despite the scrub hiding much of the landscape, Bakery Beach has changed little over the years, and 80 years later it is still possible to find odd accoutrements discarded by the former tenants, amongst the scrub.

The proposal was approved and command of the operation was given to Lieutenant-Colonel the Hon. Charles Bruce of the 1/6th Gurkhas. Shortly after nightfall, two companies of Gurkhas crept along the foot of the bluff at the northern end of Y Beach where they scaled the cliff and dug themselves in. Following a short bombardment of the Y Beach nullah by a cruiser and a destroyer, a second double company of Gurkhas then moved forward to extend the right of the captured position. By the time the Turks realised what was going on it was too late; they were now outflanked. As they retreated they were pursued by the remaining Gurkhas and two companies of Sikhs who had worked their way forward on the opposite side of Gully Ravine. In all, over 500 yards had been captured for minimal casualties in an area where it was believed no progress could be made at all. Consequently, the recently occupied area became known henceforth as Gurkha Bluff.

The French, too, had made some small advances but at heavy cost and the size of their front line had to be reduced to compensate for these losses. All the areas given up by the French were handed over to the already overstretched British.

Left: This is the rugged landscape near Y Ravine over which the Gurkhas crept on the night of May 12. It is seen here later in November with men of the West Kent Yeomanry digging shelters. Right: The Y Beach area is without doubt one of the most inaccessible today and any trip here is not made easier by the prickly scrub and intense heat in the summer months. It is relatively easy to come across the remnants of dug-outs and trenches but great care must be taken when visiting this area, particularly if you are exploring alone because of the hidden dangers.

Left: A Turkish shell explodes near an advanced dressing station close to Gurkha Bluff. This area was heavily fought over throughout the campaign and was under observation and shelling at regular intervals. Right: With the exception of the shell-burst and the Red Cross flag, this area has changed only in the amount of greenery that now binds the hillside together, often making it impossible to reach certain places. It is also exceptionally difficult to know exactly where you are in the Y Beach area as there are no cemeteries or memorials to help identify positions that have long since disappeared from any map.

It was about this time that the threat from German submarines became serious and the transport ship *Arcadian*, which had acted as Sir Ian Hamilton's HQ, was now forced to harbour at Imbros. The necessity to return it to transport duties, combined with the lack of space and safety on the peninsula, meant that from May 31 GHQ was permanently stationed ashore at Imbros, some 15 miles away.

The view from X Beach towards the island of Imbros where Sir Ian Hamilton relocated his headquarters after it became too risky to remain afloat off Gallipoli because of the threat of submarines. Although the distance between the two land masses does not appear that great, the realities and pitfalls of command from such a distance was to become only too evident.

On May 25 the first German submarine struck, as one New Zealander so matter of factly recorded in his diary: 'In the evening we helped make roads on the side of hills, then returned to rest trenches. HMS *Triumph* sunk by torpedo of Gaba Tepe in about eight minutes (12 o'clock).' The official history of the Gallipoli campaign states that the ship took 20 minutes to sink and that others ashore were far more perturbed: 'It was a nerve-racking sight, and has done none of us any good to see it.' (Senior staff officer.)

The loss of life on the *Triumph* was relatively small as first the *Chelmer* and then other small boats from the shore rushed to the scene. The Turks, who initially started to shell the rescue operation, to their credit quickly ceased and the rescue efforts proceeded unhindered.

The gradual development of W Beach was on much the same lines as that of any seaside resort at home. When the shells came from Achi Baba only, certain sites at once rose in price and were eagerly sought after by the settlers. These were the ones which commanded a sea view and were constructed on terraces cut out of the cliff overlooking the blue waters of the Dardanelles. No shells, either direct or indirect, could reach them from the land side, and the happy aristocracy of the place looked with scorn on their neighbours who were still obliged, through lack of space or the nature of their duties, to live in exposed dugouts in the valley running up from the beach.

Once the Turkish guns fired across the Straits, the situation changed dramatically. Prices along sea view fell with a horrid and disastrous slump, the hotels were almost empty, and everyone was trying to take a place in the country farther inland. The Sea View dwellers never foresaw this contingency. They only built their homes to protect themselves against shells from Achi Baba. Now they found themselves in an awkward predicament, for their dwellings, being constructed on terraces along the cliff face, could not be built up in front, and they either had to face the risk or abandon them altogether. Some fled to the top of the cliff; others had by this time become fatalists and, smoking their pipes, thought of happier days in the past and conjured up fresh hopes for the future. Others again, sunk their pride and descended into the valley once more to make terms with those whom they had lately looked down upon. Many had a working arrangement which answered very well. When the shells were coming from Achi Baba, they invited those in the valley up to Sea View, and when they were coming from Asia, they themselves descended to the valley and lived with their friends. But here again the unhappy inhabitants of Lancashire Landing were often checkmated by the Huns firing from both Asia and Achi Baba at the same time.

ELLIS ASHMEAD-BARTLETT

The Navy was desperate that the Army did not feel abandoned and, although they reduced the number of ships as a result of this new threat, they did not withdraw them altogether. However, the following day, just off W Beach, HMS *Majestic* was torpedoed. The loss of life was again fairly small; nevertheless a

The final moments of HMS *Majestic*, torpedoed on May 27.

decision to get the battleships into dock was inevitable. Unfortunately, now that naval support could not be instantaneous, the result was that the troops ashore, whose entire inventory of supplies came via the Navy, were left feeling isolated and alone. The other more serious consequence was that much of the Turkish artillery that previously could not regularly fire for fear of getting knocked out by the naval guns, was now free to shell the Helles beaches and Anzac at will. Indeed, so common was the shelling now from the Asiatic side, that the troops had even nicknamed the guns that tormented them 'Asiatic Annie' and 'Beachy Bill'.

Precautions against enemy shell-fire had to be made on the landing beaches which were used as the main storage areas for the campaign. This is W Beach, photographed in the early summer of 1915, by which time brick buildings had been constructed for the protective storage of ammunition once it was landed.

The terracing shows up very clearly on this present-day shot, as does the path that used to wind its way to the top of the bluff. It is interesting to note how much of the bank has eroded away and how little of the road that used to run down the beach now remains.

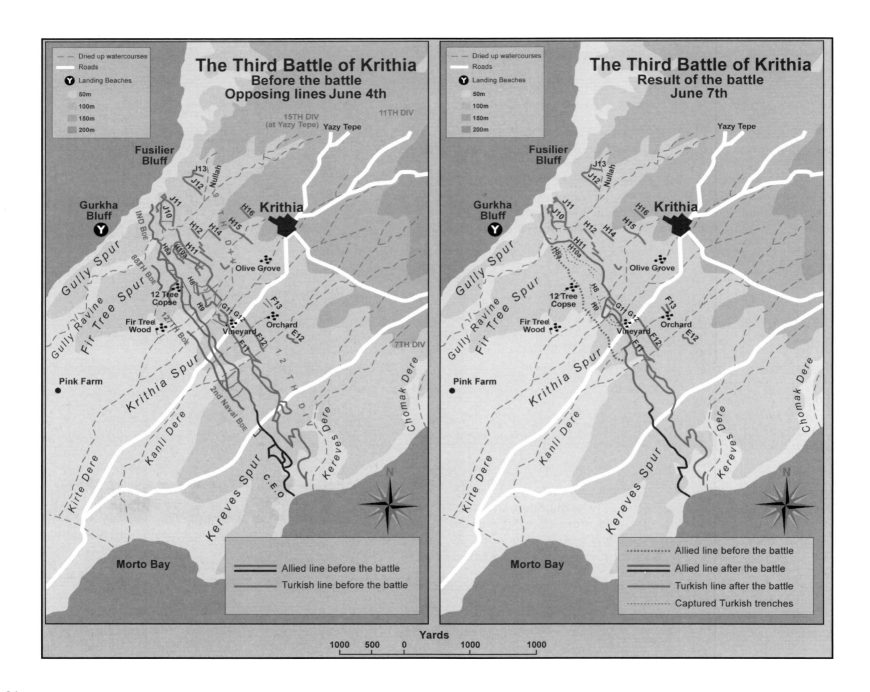

The Third Battle of Krithia
Before the battle
Opposing lines June 4th

Dried up watercourses
Roads
Y Landing Beaches
50m
100m
150m
200m

15TH DIV
(at Yazy Tepe)
11TH DIV
Yazy Tepe

Fusilier
Bluff

J13
J12
Nullah

Gurkha
Bluff
Y

H16
Krithia

J11
J10
H15
H12 H14
IND Bde
H11
Gully Spur
88TH Bde
H8a
H10a
Olive Grove
H12
Fir Tree Spur
Gully Ravine
12 Tree
Copse
H8
H9
F13
Fir Tree
Wood
127TH Bde
G11 G12
Orchard
Vineyard
F11 F12 E12
Krithia Spur
12 TH DIV
7TH DIV

Pink Farm
2nd Naval Bde
Kanli Dere
Kereves Dere
Chomak Dere

Kirte Dere
Kereves Spur
C.E.O

N

Morto Bay

	Allied line before the battle
	Turkish line before the battle

The Third Battle of Krithia
Result of the battle
June 7th

Dried up watercourses
Roads
Y Landing Beaches
50m
100m
150m
200m

Yazy Tepe

Fusilier
Bluff

J13
J12
Nullah

Gurkha
Bluff
Y

H16
Krithia

J11
J10
H15
H12 H14
H11
H8a
H10a
Olive Grove
Gully Spur
H8
12 Tree
Copse
H9
F13
Fir Tree
Wood
Gully Ravine
Fir Tree Spur
G11 G12
Orchard
Vineyard
F11 F12 E12
Krithia Spur

Pink Farm
Kanli Dere
Kereves Dere
Chomak Dere

Kirte Dere
Kereves Spur

N

Morto Bay

	Allied line before the battle
	Allied line after the battle
	Turkish line after the battle
	Captured Turkish trenches

Yards

1000   500   0   1000   1000

THE THIRD BATTLE OF KRITHIA

Following the last unsuccessful attempt at seizing Krithia, the British, who had been unable to immediately renew the offensive, had not been idle. The last few weeks had seen them digging saps and trenches, gradually bringing their positions to within 200 yards of the main Turkish defences. Although Sir Ian would have preferred to have waited until further reinforcements and munitions were available before renewing the attack, he felt that any further delay must be avoided. It was blatantly obvious to him that to sit still and suffer casualties from shelling and disease, whilst the Turkish defences became stronger by the day, would only lead to disaster further down the road. Thus on May 31 the decision was taken to launch an attack to seize the Turkish forward system of trenches across the entire width of the peninsula. The plan that was drawn up by Lieutenant-General Hunter-Weston and the French Général Henri Gouraud was unquestionably accepted and another full frontal, broad daylight attack, was to be the order of the day.

The battle which followed was to be the first on the Gallipoli peninsula that was fought under the conditions of trench warfare; that is, both sides having continuous trench systems, protected by barbed wire entanglements and strong points, or redoubts, capable of all round defence. It has to be said that the plan worked out on this occasion was not only more realistic but also much more detailed than the earlier attempts. The attack was to be divided into two waves. The first wave, which would consist of five men to every four yards, were to seize the Turkish front line as well as any outlying strong points. As soon as this had been achieved, the second wave (one man per yard), were to pass through the captured front line trenches and push on to the second and third lines of the Turkish positions. These trenches lay some 500 yards further on but nowhere were the objectives more than 800 yards from the start line. It had also been realised that consolidation of these positions had to be quick and, for this reason, special digging parties of the Royal Engineers were to be rushed forward as soon as the position was secure. These men were to repair damaged Turkish trenches and dig new communication trenches linking the old British front line to the newly-taken positions as quickly as possible. On first impressions then, this seemed to be a far more organised battle plan.

'Bathing Beach!' Swimming, although often a dangerous occupation with Turkish shells frequently exploding, was encouraged as water for washing was an unheard of commodity at Gallipoli. On the cliff-top behind W Beach are the tents of the 87th Field Ambulance, 29th Division.

Today with no Turkish bombardment and gentle sloping sand, this could be an ideal holiday location and yet it remains a quiet and reflective place, with only the occasional visitor and sunbather.

Left: Troops of the Royal Naval Division, with their officers wearing their startling (and sometimes conspicuous) white rig, making their way through a communication trench at Helles. **Right:** Although not intended as a direct comparison, this old communication trench found by the author, which still runs through part of the Helles sector which was once held by the Royal Naval Division, could possibly be the same one that features in the 1915 picture.

However, other aspects of the plan were less well considered. For instance, units were informed that the best way to clear an enemy trench was with bombing parties. The problem with this was that the only grenades that were available were of the home-made jam-tin variety which were limited to only eight per platoon. Another idea to be tried for the first time was to use armoured cars. A number of vehicles had been landed but up until now no use had been found for them. In preparation for their employment, roads were levelled and bridges repaired but, without the invention of caterpillar tracks, the initiative was destined to end in failure.

As the time for battle approached, detailed instructions were issued including for the first time trench maps showing the exact objectives for each unit. In the French sector, General Gouraud's orders to his troops were that they were to cross the Kereves Dere and obtain a footing on the far bank. If this could be successfully achieved it would secure the flank of the Royal Naval Division who were attacking to their left. Artillery support was to play a key role in the outcome of this battle as naval support would be drastically reduced because of the submarine threat, and even those ships involved would be keeping up a head of speed. To try and compensate for this, the French loaned some six batteries of guns to help support the British attack. These included some of the 75s. With a good crew these could fire about 20 rounds a minute and were loved by the Allied troops for both their accuracy and destructive power.

The main problem and, indeed, the flaw in the entire plan was that, although this was to be the heaviest barrage of the campaign thus far, there would still not be enough high explosive shells available. Of the 12,500 rounds due to be fired, nearly 11,000 were shrapnel shells that exploded in the air flinging small lead balls in all directions. Whilst these were deadly against troops caught out

Artillery support was often lacking in the campaign and, on the occasions that an effective barrage could be bought to bear, it often consisted of too much shrapnel and not enough high explosive. Thus the main Turkish defences were often still largely intact at the beginning of any Allied assault. Here British artillery goes into action during the Third Battle of Krithia on June 4, 1915.

This photo, taken from behind Sedd-el-Bahr looking towards Krithia, shows how much the scrub has taken over in places, eroding many of the small paths and tracks that once linked the tents, billets and artillery posts. The high ground — clearly evident in the 1915 photograph but now barely visible in the background between the bushes — just about gives away the location.

in the open, they caused little if any harm to strong points with overhead protection.

The attack was to begin at noon on June 4 following a four-hour bombardment that was to halt at 1120 hours. At this time, all the infantry in the front lines were to fix bayonets and cheer in an attempt to induce the Turks back into their own front line trenches, before the barrage recommenced at 1130 for a final half-hour. The attacking force was to be some 30,000 strong consisting of 20,000 British and 10,000 French troops. Figures revealed after the war indicate that they were attacking an enemy force of roughly comparable size. However, as a rule of thumb, any attacking force should be at least three times the size of that defending if it is to stand any real chance of gaining and holding much ground. Thus Gallipoli's latest tragedy was about to unfold.

In the front lines, there was an air of confidence that this time every detail had been covered and the elusive breakthrough would now be forthcoming. These thoughts were to be short-lived. As 1120 came and the artillery barrage ceased, rifle and machine-gun fire broke out right across the Turkish front line leaving few of those who were about to go 'over the top' in much doubt as to what they could expect. The conditions in those British front lines must have been horrific. Heat, noise and fear were now combined with the smell of rotting flesh as Turkish bullets burst the bloated bodies of those who had fallen some four weeks earlier during the previous battle.

The artillery stopped at noon exactly and all along the front men left the safety of their trenches, advancing steadily towards the Turkish lines. On the left, the French attack immediately

Looking towards the French lines from former Turkish positions. Taken south-east of Krithia which lies to the left, we are looking towards Kereves Dere. In the centre, one would have found the feature known as the Quadrilateral and the Redoubte Bouchet.

With the Turkish memorial near S Beach visible to the right of the thin tall trees, this photo gives a good idea of the ground over which the Allies had to attack as well as indicating the advantage of the terrain held by the Turks.

started to waiver. Here, in places, the front lines were less than 100 yards apart and, as most of the artillery had been directed further inland to avoid any 'friendly fire' type incidents, the Turkish positions lay virtually intact. The result was nothing short of a massacre. Although some troops did reach the Haricot Redoubt, with the loss of their European officers, and then coming under increasingly accurate Turkish artillery, the remaining men returned to their trenches having gained nothing. This failure of the French on the extreme right left the whole plan open to collapse but, at this stage, none of the other units knew of this set back. Indeed, many had enough problems of their own without wondering about the larger picture.

To the immediate left of the French was the Royal Naval Division which was fortunate enough to be attacking a stretch of front that had been pounded by the French 75s. However, as the French attack on their right first started to falter and then collapse, their flank quickly became exposed. The Turks, having dealt with the

A view from close to the old Turkish front lines to the south of Krithia, looking towards the Helles Memorial. These are the fields in which the Collingwood Battalion of the Royal Naval Division suffered such appalling casualties.

immediate threat of the French, were now clear to turn all their attention to this part of the front. Nevertheless, in spite of this, the men of the Anson, Hood and Howe Battalions managed to capture the Turkish front line suffering heavy casualties in the process. They were followed at 1215 hours by the men of the Collingwood Battalion who, on leaving their trenches to seize the second objective, were immediately caught in a murderous enfilade fire. Within the next few minutes, the battalion ceased to exist as a fighting force; indeed, after the battle it would be disbanded, along with the Benbow Battalion, to provide replacements for the rest of the weakened Royal Naval Division battalions. In the space of 45 minutes, this division lost 60 out of 70 officers and 1,000 out of 1,900 men, and it is a real credit to the survivors that they did reach and capture their objectives, although the heavy fire from the flank forced them to retire later in the day.

The diary of a Petty Officer of Hawke Battalion, who were relieved by the Collingwoods at 0800 hours on June 4, describes these hours in the trenches:

'Relieved by the Collingwoods at 8 a.m., the advance began at 10 o'clock. Very bad day for the Naval Division, Collingwoods wiped out. Bullock killed, Smith missing . . . Returned to trenches about midnight, communication trenches impassable with wounded. Most awful sights. 600 Collingwood casualties, 18 officers killed . . . Very hard time in Nelson Ave, cutting communication to the Manchesters, terrible sights, former officer killed. Held trench against big odds, P.O Watson and Robertson killed . . . Lieut. Stephenson wounded and 18 more casualties, hard work to relieve Manchesters, awful lack of water, unable to move wounded . . . fearful heat and flies men very satisfactory.'

Further to the left were the men of the 42nd Division consisting of the 127th (Manchester) Brigade and two battalions of the 125th Brigade. Once again, it appears that the French 75s did their work well. The men of the Manchester Territorials fought with a fierce passion that gained the utmost respect from the regular units who had viewed the Territorials arrival with some doubt. In this central part of the front, the Manchesters broke through almost the entire Turkish line. In doing so they had captured over 200 prisoners and were on the verge of breaking through to the open ground that would have led the way to the capture of Krithia

and Achi Baba. However, their right flank was becoming exposed due to the annihilation of the Royal Naval Division and the enemy trenches to their extreme left, which had been less affected by the bombardment, were now causing horrific casualties to the men who attacked there. To ease the situation, the 1/8th Lancashire Fusiliers were rushed to the right to help strengthen the flank that the remnants of the Naval Division was still holding.

The present day view from Twelve Tree Copse Cemetery looking towards Krithia Nullah and the Krithia Road. On the extreme right stands the old Redoubt Line which is about the furthest point that the Australians reached during their heroic charge on May 8. The cemetery now stands on part of the old front line which was, in fact, a series of redoubts rather than one individual strong point. On the left of the picture, not marked by any distinguishing landmarks, is the area that was once known as the Vineyard — the furthest point held by the British throughout the campaign. Thus it is possible by looking at this photograph to gauge just how little ground was gained from May 8 onwards — just the width of the overall view in the picture!

To the left of the Manchesters was the 88th Brigade which had been strengthened by units of the 86th, 87th and 126th Brigades. The shortage of shells, particularly for the howitzers whose high trajectory was ideal for the terrain was to tell as soon as the men left their trenches. The first wave of the King's Own Scottish Borderers was wiped out with very few men even reaching the enemy parapet. Their commanding officer, seeing the futility of their efforts, cancelled the second wave moments before they were due to charge.

Men of the Hampshire Regiment and the Royal Fusiliers all met a similar fate as the Turkish and German machine-gunners (mainly crew from the *Breslau*) worked overtime on their deadly task. On the extreme left of the 88th Brigade's position, the Worcestershire Regiment fought with great daring and bravery and succeeded in entering and capturing two lines of Turkish trenches. The Worcesters were now able to enfilade the Turks who were causing such horrendous casualties amongst their comrades to their right. Nearly an hour after the first men had commenced the attack, the 88th Brigade succeeded in taking most of its objectives. They had captured the Turkish trench known as H12 and advanced units had even reached the strategically-important trench H14. However Brigade HQ were either not aware or did not act upon these important gains and, as the day progressed, increased enemy fire from Gully Spur forced the Worcesters to abandon their hard-won ground.

On the extreme left of the front was the Indian Brigade which included a battalion of the Lancashire Fusiliers as well as the 1/6th Gurkhas. The barrage here had done very little damage for, as has already been explained, there were not enough guns to cover the entire front and Gully Spur had been somewhat neglected. Added to this, some guns destined to give fire support here were switched to other targets at the last moment. The net result was that what small gains were made could not be supported and both the Sikhs, Gurkhas and Lancashire Fusiliers all suffered heavy casualties.

By 1330 hours, the situation was as follows. No progress had been made on either flank, with the French, Indians and the Royal Naval Division all back at their starting positions with heavy losses. On the left of centre, the 88th Brigade had captured most of its objectives and was within about a mile of Krithia with very

Above: Turkish belt buckle and a 7.92 cartridge case taken from a dead Turk and brought back from Gallipoli by a soldier in the Essex Regiment. Below: The small buckles, shrapnel balls, and British, French and Turkish cartridge cases, were all found by the author at various points on the battlefield in 1999.

The view from the Krithia Road at a position more or less on the site of the old front lines around the Vineyard. Slightly to the left (hidden by the trees) is Twelve Tree Copse Cemetery while ahead is Fir Tree Spur. From here, the front line snaked a little to the right where one would have been found Worcester Flat and Essex Knoll, named after two of the units of the 88th Brigade who held that part of the line.

few Turks now standing in its way. The 42nd Division and the Territorials had captured all their objectives and in some places they were within three quarters of a mile of Krithia. However both the units which had made these important gains now found their flanks wide open.

Any serious Turkish counter-attack now could mean disaster for the entire Allied operation. With the reserves not deployed, this was the predicament that Lieutenant-General Hunter-Weston and Gouraud now found themselves: should they reinforce the successes of the centre, or try to secure the line by reinforcing the failures of the flanks? With only 18 battalions at their disposal, there would be no prizes for a wrong decision. Again, with hindsight it is easy to say what should have been done but unfortunately the idea of reinforcing a success seems to have been an almost alien concept to the Gallipoli commanders.

Gouraud and Hunter-Weston decided that a new attack should be made against the fortifications of Kereves Dere in the French sector and at Gully Spur on the left flank. This would inevitably leave the men in the centre, who had made such incredible gains for such hideous losses, unsupported, which would in turn force their retirement and another golden chance lost. The 1/5th Gurkhas were now sent to support the Indian Brigade at Gully Spur, whilst three battalions of the Royal Naval Division were despatched to help the French attack the emplacements of Kereves Dere.

It was less than an hour later that Gouraud informed Hunter-Weston that his forces were so exhausted that they could take no further part in the operations scheduled for that day. With the Naval Division's participation now obsolete, this attack was cancelled but the assault on the left flank by the Indians and Gurkhas was to go ahead as planned. The defences here, as we have already seen, were unshaken yet with immense bravery the troops tried once again to overcome these Turkish positions though the outcome was sadly predictable. The 1/5th Gurkhas suffered appalling casualties including every one of their British officers. The 14th Sikhs fared similarly and of their 15 British officers, they lost 12; of 14 Indian officers they lost 11, and of the 514 other ranks, 380 became casualties. To compensate for these losses, two more battalions were released from the reserves, but these same troops that could have been risked to exploit success were now being frittered away on reinforcing defeat.

Immediately following this failure, Lieutenant-General Hunter-Weston ordered all units to dig in and consolidate what ground they had gained. Alas about an hour later, a general retreat was ordered as the hard-pressed and still unsupported 42nd Division continued to fight desperate battles with Turkish reinforcements who had been rushed to the area. By nightfall on the fateful 4th, an area of between 200-500 yards had been gained on a front approximately a mile long but at the expense of 4,500 British and 2,000 French casualties.

Not that the Turks had had it all their own way as they, too, had suffered heavy casualties. Mehmed Nehad Bey, a staff officer with the southern group, said later: 'Had the British continued the attack with the same violence all would have been lost'. The German General Hans Kannengiesser, who was attached to the

Sure enough, at just before sunrise, I saw the tops of many ladders protruding from the Turkish trenches and soon over they came in their hundreds, led by a man with a large crescent flag and all shouting to Allah. My dozen or so men panicked, dropped their rifles, picks and shovels and bolted down the communication trench leaving me alone between the two sandbag barricades.

I lit one of the ridiculous jam-tin bombs which I hurled out towards the advancing Turks, when to my horror one Turk climbed on top of the further barricade and another had shoved his rifle through the loophole in the steel plate. All I could do was to dive into the sort of alcove where the steel plate was and attempt a back-handed throw of another jam-tin bomb. This bomb hit one of the top sandbags and bounced back to me, say some three to four yards behind, and all I could do was to present my rear end to receive a very unpleasant spattering of pieces of the jam-tin in my backside, legs and lower back. However I managed to light another jam-tin bomb and this was most successful, knocking out the Turk standing on top of the barricade and wounding the Turk firing madly through the loophole in the steel plate a few inches from my head.

Quickly I managed to shove out this Turkish rifle from the loophole in the steel plate and, seizing a rifle and with a full box of ammunition in my reach, I fired a very rapid 15 or more rounds a minute into masses of Turks completely filling this 90 to 120 yards of dead straight trench. My aimed bullets did frightful slaughter; at this mighty short range, every bullet must have dug into more than one Turk. Soon the rifle got so damned hot that I had to seize another until this second rifle also became far too hot and then with even a third rifle I carried on until there seemed nothing standing to hit by which time the dead and wounded Turks in that very deep wide and straight original Turkish fire trench must have numbered between 100 and 200. While I was so busy firing and handing out such a drastic killing at such short range, I recall that I was shouting and yelling like a madman.

Then foolishly I looked over the top, even climbed out to collect some of the Turkish black cricket ball bombs, when Lieutenant Young came along with some men and I started to snipe at some Turks I could see only to get a Turkish bullet hit my rifle and break up, leaving a piece stuck in my forehead and a small fragment in the wall lining of my tummy. The rest of this bullet wounded one of the Dublin Tommies who had come along with Lieutenant Young.

I then handed over this corner to Lieutenant Young and managed to get down to the Nullah to see the M.O., so that he could do something about all the jam-tin in my rear quarters and, after being somewhat patched up, I returned to the famous corner junction just as the Turks attacked again. Three of these Turks managed to drop down flat by the parapet of the now partly-built circular trench we had been digging.

Seizing a rifle, I shoved in five rounds, jumped on top of the barricade and had these three very scared and sheepish-looking Turks at three to four yards range, lying prone. I hit number one and his head was a mere shambles and then fired quickly at numbers two and three, hitting both but, as they seemed still alive, I gave each another shot. But then, of the very many Turkish bullets whistling around me, one went straight through my upper right arm, right and cleanly through the single bone, also damaging my artery and the main nerve.

It was like being hit with a sledgehammer but what was in a way worse was that I was knocked off the top of the parapet, head over heels, and landed with the rifle on top of me.

LIEUTENANT GREVILLE CRIPPS
(describing the Turkish counter-attack
on the Royal Dublin Fusiliers on July 5)

Nothing can convey to you how dreadful is the sight of a suffering badly wounded man — nothing can convey it to you. I heard two short surprised coughs and saw a man bend and fall. A friend darted to him, opened his tunic and said to him, 'You're done Ginger, you're done: they've got you.' This frankness really seemed the most appropriate and sincere thing. They bandaged him up. While I was with him he said some remarkable things. 'Shall I go to Heaven or Hell sir?' I said with perfect confidence, 'To Heaven.' He said: 'No tell me man to man.' I repeated what I had said. A little while later he made up a beautiful prayer — 'Oh God, be good and ease my pain — if only a little.' All the while it was unbearable to see what he suffered. And then, slowly drawn out: 'I didn't mean to groan, but' — in a long-drawn-out groan — 'I must.' I went to see him in the morning. . . . Passers-by stepped over his body as they went on their way.'

LIEUTENANT JOHN ALLEN
13TH WORCESTERS, KILLED IN ACTION JUNE 6, 1915

John Allen is buried in Twelve Tree Copse Cemetery.

Left: The Indian troops at Gallipoli played an important — if very often overlooked — role as their small AT carts were not only used in the delivery of supplies but also for the removal of the wounded. Although transporting supplies is normally considered a 'safe' job, it must be remembered that at Gallipoli, from the moment stores were landed, they were within range of the Turkish guns and all the known supply routes were constantly and randomly shelled making it one of the more riskier tasks within the peninsula. Here, Indians can be seen exercising their mules while a shell bursts on the ridge to the left of Achi Baba — the high peak to the right. Right: Today, the fields in this area have all returned to arable farming, the ploughing often turning up relics from the campaign, although one must be careful to avoid live ammunition and be thoughtful towards the crops.

Left: The Howe Battalion resting on Drake's Hill in June 1915. The Royal Naval Division was one of the hardest hit at Gallipoli, causing two battalions to be disbanded to make up the numbers in the others. Many RND men were ex-sailors who volunteered for duty ashore, going into action having received less infantry **training than most other units. Even so, they fought with great bravery and tenacity and were often only evicted from captured positions due to depleted numbers and inadequate reinforcement. Right: On the top of the hill many of the one-man foxholes can still be traced; the peak of Achi Baba stands in the distance.**

Turkish 9th Division, wrote that 'I felt that another energetic attack by the English would have had the worst results'. However the British and French, having come so close to the breakthrough they desperately needed, were now too weak to even contemplate any further offensive action. As a consequence, this gave the Turks ample time to prepare new defences and put more reinforcements in place.

Throughout the evening of the 4th — and indeed into the 5th and 6th — the Turks desperately fought back in an attempt to regain their lost positions. Meanwhile the wounded were gradually being cleared, largely thanks to the efforts of the overworked stretcher-bearers who were ably assisted by the Zion Mule Corps. These men worked tirelessly, bringing ammunition forwards and taking the wounded back to the beaches.

Major-General Beauvoir de Lisle, the new commander of the 29th Division, chose this day to arrive from France; what he made of the scenes that greeted him is unfortunately not recorded.

While the wounded were slowly being cleared, there was still no time to bury the dead. Many bodies lying in exposed positions would never be recovered and even to this day many men have no known grave. Others, like a company of King's Own Scottish Borderers who were wiped out, were cleared simply by being thrown over the parapet on either side of the trench. By a general lack of compassion and foresight, it fell to a newly-landed platoon of the KOSBs to bury them and, as their first job on the peninsula, a crueller welcome can hardly be imagined.

On June 6, a fierce Turkish counter-attack developed but 2nd Lieutenant George Moor of the Hampshire Regiment succeeded in stemming a British retreat before rallying the surviving men (who had lost all their officers) into retaking the lost trench, thus saving a complete collapse of the line. For this action he was later awarded the Victoria Cross.

As the 6th passed into the 7th, the fighting that is attributed to the Third Battle of Krithia came to an end, but with it came the realisation that any wearing down of the enemy and break-out from the south was now virtually impossible. Although the politicians in London had finally agreed to send reinforcements, it was certainly not a foregone conclusion that landing them at Helles would ensure victory. Now something or somewhere new was needed.

Left: The 22nd Battalion, AIF, which had just arrived from Egypt, photographed making its way to the front line at Anzac on June 9, 1915. Right: A descent of mammoth proportions, through scrub which had not been penetrated for 80 years, resulted in the author finally reaching the area close to where the original photo was taken. Numerous reminders of the past remain in this area but one must be very careful; it can be exceptionally easy to get down the hill but returning to the top is an entirely different story!

JUNE AND JULY — SMALLER OFFENSIVES AT HELLES PREPARATIONS AT ANZAC

After much debate, the decision was made in London to reinforce the Dardanelles operation with three fresh divisions consisting mainly of men from the 'New Army'. These were volunteers from all walks of life who at the outbreak of the war had answered Kitchener's call to arms.

The problem facing GHQ on Imbros was that although this was good news in itself, they could not arrive until the second week of July at the earliest so any thoughts of further major attacks would be impossible before then. Meanwhile the orders given to the Helles sector were for limited offensives only on narrow fronts that could be heavily bombarded by all available guns. The lessons of the last two major offensives here had finally been learned in as much as the commanders now realised that if success could not be achieved on the flanks, then little overall success could be expected.

At Anzac the situation was somewhat different. It was already realised that the northern flank was the most likely place for any break-out to be successful so it was decided that no further attacks were to be made here until the fresh troops were in position. Instead, the troops got into a routine of sniping, digging and attacking as diversions during the British and French attacks in the south. All this was a bid to convince the Turkish command that the Anzac beach-head was purely a side-show to the Helles front and that the next serious blow would be coming from here.

To keep up this pretence, both the British and French commanders started drawing up plans to keep the Turks guessing, as well as trying to snatch an advantageous position when and where they could. The first of the attacks under this new tactic took place in the French sector on June 21. The plan was to attack on a front of about 650 yards and seize a number of troublesome

Gully Ravine is a natural feature about three miles in length running roughly south to north. It was the obvious way to get men to the front as the Turks could not see into it and the steep sides protected if from all but the most accurate artillery fire. In this 1915 picture we can see the entrance to Gully Ravine from Gully Beach. The area around the beach was probably one of the most photographed locations on the peninsula as this was where many of the troops were bivouacked before moving up to the front. Opposite page, top: Today Gully Beach remains virtually deserted and receives few visitors; thus it has changed little. It is a place of strong memories as the presence of the lost battalions who marched up the ravine never to return still seems to hang in the air, giving it an almost ghostly feel. The greenery today hides many of Gully Ravine's features though the rock face on the left of the picture remains distinct, as does the 'main road' which runs through it. As can be seen, the scrub gets thicker the further you advance up the ravine. What cannot be seen though is the oppressive heat and stillness that awaits anyone who ventures further along Gully Ravine.

redoubts as well as the crest of Kereves Spur — or Hill 83 as the Turks called it. On the whole this attack was successful. It had started early in the morning though it was nightfall before all the units were able to link up and make the position defendable. They had managed to secure the ridge of Kereves Spur which, in turn, meant that troops moving up the gullies to the centre of the French sector were no longer under observation from the Turkish spotters who were the former residents of this position. Neverthe-less the price for these limited gains had been high for both sides. The French had suffered some 2,500 casualties and, whilst no accurate figures are available for the Turkish side, it is believed that they lost at least 6,000 men on this day. The most important factor though, other than the greatly improved morale of the French, was the proof that with heavy and concentrated artillery fire, even the most fearsome of Turkish strongholds were not impregnable.

Left: The lower slopes of Plugge's Plateau, overlooking Anzac Cove, housed the divisional HQ of the Australians and New Zealanders. Right: Whilst the top slopes have remained largely unchanged, the bottom is now overgrown and almost impenetrable. It seems impossible to imagine that lines of horses and mules together with an army headquarters was once based here.

Left: The French depot at Sedd-el-Bahr on V Beach, was a centre for the arrival of supplies and, as such, it was often targeted by Turkish guns positioned on the Asiatic side of the Dardanelles. To help minimise casualties, the French posted a bugler to sound off when the distant report of the Turkish guns was heard, thus giving a warning of about 20-30 seconds to take cover. Right: Today, the empty and derelict castle still makes this an easy place to identify. The large parts that are now missing were dismantled by returning Turkish civilians to rebuild houses in the village.

Left: While the French used V Beach as their main landing area, the British used W Beach (or Lancashire Landing as it is probably better known). Seen here, in the summer of 1915, the closely-packed stores are an inviting target as a shell could scarcely fail to hit something. Right: The actual beach where the Lancashires landed is strangely not one of the most visited locations on the peninsula. It became a Turkish military base after the war and remained a restricted area until fairly recently. Today it is possible to drive right onto the beach to view a largely timeless vista, save for the memorials on the skyline.

The next attack in this series of operations went in on the opposite flank around Gully Ravine on June 28. It was, coincidentally, the same date that Mustafa Kemal was planning an attack in the Anzac sector near Russell's Top. Following the Anzac feint that cost them some 300 casualties, Kemal was forced to postpone his own attack until the 29th. After a brief bombardment, the Turks advanced with the usual cries of 'Allah!' 'Allah!' but they were quickly beaten back as one New Zealander recorded in his diary: 'At midnight and until 4 o'clock the Turks attacked left flank but were severely repulsed. They got into several saps, but were quickly bombed and shot down. Turks then bombarded us fiercely at daybreak. A brass cap of a shell tore a hole 6in by 4in through my bivouac sheet and landed within a few inches of my head, also making 6 holes in my towel!! . . . Turks losses today 300 killed and 6 captured. Australians 6 killed and 30 wounded.'

These figures compare remarkably well with the Official History of the campaign that records Turkish losses at about 800, with 13 captured, whilst the Australian casualties are said to have been only 26.

Following this attack and the ease with which it had been repulsed, the Turks seem to have gone into an almost shocked-like state. Firing around Russell's Top died away to nothing and, at one point, although only for a short period, it was possible to stroll around areas where it would normally have meant certain death during daylight hours.

Meanwhile, at Gully Ravine things were hotting up. Sir Ian had been anxious to build on the French success of June 21 at the earliest possible moment but the whole reason for their success — the artillery — was now the hold up. All the French guns that were to support the British advance, as well as the British guns that had been lent to the French, now had to be repositioned to be able to give adequate fire support at Gully Ravine. The attack here was to take place across a front of nearly 700 yards and was to proceed up Gully Ravine as well as across Gully Spur. The aim was to capture an as-yet-uncompleted trench system designated J12 and J13, as well as H12 and H12a on Fir Tree Spur. The defences here were undeniably strong but, because of the terrain, the trenches were not deep and therefore did not offer the protection from a howitzer barrage that a trench on the Western Front might have given.

Like a scene from a Cecil B. DeMille epic, Maoris and Australians draw a water tank up a steep slope from Anzac Cove.

The author found the same ridge today while making the ascent to Plugge's Plateau Cemetery. An idea of what a logistical nightmare the Gallipoli campaign must have been is that everything landed here had to be moved by hand or mule, including all large equipment. Steve Newman comments that 'on the scorching hot day I made this climb, I was glad of having nothing more to carry than a couple of cameras — what it must have been like in the summer of 1915 is best left to the imagination.'

Indian AT mule carts moving supplies near Gully Ravine.

But for the increased vegetation and the decrease in human occupants, the scene here has changed little since 1915 and one is almost awaiting one of the faithful carts to come around the corner! Many old dug-outs and one-man shelters lie in these hills which have helped to speed up their erosion.

Lieutenant-General Hunter-Weston, who was now in command of VIII Corps, appointed Major-General de Lisle to command the operation. He was given an almost free hand in the planning and consequently it was decided to use up almost a third of the entire supply of artillery shells available to support this one attack. This would make the shell per yard ratio the highest yet on the British section of the front. Some 16,000 rounds, nearly 5,000 more than was actually sanctioned, would be fired and by the end of the day only 22,000 shells remained in stock in the entire southern sector.

Major-General de Lisle planned the operation most thoroughly, realising that many of his officers were only recently landed and were yet to get their bearings properly. The barrage was to commence at 0900 hours and be joined at 1020 by field artillery that would cut any wire entanglements that the Turks might have erected. At 1045, the barrage would move off the stronghold known as Boomerang Redoubt and at this moment it would be charged by a battalion of the 87th Brigade. At 1100, the entire barrage would cease and the remainder of the 87th Brigade would attack the first three lines of defences around Gully Spur and Gully Ravine. At the same time the 156th Brigade was to assault its objectives near Fir Tree Spur whilst the Indian Brigade advanced along the cliffs to protect the left flank.

If these objectives were successfully taken, the 86th Brigade were then to attack J12 and J13 and try to occupy a nullah that ran off Gully Ravine. On reaching J13, the Indians would then spread out from the cliffs and occupy an east-facing trench called J11a. The units were to attack in three waves: assaulting parties first followed by supports and reserves. All were to leave their heavy packs behind because of the intense heat, and instead a triangular piece of biscuit tin was to be attached to the back of each man so that artillery spotters could see how far the troops had penetrated. In theory this may have seemed like a good idea but, as casualties mounted, artillery spotters were unable to tell the difference between men taking cover and those who had been killed. The end result was that the spotters often saw triangles reflecting near objectives that belonged only to the dead. From the distance at which they were observing, they frequently believed that these casualties were men holding positions that in reality were still firmly in Turkish hands.

June 28 turned out to be another sweltering day but, having seen and heard the barrage, the men preparing to go over the top were confident of success. The first men to charge were those of the Border Regiment who stormed the Boomerang Redoubt and then Turkey Trench. Although suffering losses they succeeded in capturing not only the strong point but over 100 prisoners. Then at 1100 hours, as the guns increased their range to target Turkish positions to the rear, the troops on both sides of Gully Ravine started to push forwards.

On Gully Spur itself, where the artillery barrage had been centred, men of the 87th Brigade swept through the first two lines of Turkish defences unhindered.

However to the right of Gully Ravine, on Fir Tree Spur, where the barrage had not been as concentrated, things were not going

A heavy barrage is bought down on the Turkish lines on the left of the front near Krithia.

as well. The Royal Scots made a gallant charge and succeeded in taking the first two lines of the Turkish defences but they, in turn, lost most of their officers including their commanding officer who was mortally wounded. To the right were the men of the Scottish Rifles. On their stretch of the line not a single high explosive shell had fallen and the resulting casualties that the unshaken Turkish troops were to inflict were predictably horrendous. Within five minutes, this regiment lost 25 of its 26 officers and over 400 men before the remnants of the shattered unit pulled back to their starting positions. Over on the extreme left, some men managed to make contact with the Royal Scots and then joined them in defending the old Turkish front line which they had somehow managed to overrun.

Major-General de Lisle, realising all was not going well on the right, ordered two further companies of the Scottish Rifles forward to renew the attack but without artillery support this was doomed to failure. After suffering the same fate as the initial wave, these men were soon back in their own front line, having gained nothing but heavy casualties. On Gully Spur, things had gone much better but, after gaining a lot of ground including trenches J12 and J13 that led to the all-important nullah, the Turks were now fighting back hard. Following a barrage, the Turks sent in bombing parties who made some inroads into the British gains.

The Gurkhas and the Royal Munster Fusiliers then counter-attacked and succeeded in recapturing the edge of the nullah after some heavy fighting. By nightfall the position had changed hands again as the Turks captured the nullah after fierce hand-to-hand fighting. Major-General de Lisle, realising the importance of securing the nullah, sent further troops through Gully Ravine to try and outflank the Turks who were now holding the extreme end of J12. These troops became increasingly exposed as they worked their way up the ravine but, even after losing all their officers, the men made valiant further attempts to take J12 but all to no avail.

On the right, the failure of the Scottish Rifles to make any headway against the Turkish positions left de Lisle little option but to send the 88th Brigade up to the line. They were to try and take the heavily defended positions here after a bombardment that was in effect only a token effort. Predictably, the men of the Essex Regiment and the Royal Scots fared no better than the 156th Brigade who had suffered so heavily here earlier. On hearing of the losses

Left: French soldiers at Helles digging what appears to be either a reserve line or more graves. Right: Where once men toiled, only fields of ripening wheat now stand. Just visible on the extreme right of the picture is the Turkish memorial to the Gallipoli campaign — which today is known to the Turks as the Canakkale War.

It is a battle of which Turks are justly proud bearing in mind the awesome reputation of the Royal Navy and British Army of the time. Whilst some accounts rather lavishly describe the Allies as being driven into the sea, it is perhaps fairer to reflect on the bravery and endurance of all participants.

from these units, Major-General de Lisle ordered up a battalion of the Hampshire Regiment to relieve the beleaguered remnants holding this section of the front line. Tactically, at least on the left, important gains had been made but the casualties for the day were once again horrendous, some 3,800 men having joined the growing casualty lists with over 1,350 of these coming from the 156th Brigade alone — nearly half their entire complement.

Whilst all this had been going on, the French had made a bold attempt to seize the defensive works known as the Quadrilateral. This position had been the main reason that their successes of June 21 had not been exploited further. Following a barrage that lasted little more than an hour, French Colonial troops managed to storm the works whereupon they defied fierce and determined Turkish counter-attacks. Lieutenant-General Hunter-Weston was delighted by this news as it removed the main obstacle of an advance by the British right, and he immediately started to plan the advance on Achi Baba although it was agreed that little more could be done until the 52nd Division were landed.

The Turks, having realised the threat now posed by the Allied gains made on both flanks, started to organise counter-attacks. The first was against the Gurkhas near Gully Spur on the night of June 30 which regained a little ground but cost them heavily.

The following night the Turks attacked again. At first, they gained ground but a bold response by men of the Inniskilling Fusiliers recaptured all that had been lost. It was thus even more unfortunate that muddled orders received by the Inniskillings led them to believe that they were to fall back to a nearby barricade whereupon the Turks quickly occupied the deserted position.

The following night (July 2), believing that the Inniskillings had been forced to withdraw and encouraged by his recent success, a local Turkish commander ordered an attack right across the salient that had now formed. At about 1800 hours, scores of Turkish soldiers could be seen advancing near Fusilier Bluff but this attack was stopped in its tracks by the guns of HMS *Scorpion* which was lying just of the coast. A little more than an hour later the Turks renewed this attack but the terrain over which they were

Life in the trenches on the peninsula. Above, using an SMLE fitted with periscopic sniper equipment to prevent exposing the firer to counter-fire and, below, general living conditions in the front line. Note the shaved head to reduce the misery of the ever-present lice, and the wooden box periscope lying on the sandbags on the left.

to cross was very exposed and they had to cross 400 yards of open ground before reaching the British lines. As had happened at Anzac on May 19, the Gurkhas were falling over themselves to get a piece of the action in the firing line. Added to this, British shrapnel shells were taking a huge toll on the advancing infantry, the result was that very few Turks got nearer than 50 yards of their objective. Patrols sent out that night reported that the ground was literally carpeted with the dead.

The Turks were now becoming increasingly alarmed at the situation in the southern sector and three more divisions were rushed to the area with the intention of launching an offensive against the whole British front. The date for this operation was set for July 5.

At dawn on the 5th, following a bombardment that had had little effect, the Turks began to advance but, as wave after wave appeared, they were mown down in their hundreds. Almost immediately, when it became apparent that the attack was destined to fail, Turkish officers could no longer persuade their men to leave the trenches. Only in one place, on a front held by the Anson Battalion of the Royal Naval Division, did the Turks penetrate the British front line and even here they were quickly driven back for little loss. Between June 28 and July 5, the Turks lost nearly 16,000 men and it was admitted by them to have been the most costly action so far on the peninsula. Nevertheless, as we have already seen, the British and French were not in any state to launch a counter-offensive and so the Turks were given ample time to re-organise their line and bring more fresh troops to the area.

In front of the British lines lay a sea of carnage which, in the stifling heat, quickly became a huge health hazard. A Turkish request for an armistice was refused, the reason for this being that the British believed that any fresh Turkish troops, which they thought would soon arrive in the area, would not attack over their own dead. On balance, this seems somewhat unlikely as the Turks rarely showed the same respect for their dead as the Allies showed to theirs. Maybe if the commanders had been forced to live alongside thousands of decaying corpses, a cease-fire would have been forthcoming.

Although the British and French wanted to exploit the weakness in the Turkish lines, they were powerless to do so. Supplies

This is the slope where Gully Ravine meets Gully Beach, which housed various HQs throughout the campaign, as well as being an important communications route. Over 80 years later, many of the cliff faces around the ravine have become far less steep than they were in 1915. Note also how the open water source of 'then' has become the tidy rock-lined well of 'now'.

of artillery shells were critically low and it had already been proven time and time again that any advance without adequate support from the big guns only ended in a futile loss of life. Yet even if the artillery had been ready, it is doubtful that the men of the Royal Naval Division, who had been holding the sector of the line that joined the French sector, could be asked to go over the top again. After nine weeks in the trenches, both officers and men were suffering from total mental and physical exhaustion, not to mention dysentery. This division was now only a shadow of the fighting force which had originally landed and it had to be subsequently withdrawn from the front for a rest.

The 52nd Division, whose final brigade was landed on the morning of July 3, were now to spearhead the next attack. Of the four brigades in this newly-landed division, only the 156th Brigade had seen front line service. This had been during the attack on June 28 when it suffered 50 per cent casualties, an action from which it was still trying to recover. Added to the 52nd Division were some troops from the 13th Division who were only to be used for defensive purposes. They had been sent across from England to take part in the 'great new offensive' and Sir Ian was keen to keep them fresh and at full strength.

So it was that the third attack in this series, this time to advance in the centre to straighten the line, was delayed and delayed until a date was finally set for July 12. The attack was to take place on the right of the British front, between the Krithia Road on the right and Achi Baba Nullah on the left, with the right flank in the French sector near the Rognon system of defences. Rather surprisingly, the attack on the British front was to be carried out in two phases. The first on the right was to be at 0735 hours whilst the second was to come some nine hours later at 1650 to enable the artillery to accurately concentrate on each section of the line at a time. Contingency plans had been drawn up so that if the first phase was immediately successful, the second could go ahead straight away. The French would attack at the same time as the British, the combined manpower amounting to about 12,500 troops.

Just before the battle commenced, thanks to some accurate aerial reconnaissance, the objective of the 157th Brigade, a Turkish trench designated E12, was found to be barely deep enough to conceal a man lying down. It was therefore realised that the chances of holding this against determined counter-attacks were not good so orders were amended at the last minute to instruct only a few look-out posts to occupy E12. Instead, the main force, was now to take shelter in the much deeper E11 that ran about 150 yards in front of E12. Unfortunately this change of plan was not received by all the officers taking part and, to add to the confusion, orders were given for all maps to be left behind to prevent them from falling into enemy hands. As a security measure this seems to have had far more to lose by the confusion it caused for the British were only using copies of captured Turkish maps!

The morning of July 12 was breathless and sweltering, typical for Gallipoli at that time of year. As the barrage ended the British and French troops moved off. Men of the Royal Scots Fusiliers were the first to reach the trenches where the high explosive shells had done their work but from here on it was not so easy. Groups of Turks stubbornly defended the labyrinth of unfinished earthworks that were now choked with the dead and wounded. The Royal Scots fought on bravely and, in spite of losing all their officers bar one and 50 per cent of the rank and file, they still succeeded in making contact with the French on their right.

The men of the King's Own Scottish Borderers were attacking to the left of the Royal Scots. After quickly taking the first two trenches, they pushed on towards their final objective: trench E11. However, it turned out that this had not been completed and the KOSBs were destined to lose over 60 per cent of their strength, including their commanding officer, trying to establish themselves in a trench that offered no cover.

Meanwhile, the French were suffering too. They had succeeded in linking up with the Royal Scots in a Turkish reserve trench and had made limited gains against the Rognon defences. Little of this was known at HQ where contradictory messages reporting some successes were filtering through. The question now was: had the operation been a complete success and, if so, should the planned afternoon attack go ahead straight away or later on as scheduled? However, by the time the position had become clearer, there was no point in sending the men in the second phase over the top without a bombardment to assist them. This meant that the afternoon attack was to go ahead as originally planned. Indeed, the French, having gained some ground and seen the British do the same, were now enthusiastic to renew the

Corporal William Smith, B Company, 1/4th King's Own Scottish Borderers. Missing in action July 12, 1915, aged 21. He is commemorated today on the Helles Memorial and in the memory of his family through this memorial card.

offensive. They, too, now promised troops for the afternoon attack that was scheduled for 1650 hours.

The softening up barrage lasted about an hour and was then followed by an assault by the 157th Brigade. The 1/7th Highland Light Infantry succeeded in pushing through all three lines of Turkish defences and it was only when they reached their objective — the trench E12 — that they discovered that it was little more than a shallow ditch that had been virtually destroyed by the barrage. The men of the 1/7th Highland Light Infantry tried to hold this feature but, as casualties mounted in this exposed and undefendable position, they were forced to retire to E11.

In the centre, the Argyll and Sutherland Highlanders succeeded in not only capturing part of E12 but also two further trenches in advance of this position. On the extreme left, around Achi Baba Nullah, men of the 1/6th Highland Light Infantry, supported by men from the 1/5th Battalion of the same regiment, managed, after some tough fighting, to secure the gains made on the left. Once the position was consolidated, men from the Royal Marine Light Infantry took over and the Scottish troops withdrew. Over on the right, the 155th Brigade and the French had made only slight gains.

The British now bought up what reserves they could muster to take over the old front line and help repel any Turkish counter-attack that might be forthcoming. A Petty Officer of the Royal Naval Division records the scene: 'Terrific bombardment by land and sea. Advance commenced at 9.30 very successful so far. Turkish trenches absolutely indescribable. Awful slaughter from monitors fire. Dead actually six deep in places. Terrible sights near redoubt which was taken and lost six times before finally resting with the KOSB. Absolute field of death.'

As the morning of July 13, dawned, one strange incident occurred that added to the confusion at HQ and nearly led to the entire previous day's work being undone. Following the dawn stand-to, an order was passed along parts of the front to start thinning the line. Thinking that a general withdrawal had been ordered, the trickle soon became a torrent as men clamoured not to be left behind with the result that for a time the front line was unmanned. Luckily, the Turks did not realise the advantage and officers from various regiments quickly rallied their troops to reoccupy the front line trenches before they realised what had happened.

Lieutenant-General Hunter-Weston received exaggerated reports of this incident and became hugely worried about a Turkish position in the 52nd Division's sector that had not yet been taken. He therefore asked Sir Ian if he could renew the offensive that afternoon, using the worn-out troops of the Royal Naval Division and Royal Marine Light Infantry. With permission granted, the new attack was set for 1630 hours. The battalions chosen were the Chatham, Nelson and Portsmouth from the aforementioned divisions. Alas, none were issued with amended trench maps and no one saw fit to explain to them that the trench E12 on this part of the front was incomplete and therefore impossible to defend. To make matters worse, it was decided that because the communication trenches were so clogged with casualties, the troops would start their attack from the old British front line. This ill-thought-out plan meant that they would be exposed to Turkish fire for far longer than was otherwise necessary.

The troops, who did not receive these orders until 1500 hours, were still some 20 minutes away from their start line when the short bombardment came to an end. By the time they were in a position to start their attack, the Turks had recovered and were ready and waiting. On the right the Chatham Battalion made no headway at all while the Portsmouth Battalion, who were attacking the centre, came under heavy shrapnel fire. By the time they reached the most advanced of the British trenches that were held by the 1/7th Highland Light Infantry, they had already suffered severe casualties. Still they pushed on and gallantly succeeded in taking E12 for the second time in 24 hours. However, as we have already seen, this trench was untenable and the few survivors were quickly forced to withdraw.

An even more bitter blow was about to befall the men of the Nelson Battalion who had been ordered to take E12a and E12b. Having suffered the same shrapnel ordeal as the Portsmouth Battalion, as well as machine-gun fire from the flanks, they eventually reached their objective. However, as they leapt into the newly 'captured' trench believing they had achieved their goal, they soon discovered that it was already held by men of the 52nd Division. Headquarters had got it seriously wrong. This advance to capture a position that had been already taken — added to the futile attack by the Chatham and Portsmouth Battalions — cost some 500 men and 24 officers, including both Royal Marine Light Infantry commanding officers.

Whilst the British and Commonwealth dead lie in over 30 cemeteries scattered across the peninsula, the French have been concentrated almost to a man in the cemetery that overlooks Morto Bay. Although some lie in individual graves, others are massed in five large ossuaries situated around the base of the tower — a feature of many French war cemeteries.

Meanwhile, the French attack had been successful. Although little ground had been gained on the British flank, the centre of the French line had at last succeeded in pushing the Turks back to the final defendable position on Kereves Dere.

Reinforcements were sent up to the line throughout the night of July 13 and by dawn on the 14th most of the gains had been secured. The two day's fighting had cost the Allies some 4,000 casualties, while the Turks suffered around 9,000. More importantly for morale, was the fact that the Turks had been soundly beaten and evicted from trenches that they had been improving and strengthening for weeks. However, so tired and under-strength were both the British and French that these gains could not be immediately exploited.

With this battle finished, there came the conclusion of the 'limited' offensives that had been ordered since the close of the Third Battle of Krithia in early June. In spite of some 12,500 Allied casualties and over 30,000 Turkish, little had been achieved to improve the tactical position of either side. It is true the Allies had made some important gains which, if exploited, could well have led to victory. The commanders, however, were fully aware when they launched these attacks that they could not support any sustained offensive; therefore the gains to casualties ratio, and wisdom of them, have to be called into question.

Now, a major new offensive was planned in the Anzac sector from where Sir Ian believed any break-out would have to come. Fresh troops were arriving all the time but, following the events of April, security was now acknowledged to be an important issue. This was to herald the most critical stage of the campaign since the initial landings over three months previously. As one diary extract written in July (which also shows that security was still not as tight as Sir Ian may have hoped) enthuses: 'Rumoured new landing at Suvla, object to cut off supplies from reaching Achi Baba. Great possibilities if landing is successful. Could be the turning point of the entire campaign.'

NEW ARMY, NEW HOPE, NEW OFFENSIVE, OLD LEADERSHIP.

Above: View taken looking southwards over part of the Anzac sector showing No. 2 Outpost, the Sphinx and Plugge's Plateau. Below: Today New Zealand No. 2 Cemetery (rather confusingly just 100 yards from No. 2 Outpost Cemetery) nestles in the fold of ground in the foreground whilst the buildings behind are the workshops of the Commonwealth War Graves Commission. The distinctive outcrop is the Sphinx whilst to the right we can see Plugge's Plateau and then finally the headland of Ari Burnu.

THE PLAN

The original plan formulated by General Birdwood that had been adopted by Sir Ian Hamilton had been somewhat enlarged because of the news from London that a fourth division was being released to take part in the make or break August offensive. The politicians who had backed the scheme, albeit in some cases very reluctantly, now realised that anything less than success at Gallipoli could possibly spur other eastern countries to rise against the British, having seen that Great Britain was not invincible.

The new operation was set to take place in two stages. The first assault was to come from the Anzac sector at night, the aim being to capture Chunuk Bair and the following morning to seize Battleship Hill, 400 Plateau and Baby 700 before moving on to Gun Ridge. As more ground became available, extra troops were to be landed to reinforce the offensive which was given Maidos (an objective of April 25) as its goal. Success here would, as the original plan intended, cut off the Turkish troops holding back the British in the Helles sector.

The launch had originally been scheduled for July but, due to delays in troops arriving and becoming acclimatised, it was to be August before the number required would be in place to give the plan a reasonable chance of success. However these extra few weeks also gave the Turks a chance to strengthen their defensive positions on the northern flank. This was done to such an extent, that the British commanders were forced to rethink.

The main problem now facing the Allied command was that of space. The number of troops required to capture the objectives already mentioned outweighed those that could be physically housed on the narrow scrap of land held by the Anzacs.

Added to this, all the extra troops would have to be hidden from Turkish observers to avoid alerting them to the imminent new offensive. It became clear from all this that the only possibility of the operation being a success was to mount a second landing that could quickly link up with Anzac. It was hoped that not only would this throw the Turks into disarray but it would also supply the extra space required for the landing of both troops and supplies. To the south of Anzac, the possibility of landing successfully was virtually nil. All the suitable beaches were protected by wire entanglements and defended by machine guns and no one wanted a repeat performance of the abortive landings on W or V Beaches. So it had to be to the north where the virtually undefended Suvla Bay, less than five miles from Anzac, became the favoured location. The only defensive positions at Suvla were some small outposts that doubled up as look-out posts for Turkish artillery spotters. Over the past few months, Anzac troops had regularly raided these outposts in an attempt to cut down the accuracy of the Turkish shelling. In all these raids, the losses had been small, reinforcing the belief that this area was only lightly defended.

The geography of the location, as with most of the peninsula, lent itself to the defender. The plan was, however, to quickly seize the high ground that surrounds the Suvla plain on three sides which, if executed promptly, would see the British entrenched on the high peaks before the Turks were able to get troops in to the area in any strength. This, in turn, would make the British the defenders of this easily-held position and would also mean the Turks would be unable to oversee the beach-head. A secure beach-head would then allow supplies and more troops to land quickly and a major push inland to become a real possibility. The whole idea relied on speed of action and initiative, things that had often been sadly lacking in Allied strategy thus far.

To the north of the landing area, running west to east, is the ridge known as Kiretch Tepe. This joins with the south-oriented Tekke Tepe that at nearly 900 feet and less than four miles from the coast is probably the most dominant feature. The final ridge, slightly to the south of the main landing area, is that of the Anafarta Spur. This starts near the coast with a cluster of hills, known to the British as Chocolate Hill, Green Hill and Scimitar Hill, before it forms an undulating ridge known as the W Hills that peak at a maximum of about 350 feet.

The landing itself was to take place near centre of the curved Suvla Bay, just to the north of what was to become known as 'the Cut'. The Cut is itself a small inlet to the Salt Lake which, while flooded in the winter months, dries out completely during the summer.

To help with the landing, motor lighters were being brought in from England which would allow troops to get ashore far quicker than they had been able to on April 25. The lighters were the forerunners of the modern landing craft and they could sail in only a

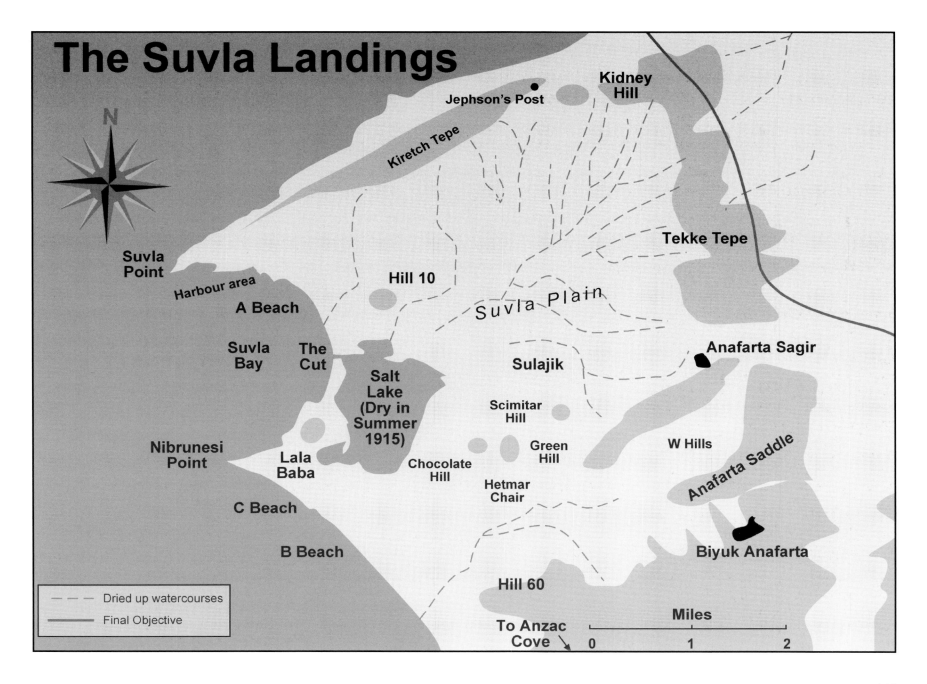

The Suvla Landings

Jephson's Post

Kidney Hill

Kiretch Tepe

Tekke Tepe

Suvla Point

Harbour area

A Beach

Hill 10

Suvla Plain

Suvla Bay

The Cut

Salt Lake (Dry in Summer 1915)

Sulajik

Anafarta Sagir

Scimitar Hill

Nibrunesi Point

Lala Baba

Chocolate Hill

Green Hill

W Hills

Anafarta Saddle

C Beach

Hetmar Chair

B Beach

Biyuk Anafarta

Hill 60

To Anzac Cove

- - - Dried up watercourses

——— Final Objective

Miles

0   1   2

View from the Nek looking northwards to Suvla Bay, the Salt Lake and Kiretch Tepe ridge.

few feet of water. In addition, the Navy had received a quantity of torpedo netting and, with this strung across the bay, it was confident of being able to give unhindered fire support without the fear of losses to German submarines. Anzac troops had already been ashore to the south of Suvla to search for and destroy Turkish guns believed to be in the vicinity. Following favourable reports from these troops throughout June, Sir Ian decided that this area should also be used as a landing beach.

The *Mauritania*, the sister ship to the ill-fated *Lusitania*, arriving at Mudros harbour. Many former luxury liners (including the *Olympic*, the sister ship of the *Titanic* and the *Britannic*) were used to ferry troops from Britain. Their speed was often the only defence against German submarines.

As June passed into July, with fresh troops arriving all the time, London also released a further two divisions although these would not arrive in time to take part in the initial landing. Sir Ian feared that with every day's delay the Turks were improving and strengthening their positions, and it was with this thought in mind that he decided to start the attack without waiting for the additional troops to arrive.

His immediate strength of four fresh divisions would, he believed, be sufficient. Two of these divisions would join the troops already ashore at Anzac whilst the third would land at Suvla and on the following day be reinforced by the fourth. This would then form IX Corps which would be under the command of Lieutenant-General Sir Frederick Stopford. On leaving London, Stopford was so weak that he could not carry his own briefcase making him a strange choice for a command that was crying out for a dynamic commander. It is from his appointment that one of the most contentious issues of the entire campaign arises with many people blaming him for the Suvla landings ending in failure. Others will point out in his defence that he only ever received suggestions and ideas, never direct orders, regarding the capture of specific objectives. The truth probably lies some where in the middle. Due to a security clamp down which was verging on paranoia, no one was being properly briefed, and this included the unfortunate Stopford.

Under the weight of men and equipment, landing both by day and night, the sorting of supplies in Mudros harbour was becoming a shambles. The men ashore started calling it 'Imbros, Mudros and bloody chaos'; meanwhile, boats still continued to arrive, haphazardly loaded. It was not until an Inspectorate-General was appointed on the orders of Sir Ian that matters started to improve. Brigadier-General The Hon. Herbert Alexander Lawrence and Major-General Sir Edward Altham, must take the majority of the credit for the vastly improved situation.

In mid-July plans were afoot to make sure that any wounded would not have to go through the ordeal that many men suffered on April 25. Surgeon-General William Birrell, had been appointed as Medical Services Director and, on being told of the new offensive, had worked night and day to ensure medical attention would be sufficient. One bone of contention was that Birrell was working on a figure of 30,000 casualties in the first three days but Sir Ian reduced this number to 20,000. Another was that a new system had been put in place giving three different officers command over certain stages of a wounded man's journey but unfortunately nobody was quite sure where one person's area of responsibility ended and the next started. Nevertheless, the positive side of all this medical reorganisation was that some 300 extra doctors and nurses had been allocated to both Mudros and the hospital ships which were to anchor off the beach in pairs. As the wounded arrived on board they were to be classified by the nature of their wounds. Lightly wounded men were to be placed on trawlers waiting on the far side of the ship from where they would be moved to nearby temporary hospital ships that were equipped just for dealing with light wounds. The more seriously wounded would remain on board the hospital ship until it was full. As soon as this happened, it was to steam full speed for Mudros. On leaving, an empty hospital ship returning from Mudros would take over the berth just offshore. Six hospital ships were to continue this shuttle service until enough territory had been taken to allow proper medical facilities to be set up ashore.

Although the logistics were gradually being sorted out, the plans for the landing were still to be finalised and, indeed, the date

One of the hospital ships leaves Mudros for Gallipoli (above) to collect wounded. The snapshot (below) shows seriously wounded men being loaded onto the deck of the *Grantully Castle* — some 90,000 men were evacuated sick.

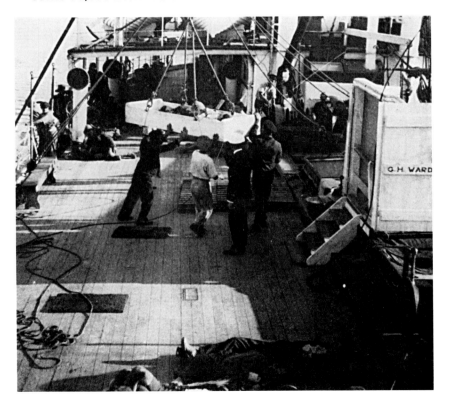

was still to be set. Approximately three to four days would be required to get the two divisions ashore at Anzac without arousing Turkish suspicions. This, combined with the necessity for adequate moonlight, led to the landing being scheduled for the night of August 6/7. The moon on this night would rise two hours after midnight, assisting the troops who by then would be ashore, the pitch black prior to this helping to cover the initial landing.

To the south at Helles no fresh troops were to be put ashore, the plan here being purely defensive, apart from some feint attacks to divert reinforcements away from Anzac. At one stage, Sir Ian had wanted the 29th Division to be attached to IX Corps as he felt that their professionalism and experience would help the men of Kitchener's New Army in taking their objectives. Sir Ian was eventually talked out of the idea by some of his staff officers who thought the strain on men being ordered to land twice on a hostile shore would be too much. As will be seen, even though these troops were exhausted and understrength, landing them may well have tipped the scale in Britain's favour yet most of the officers and men who had gone ashore on April 25 were by this stage either dead, sick, or wounded.

The New Army was comprised of men who had volunteered in 1914 in answer to Kitchener's call for new recruits. Many had enlisted with their mates from their home towns and whilst this made for a great 'team spirit', it did have its down side. When casualties were heavy — as they would be at both Gallipoli and later on the Somme — it would all but wipe out the menfolk from one area. However, these troops of the New Army were eager to see action and prove themselves and, after some ten months' training, they now felt ready. Most of these units were led by regular officers but this was, in many ways, a false economy as the majority were over 50 years of age and veterans of wars that, in scale and types of weapons used, might well have been from another era.

Thus it was that the men of the First New Army, or 'K1' as they were commonly known, would spearhead the landing at Suvla without the benefit of having the support of troops who had been underfire before. Added to this, the tight security that surrounded the entire operation meant that no one had been trained to attack at night and seize a range of hills that had not been accurately reconnoitred. Sir Ian however insisted upon this secrecy, even to

The remains of the trenches at Lone Pine looking towards Chunuk Bair with Lone Pine Cemetery on the extreme right. This photo was taken by a member of the Imperial War Graves Commission during their work on the battlefields after the war.

An indication of just how well nature heals its scars can be gauged from this picture. The cemetery is just out of view on the right whilst Johnston's Jolly Cemetery lies on the left. Further up the hill can be seen the Turkish cemetery which marks Quinn's Post, whilst higher still are the Nek and Baby 700 and, surmounting them, Chunuk Bair.

the extent that many of the senior officers did not know the true objective until the last minute. It is rather strange therefore that in a number of diaries of ordinary soldiers already on the peninsula, many start mentioning the rumours of a landing at Suvla as early as the middle of July. In many ways this proves that the security was not as tight as was hoped and, by not briefing his officers properly, Sir Ian was hindering rather than helping the situation. A lot of officers would be set ashore at Suvla having just been given an out-of-date map with no idea of the geography of the area or what their objective really was.

As July moved into August, the final plan on which the entire campaign now rested was completed. At Helles there would be a feint along about a mile front, once again divided into morning and afternoon phases. The objectives were very limited and only in the case of a miraculous breakthrough were any reinforcements to be put ashore.

At Anzac the plan was far more complex. The operation was to begin with an attack on the heavily defended Lone Pine position. Although primarily a diversion, any ground gained here would be invaluable if the advance went as planned. As night fell, silent attacks on Turkish outposts guarding the entrances to the gullies that led to the heights of Sari Bair were to be carried out by Maori troops. The total surprise and silence of this action would be a key to the success or failure of the whole operation. If all had gone well up to this point, the next and most important stage of the operation was to take place. The main assaulting columns would now advance and try to seize the heights of Hill (Point) 971 (Koja Chemen Tepe), Hill Q and Chunuk Bair. It was hoped that these positions could be seized before dawn at which time the right-hand flank could sweep down and capture Baby 700 and Battleship Hill. This was to be supported by a simultaneous attack by troops from Russell's Top attacking The Nek. The whole plan was reliant on things going well throughout each stage; any hold up could cause major problems or possibly the complete failure of the whole endeavour.

Meanwhile, shortly after 2200 hours, the first troops would be landed at Suvla just to the south of Nibrunesi Point. The 11th Division, who were to be first ashore, had received strict instructions as to their objectives. One battalion was to seize the small hill close to the coast known as Lala Baba whilst the second was to march around the bay and take the Turkish outpost near Suvla Point. As soon as this position was captured, the battalion was to push on to the Kiretch Tepe ridge and clear the crest, thus securing the northern flank. A further two battalions were to be despatched against Chocolate Hill and the W Hills and, having secured these positions, they were to then proceed to the Tekke Tepe ridge. If all these objectives had been taken by first light on the 7th, two brigades of the 10th Division, which were to be landed at dawn, would advance towards Anafarta Sagir and help the Anzac troops with their assault on Hill 971.

Unfortunately, the plan for attacking Chocolate Hill and the W Hills had, through lack of reconnaissance due to the security paranoia, a fatal flaw. Troops landing to the south of Nibrunesi Point were being asked to march away from their objectives and around the dried out Salt Lake and attack Chocolate Hill from the north. The reason for this strange route was twofold. Firstly, there were fears that the southern approaches were defended with wire and prepared positions, whereas the northern approach was known to be undefended since Anzac troops had wandered around this area in their attempt to destroy a Turkish gun back in June.

The second reason for taking such a circuitous route was that no one was actually sure whether the dried out Salt Lake could

Looking across the Salt Lake towards Lala Baba from Chocolate Hill today. It was over this flat, exposed land that the men of the 2nd Mounted Division marched under accurate Turkish shrapnel fire to take part in the assault on August 21.

support infantry. It was feared that if it was not completely dry the troops might become bogged down in a muddy quagmire. Security restrictions had banned reconnaissance aircraft from overflying this area for fear of arousing Turkish suspicions. The idea of landing a small party to check out the state of the lake had been suggested but had been rejected for the same reason. The truth was that the bed was dry and easily crossable and the prepared positions that were feared on the southern side of the hills consisted of nothing more than some rusty wire and a few Turkish troops who were under orders to retire if any serious landing was attempted. This lack of understanding over the limits of inexperienced troops marching at night through hostile terrain, combined with the absence of any reconnaissance, was a severe miscalculation on the part of the planners.

The whole plan depended upon surprise rather than superiority in numbers; the other important factor being that of speed. If the high ground could be seized quickly, the plan stood a good chance of success. However, speed — the very thing that would make the plan a success — was also to be its Achilles Heel.

The Turkish viewpoint from the heights near Chunuk Bair, showing the maze of gullies and ravines as well as the commanding view that this position enjoyed. Looking up towards Suvla Bay, a British destroyer is visible just off the coast.

AUGUST 6-7 — THE REALITY

The August offensive, although chiefly based around the Anzac sector, did in actual fact start in the Helles sector. At 1420 hours on August 6, the bombardment commenced against the Turkish front line positions between Gully Ravine and Krithia Nullah. Following this barrage, which slowly increased in ferocity over the next hour, men once again dragged themselves out of their trenches and into battle.

Achi Baba as seen from the site of No. 17 Field Hospital sited on the high ground behind Lancashire Landing Cemetery.

Today golden wheat fields show the way to Achi Baba.

The dust that had been thrown up during the barrage made visibility difficult, especially for the staff officers watching the attack unfold from W Beach. The Turkish guns that had recently been amassed nearby immediately replied and casualties quickly mounted. As the attack progressed, the observers believed all to be going well. They had seen some men reach the Turkish positions and enter them and they could even see some of the reflective triangles the men were wearing near the parapet of the Turks' second line of defence. However, these markers, were worn by both the living and the dead and those visible in the advanced positions were all being worn by the latter. Assuming the attack to have been a success, the order was now given to send in the 1st Munsters (under Guy Geddes of April 25 fame, now holding the temporary rank of Lieutenant-Colonel) to help consolidate the 'gains' yet headquarters was at the same time mystified as to why they were receiving no reports of the advances made. The truth, sadly, was that almost every officer whose job it was to relay information was now lying dead in a hot, dusty and confused no man's land.

For a while, this lack of information was ignored by HQ but eventually the news reached them from the wounded now trickling back that the whole attack had once again been little more than organised suicide. The 1st Munsters eventually reached the front line with little more than 50 men still on their feet. On seeing the situation, Geddes wired HQ asking instructions but, with cold brutality and stubbornness that was so often the hallmark of the campaign's leadership, these few men were also ordered to their deaths. It was not until some time after the men were due to have attacked that the assault was cancelled but fortunately Geddes' refusal to needlessly sacrifice his men had saved their lives. The next order he received made no mention of the doomed attack; instead, he and his men were ordered to 'get as much sleep as possible' while the plans were reconsidered.

Under the cover of darkness, an advanced scouting party of the Manchester Regiment had discovered that their objective had been untouched by the shelling and was instead bristling with Turks. Consequently, the attack on this sector of the line was cancelled but the 88th Brigade, consisting of the 4th Worcesters, 2nd Hampshires, 1st Essex and 1/5th Royal Scots (reserve), had no such luck. Their attack went ahead as scheduled and, at a cost of some 2,000 casualties from the 3,000 men involved, they made no gains at all.

Contemporary panorama of part of the ground covered by the Anzac advance on the night of August 6/7. This photograph was taken looking across towards Suvla Bay. Kiretch Tepe can be seen faintly in the distance with the Salt Lake in front.

Today the view from a position between Walker's Ridge and the Nek has changed little and one can see Lala Baba quite clearly at the mouth of the Salt Lake. Both Chocolate and Green Hills also show up further round. In the foreground to the left can be seen the CWGC workshops close to the shoreline.

The following morning, along part of the line near the position known as the Vineyard that was held by the 42nd Division, the attack was renewed. The 1/6th and 1/7th Lancashire Fusiliers made some small gains but again at a terrible price. Into the night isolated units desperately clung to hard-won ground but one by one they were forced to retreat, all except for a small party near the Vineyard who somehow managed to cling on to their position. Yet this small gain had not only cost a further 1,500 men but it had also failed to keep the Turkish reserves occupied in the southern sector. Following this setback, further offensive action in the Helles sector was abandoned as any further weakening of British strength through more casualties would seriously jeopardise the ability to be able to hold on to the existing positions if the Turks launched a fierce attack.

At 1730 hours on August 6, just as the 88th Brigade had completed its task of being massacred at Helles, troops of the 1st Australian Brigade were preparing to attack at Lone Pine. The Turkish positions here looked out over flat approaches with perfect fields of fire and it was viewed by the Turks as one of their most secure positions. This confidence was well placed but the Australians about to attack here were keen to prove themselves worthy of the Anzac name.

To help the troops reach the Turkish emplacements with minimum casualties, tunnels had been dug under no man's land. As soon as the attack started, the concealed exits were opened and Australian troops poured from them. Most of the men reached the Turkish positions without having come under serious fire but it was from here that the problems really began. Although aerial reconnaissance had provided accurate trench maps of the area, the inexperience of interpreting the same had meant that no one had realised that the trenches were covered with heavy roofing made from pine logs. Some of the most brutal fighting of the campaign now took place as the Australian troops desperately sought a way into this labyrinth. In some places, they tore holes in the roofs before jumping in and setting about any Turks they met whilst others, joined by men approaching from the proper entrances to the tunnels at the rear of the strong point, started to clear the enemy from that direction. In places, the intermixed dead were five or six deep and every traverse and corner brought with it the expectation of a horrid death. By 1830 hours the centre of

A front line Australian trench after the attack on Lone Pine, with dead and wounded lying in the foreground. A soldier watches anxiously from the shelter of the sandbags as a comrade makes his way over the top of the trench with just his legs visible.

One of the captured Lone Pine trenches shortly after the struggle to take it. On the parapet can be seen the dead from both sides, the Australians still wearing their white armbands to help with recognition. Standing in the foreground is an officer of the 2nd Battalion.

the stronghold had been reached and half an hour later orders were given to the 1st Battalion to help with the consolidation of the position.

On hearing of the incredible 'scrap' that was going on at Lone Pine, many men in reserve areas scrambled to join in — a credit to the Anzac spirit. This onrush was only halted when military police were posted to stop it but even the MPs could not deter some who, for either cigarettes or cash, managed to 'join' a unit that was being sent up to Lone Pine. Many deeds of gallantry throughout this action doubtless went unrecorded as all the witnesses were killed but, even so, seven Victoria Crosses were awarded for this one battle and the Lone Pine action became one of legend.

The only negative side was one of misfortune. Reserves of the Turkish 9th Division had been called to assist the defenders of Lone Pine but their orders were later cancelled. However, through a cruel twist of fate, this led to these troops being on the northern flank near Chunuk Bair; exactly where the main thrust of the New Zealand, and indeed, the Allied offensive, was about to emanate.

As the southern flank around Lone Pine settled into the 'routine' of fierce Turkish counter-attacks, the New Zealanders to the north were getting ready for their night assault against the heights. The attack to seize the heights of Hill 971 (Koja Chemen Tepe), Hill Q and Chunuk Bair was not only the catalyst of this new offensive but also central to the entire campaign. The plan that had been drawn up to overcome these huge obstacles was both intricate and detailed, the only problem being that it was probably too detailed and the margin allowed for errors too small. Mistakes were to be, perhaps unsurprisingly, a common feature in the night advance towards the heights. The plan consisted of a left and right covering force which were to capture the lower foothills. Following on were the two main assaulting columns which would 'overtake' these forces and then push on towards their objectives. The main problem was that the two columns, (left and right as we shall now call them), were to advance along unknown routes at night. Added to this, the Greek guides were at best unreliable and at worst more of a hindrance than a help. Some officers and NCOs had been allowed the freedom of Anzac and the use of a destroyer offshore to view the terrain but, as a preparation for a night march with tired troops, this was probably of little practical use.

The first troops to advance were those of the right covering force. This body, consisting of the Wellington, Auckland, Canterbury and Otago Mounted Rifles, as well as a Maori contingent and some engineers, was approximately 2,000 strong. The plan here was for the Wellington and Auckland Regiments to take Old No. 3 Post, Destroyer Hill and the Table Top, while the Otago and Canterbury Regiments, assisted by the Maoris, were to take Bauchop's Hill and force the Turkish units there back across the Aghyl Dere.

The defences around Old Post No. 3 were known to be strong on its western face but to the south they were light and it was from this direction that the men of Auckland and the Maoris were to attack. The plan here had been carefully worked out. At 2100

The cemetery at Lone Pine (above left) and the Lone Pine Memorial (above right) recording the names of nearly 7,000 Anzacs who have no known grave. It was so named after a solitary pine tree that once stood here on the southern end of 400 Plateau. Today a single pine again stands sentinel; this time, however, deliberately planted in the middle of the cemetery. Progenies from the original tree survive today in Australia at Melbourne (below left) and Mulwala, New South Wales (centre), and Te Aroha on North Island, New Zealand, (below right), all planted in memory of ' departed comrades'.

Before the August offensive, the left of the Anzac line lay around a group of outposts called Nos. 1, 2 and 3. This soldier's snapshot shows Anzac dugouts at Outpost No. 2.

Other than the introduction of the beautifully-maintained No. 2 Cemetery, and the disappearance of both the tree and telegraph pole, little has changed today in this out-of-the-way spot.

hours exactly, as it had done every other night for the past few weeks, a destroyer would train its searchlight on the position and commence firing. Just before the scheduled conclusion of its brief barrage, at around 2130, the New Zealanders charged forward. Following the routine of the past few weeks, the Turks were still expecting another five minutes' grace and so were completely surprised and quickly overwhelmed, the position being taken with barely a shot being fired.

Shortly afterwards, one squadron of the Wellington battalion took Destroyer Hill after a brief but violent struggle while the remainder of the regiment succeeded in taking Table Top. However the ascent had been a lot steeper than anyone had expected and it was gone midnight by the time the position was secure.

Meanwhile, the Canterbury and Otago units had found the slopes of Bauchop's Hill more heavily defended than had been expected. Although forced to fight in small and isolated groups,

they had still secured this valuable position by around 0100. The Otago's suffered most heavily during this action losing around 100 men out of the 400 who were employed.

The left covering force, consisting of the 4th South Wales Borderers, 5th Wiltshires and men of the 72nd Field Company, Royal Engineers, were making their way towards their objectives as the New Zealanders were taking Bauchop's Hill. After some brief delays, these men captured silently, with the use of the bayonet, a Turkish post at Aghyl Dere. From here they pushed on towards Damakjelik Bair where they were to take another Turkish post, thus securing the northern flank for the main assaulting columns. On reaching the strong point they found it was far more heavily defended than anyone had expected but nevertheless they attacked and, whether out of fear or complete surprise, the Turks surrendered without much of a fight. By 0100 hours, the position was secure and some 200 prisoners had been taken. The first

Left: The grave of Commander Edward Howell Cater who, as beach landing officer at Anzac, was responsible for directing both incoming barges and Anzac fatigue parties. He was killed by shrapnel whilst trying to help the crew of a small boat which had been hit by enemy fire. **Above:** Commander Cater is buried in Beach Cemetery, one of the most beautiful on the whole peninsula. Note the incorrect date of death on the original grave marker which should be August 7.

phase had gone well; the route was now completely open for the more distant objectives of the main assaulting columns, that is if they could manage to find them on this the darkest of nights.

The right assaulting column had been scheduled to start its advance shortly before 2300 hours with the aim of being on top of

Above: The view in 1915 from No. 2 Outpost looking towards the Sari Bair range. Below: No need to avoid snipers today at No. 2 Outpost. In the foreground, just to the left of centre, can be seen Table Top, whilst behind and to the right flanked by trees are the memorials on Chunuk Bair. To the left of this can be seen Rhododendron Spur.

Chunuk Bair an hour before dawn. This force consisted of the New Zealand Infantry Brigade, the 26th Indian Mountain Brigade and a company of New Zealand engineers. Upon hearing firing ahead of him, Brigadier-General Francis Johnston (commanding this force) ordered a halt and it was nearly midnight by the time his column was moving again. The Otago Battalion, who were advancing a little to the north had also been delayed. This was due to having to round up Turkish soldiers who were keen to surrender on the newly-captured Table Top position. Some time was lost but by 0230 the column was once again advancing. Soon after this, the Otagos were supposed to link up with the Canterbury Battalion but the latter had failed to arrive so the Otago's, now within 1,300 yards of the summit of Chunuk Bair, halted. It turned out that the Canterbury Battalion had got hopelessly lost and at dawn they found themselves back at their start point! As the morning light grew stronger, Brigadier-General Johnston's refusal to advance to the summit without this fourth battalion inadvertently started a chain of events that gave the Turks time to rush reinforcements to the top of this crucial crest.

If things were not going well with the right-hand column, much the same can be said of the left, which without doubt had the harder task. The left assaulting column, which had been detailed to seize Hill 971 and Hill Q, began the advance shortly after sunset by a circuitous but lightly defended route with the hope that it would be on top of its objectives by dawn. The column consisted of the 4th Australian Brigade, 29th Indian Brigade, 21st Indian Mountain Battery and the 2nd Field Company of the New Zealand Engineers. The plan was to march via No. 3 Post, around Walden Point and then work up Aghyl Dere. From here, the Indian Brigade would move on Hill Q while the Australian Brigade continued towards Abdul Rahman Spur and then on to Hill 971.

The operation did not start well and it was to be some four hours before the end of the column passed the start point due, in part, to a local guide recommending a short cut that turned out to be a gorge housing Turkish snipers. Whilst these were dealt with time was ticking away. Throughout the night progress was slow, most units spending more time lost and trying to get their bearings than advancing. Shortly before first light it was clear that obtaining their objectives would be beyond them. The 4th Australians had not even reached Abdul Rahman Spur and were

so fatigued that their officers could not encourage the men to go any further. This was in spite of the fact that all opposition had died away and the way to Hill 971 was more open than even the most optimistic of commanders could have dared hope for. Other units had also got hopelessly lost and intermixed. The 1/5th Gurkhas were not to be seen until long after daybreak when they were eventually spotted advancing up Chamchik Punar towards Hill Q. Some members of the 2/10th Gurkhas, having made a wrong turn, now found themselves linking up with the New Zealanders on Rhododendron Spur.

The best efforts, however, were by Major Cecil Allanson and the 1/6th Gurkhas. Throughout the night they had made slow but steady progress and by dawn were less than a 1,000 yards from the summit of Hill Q. With first light came the realisation to the Turks of just how close the Allies were to seizing this important high ground; the race was now on.

Meanwhile, throughout the hours of darkness, thousands of fresh troops had been coming ashore at nearby Suvla Bay. Within 30 minutes some four battalions had been landed, most not even getting their feet wet. Of nearly 10,000 men who came ashore, only one became a casualty — a sailor who stopped a bullet from a lone Turkish soldier who, having fired, disappeared into the night.

The 7th ~~South~~ North Staffords and the 9th Sherwood Foresters quickly moved to the east to guard the right flank while the 6th Yorkshires and the 9th West Yorkshires made for the small hump called Lala Baba. The two companies of the 6th Yorks who were to start the assault were, in fact, also the first New Army troops to go into any attack in the Great War; they would not be the last. The troops now spoiling to give a good account of themselves had not had the best preparation for going into combat. They had already been on their feet for 17 hours; only ever taken part in one aborted night march; were suffering from reactions to recent inoculations, and had only been given inaccurate maps a few hours before — certainly not, the ideal way to enter a war.

As the Yorkshiremen started to advance on Lala Baba, a red flare was fired by the Turks signalling their awareness of the landing. Every second that was lost from that moment on was irretrievable. The Yorks charged up the small mound, suffering heavily as they did so. Particularly hard hit were the junior officers

whose white armbands made them easier targets. Even on gaining the hill, the casualties did not stop as odd Turks took cover in the trenches and scrub to snipe at the British who were by now all around them.

It was from this point that things really started to go wrong. Instead of advancing on Hill 10 as should have been the case, there was now no one left standing who knew what the orders were as most of the officers, including Lieutenant-Colonel Edward Chapman and Major Archibald Roberts, had fallen. Meanwhile, the 9th West Yorks, who were supposed to be right behind them, had become involved in a skirmish all of their own and were making slow progress. Under such circumstances, it is understandable that many of the men who had just seen friends killed or wounded, and had no idea of what was expected of them, just sat down to await orders. Nevertheless, it was not long before the West Yorks fought their way to Lala Baba and met up with the 6th Yorks, who still had not moved.

Orders were eventually issued to try and join up with the men of the 34th Brigade who were by this time coming ashore on A Beach but the link-up was not quick in coming as the men had been landed in uncharted waters. Many of the lighters grounded far out to sea, forcing the men — at least those who could — to swim ashore carrying nearly 200 pounds of kit and all this while under a withering fire from the Turks. On top of this, the 11th Manchesters and the 9th Lancashire Fusiliers had come ashore in completely the wrong place but none the less started

The hill called Lala Baba where the first British volunteers of 'Kitcheners Army' saw action in the Great War. In this photo taken in the summer of 1915, the hill at the mouth of the Salt Lake forms the backdrop to a Maurice Farman MF11 'Shorthorn' that has made a forced landing and lies almost surreally in the foreground.

After an expedition that most mountaineers would have been proud of, the former location of the aircraft was finally discovered by the author. Little evidence of the British tenure at Suvla remains, apart from when the fields are ploughed when relics of the battle come to light.

Left: Hill 10 Cemetery just after the Imperial War Graves Commission completed the erection of permanent walls and uniform — yet temporary — grave markers. We are looking towards Suvla Point and the start of the Kiretch Tepe ridge. Right: An idea of how quickly Suvla has hidden its scars is apparent from this shot.

Apart from the height of the trees, perhaps most surprising is the fact that the original — and presumably only temporary — barbed wire fence has survived and still protects the cemetery today, visible in the foreground of the 1919 shot and to the right on our modern day comparison.

to push forward. It is much to the credit of the 11th Manchesters that by daybreak they had advanced some two miles along the Kiretch Tepe ridge before stiff Turkish resistance halted them. The 9th Lancashire Fusiliers were facing further problems as they desperately tried to find their first objective, Hill 10. They had been told that when they landed it would be directly in front of them but as they had been set down too far south, all they could see in the pitch dark was the outline of the Salt Lake. The officers and NCOs were particularly exposed as they searched for one another and tried to reorganise their men, and they suffered terribly. By noon the following day, the Fusiliers had suffered 60 per cent casualties amongst its officers and some 20 per cent of the rank and file.

By 0300 hours the situation was little short of a shambles. Many men were still grounded out to sea; the Lancashire Fusiliers were roaming around looking for Hill 10 and less than half a division had been landed. The scheme for taking Chocolate Hill and the W Hills was fast becoming impossible due to the decision not

to land the troops intended for this assault on B Beach. At Lala Baba, having tried to make contact once and failing, no further attempts to link up with A Beach were made. There were now six battalions sitting idle while the approaches across the Suvla Plain and on towards the high ground behind lay completely open.

At 0330 hours the Lancashire Fusiliers attacked and took a sand dune that was firmly believed to be Hill 10. Unfortunately it was not but, as they reached the top of this small feature, fire from the real Hill 10 poured down on them inflicting further casualties. By now the whole scene was bedlam. In some places, British units were firing at British units, whilst elsewhere men just sat and awaited orders from commanders who were not even aware they were there.

Meanwhile, on Imbros, Sir Ian waited desperate for information. Cables had been laid to ensure signals could be received promptly but the only message received was sent by a bored telegraphist to his mate on Imbros: 'A little shelling at A has now ceased. All quiet at B.' Although not an official message, and not

View taken from the reconstructed Australian front line at the Nek. Although positioned fairly accurately, the trenches here are far roomier and less claustrophobic than they would have been in 1915 (not to mention the absence of a foul smell). In front can be seen the Nek Cemetery which is situated on part of the old no man's land where the 10th Light Horse suffered such hideous casualties during their attack on August 7.

We had no horses at Anzac. We were serving as infantry and we were all crawling with lice, thirsty, hungry and completely browned off. One of our Generals came up to inspect us in our trenches in front of Lone Pine, and he was a fatherly sort, always used to ask the blokes about their family and stuff like that. He spoke to all the troops and he said to one soldier on the firing step, 'Don't forget to write home. How is your father?' The bloke answered: 'He's dead.' A bit later the General coming back along the trench asked the same question to same soldier, 'And how is your father?' And the bloke said, 'He's still dead, the lucky bugger.' We all laughed. I don't know what the General thought! But the tale went the rounds.

CORPORAL G. GILBERT
A SQUADRON, 13th LIGHT HORSE

addressed to anyone in particular, Sir Ian understandably took it to mean that the landing had been virtually unopposed.

The problems he now faced were with his own side. On board the *Jonquil*, which was now moored in Suvla Bay, Lieutenant-General Stopford and his General Staff brought their mattresses up on deck to sleep. As he settled down for the night, the General confided his grave concerns and doubts over the whole venture although it appears that it did not occur to him to send a staff officer ashore to find out the true situation. Instead, he and his staff were probably the only men — on either side — who were going to get a good night's sleep.

As dawn broke, the men of the Australian Light Horse prepared for their attack on the Nek. The bombardment that was supposed to finish at 0430 actually ceased at 0423 leaving the men wondering whether this was a tactical ruse or a terrible mistake. It was in fact a terrible mistake. As the Turks flooded back into their front line trenches few of the men about to go over the top doubted what lay in store for them. It should be remembered that this attack was supporting the New Zealand units which, it was hoped, would be on top of Chunuk Bair by this time. If that had been the case, and those same New Zealanders had now been working down over Battleship Hill and on towards Baby 700, the attack may have stood a chance. But as we have seen, the troops involved in that night action had failed to take the high ground; consequently the attack on the Nek should have been cancelled straight away. However, it was not and the bravery shown by the Australian troops here defies description.

The attack began at 0430 hours, the men who led it being immediately cut to pieces. Lieutenant-Colonel Alexander White and all his nine officers were killed instantly and within seconds not a man remained standing. Undaunted, the second wave leaped over the parapet and met an identical fate, save for one man carrying a marker flag who reached the Turkish front line only to be killed there. The commander of the third wave from 10th Light Horse, on seeing the result of the first two attempts,

Above: No man's land at the Nek over which the Turks charged on June 29 and the 3rd Australian Brigade on August 7. It is strewn with numerous dead. The Turkish trenches and wire can be seen in the middle distance along with a bomb-catcher on the right. The stench is almost palpable. Left: Taken from the wall of the Nek Cemetery, it is easy to see that this is the same place. Less easy on a bright vibrant summer's day is to imagine the carnage that once took place here. From the Nek it is possible to look across the old Anzac positions in almost every direction which today makes it one of the favourite spots for tour guides to explain the complexities of Anzac and let visitors to the battle-field gain their bearings. This massacre of the 8th and 10th Light Horse is reproduced (although wrongfully showing it as a diver-sion to the British landings at Suvla) in the 1981 Australian feature film *Gallipoli* starring Mel Gibson and Mark Lee.

Left: The plan at Suvla — although never adequately stated — was to gain possession of the high ground that surrounds the plain which could then be used as a beach-head without Turkish artillery spotters being able to overlook it. However, with the Turks maintaining their hold on the high ground, and able to survey the British right under their noses, any movement was liable to attract the prompt attention of Turkish artillery. Here a shell explodes next to a terrified mule near West Beach. Right: No explosions at Suvla today! All around this area lie scattered pieces of debris connected with the campaign, mainly pieces of broken rum jars, although it is still possible to find pieces of shrapnel and the occasional spent bullet.

sought clarification that they were still to attack. His commanding officer, Lieutenant-Colonel Noel Brazier, saw the futility of this action, and tried to persuade headquarters that it was pointless to commit the men to certain death, but to no avail. Convinced that some Australians had reached the Turkish trenches and were in need of support, the third wave was ordered to advance over the bodies of their dead and dying comrades, only to suffer the same fate. Before Brazier could stop them, half the fourth wave had started, and they, too, were mown down. In the space of just a few minutes, some 650 brave men of the Australian Light Horse had been added to Gallipoli's ever growing casualty list. Added to these were some 70 men of the Royal Welsh Fusiliers who also became casualties whilst attacking from Monash Gully. They were attacking in the hope of supporting the New Zealanders who were at this time, still nearly a mile away on Rhododendron Spur.

An attack by the 1st Light Horse around Pope's Hill, after initially achieving a little success, soon petered out. With no support 150 of the 200 men engaged were lost before the survivors retired.

All of these attacks were futile and wasteful. What makes it even worse, is that Turkish records show that only two mountain guns and some 20 men stood between the three battalions of New Zealanders and Chunuk Bair. However, trying to follow the orders he was given, Brigadier-General Johnston still waited for the arrival of his elusive fourth battalion completely unaware of the shambles around him

If the delay in advancing on Chunuk Bair was wasteful, the stagnation at Suvla was verging on the criminal. At 0530 hours, Hill 10 was still in Turkish hands whilst the 34th Brigade were wandering around seeking some kind of purpose. For some unknown reason, the 5th Dorsets and 8th Northumberland

After its capture, Chocolate Hill became an important reserve line for both stores and troops. Here men of the 53rd Welsh Division go about their business.

Taken from part of the Salt Lake that had already dried out, little can be seen to have changed today at Chocolate Hill — which in general is true of most of the Suvla area.

Fusiliers were ordered to dig in near the beach; Lala Baba had now become the 'rest area' for almost the entire 33rd Brigade. All the while, the Turks were pulling back and organising defensive positions around Chocolate Hill and the W Hills. Had a general advance been mounted now across the Suvla Plain it would certainly have captured vital high ground but almost everyone at Suvla seemed ignorant of the importance of a quick response, so

no one moved. Major-General Frederick Hammersley, the General Officer Commanding 11th Division, did originally order a vigorous push on Chocolate and W Hills but after his HQ received a direct hit, his orders became both contradictory and confusing.

All the time the chaos was mounting ashore, it was being increased by the late and confused landing of the 10th Division. Lieutenant-General Stopford, though, still remained aboard ship reasoning that he could exercise more control from there but, as no line of communication to the shore had yet been set up, it is hard to imagine an officer in command of such a large operation being less in control. With Hammersley's confused orders continuing to contradict reports reaching the Brigade Commanders, little was ever likely to be achieved under these circumstances.

It was now decided that the 34th Brigade were too tired and 'done up' after their exertions through the night to take part in any further offensive action. With their removal, and no one knowing who was giving out the orders, the men just sat down and waited. Meanwhile, their officers argued with anyone who would listen about what they were supposed to do next. After much wrangling, an attack was ordered for 1730. The idea of seizing the W Hills had been dropped in favour of an attack on Chocolate Hill, a task that could have gone in unopposed if it had been organised sooner. The 6th Lincolnshire, the Border Regiment and three Irish battalions started the attack almost simultaneously and, as darkness fell on the 7th, Chocolate Hill was captured. However, the Turks, who were now on the run, were not harassed any further. The five battalions which had taken Chocolate Hill were now hopelessly intermixed and they also waited for further instructions. As no scouts were sent out, contact with the enemy was lost. It was bad enough that the attack here on the right of Suvla was some 18-20 hours behind schedule, yet the situation on the left was by now even more appalling.

Most of the units who had been landed on the left flank were supposed to have been ashore at around 0800 but the majority were not ready to move off the beach until the late afternoon. A thunderstorm and the uncharted waters at this location did not help but they are certainly not the only reasons that the attack was running so far behind schedule: another problem was that of water, or rather the lack of it. Some troops who had pushed inland were now returning to the beach for replenishment whilst the two

Left: An Australian on Walker's Ridge carries a wounded comrade out of danger during the summer of 1915. Right: The view from the upper slopes of the ridge looking down towards the long sweep of Ocean Beach is largely unchanged. It is possible to explore many of the old trenches that still remain in this area, although most have now been eroded by time and weather and are very much shallower. The small hill of Lala Baba shows up clearly at the mouth of the Salt Lake whilst behind it can be seen the ridge of Kiretch Tepe — one of the main objectives of the landing at Suvla.

seaborne lighters carrying thousands of tons of water, had grounded far out to sea. This shortage of water took over as the main focus of attention with any thought of attacking the Turks secondary.

It was now that the accurate reports from Anzac — of tranquillity at Suvla and a Turkish withdrawal — were in vast contrast to Lieutenant-General Stopford's view of events from his position offshore. In his first message to Sir Ian, after stating that by 0730 hours Hill 10 had not been taken, he ended by saying that, 'as you see, we have been able to advance little beyond the edge of the beach'. Although his message was basically true, his implications were because of enemy action rather than the incompetence and lack of leadership that was really holding up proceedings.

If Sir Ian was disheartened on receiving this message, he did not show it for in his reply he sent a weak message of support, encouraging a rapid advance but stopping short of actually ordering it.

By 0700 hours on the 7th, General Liman von Sanders had quite rightly guessed that the Suvla landing was not a diversion but the main thrust. So now, having already released three battalions from Bulair, he ordered forward additional units to the Suvla and Anzac sectors although he realised that it would still take some 30 hours for these decisive reinforcements to reach the area. The race was now on.

Meanwhile, the battle for the heights of the Anzac sector continued to rage. There had been a brief lull following the destruction of the Light Horse at the Nek but shortly afterwards renewed efforts were made to try to redress the balance. At last, Brigadier-General Johnston decided he could wait no longer for his missing battalion for the window of opportunity was already being closed as Turkish soldiers started to amass on Chunuk Bair. His first attack here secured the feature known as the Apex, approximately 400 yards from the summit. Johnston wanted to wait till nightfall before renewing the advance but, on hearing this, General Godley insisted the attack be renewed at 1030 following a 15-minute barrage.

The attack went ahead following an accurate bombardment but the New Zealanders, who had been joined by elements of the

2/10th Gurkhas, ran into a storm of return fire. For the cost of over 250 men they managed to take the Pinnacle which lay less than 300 yards from the crest. However, Johnston reported to Godley that no further action was possible until nightfall and this time Godley agreed.

The other assaulting column, which was meant to capture Hill Q and Hill 971, had also not been able to reach their objectives. Realising the critical situation he faced, Major-General Cox commanding the 29th Indian Brigade secured the 39th Brigade as reinforcements. Part of Kitchener's New Army, the brigade consisted of the 9th Royal Warwicks, 7th Gloucesters, 9th Worcesters and the 7th North Staffords. In the end, however, only the 7th Gloucesters found their way to join up with Cox's troops while the rest got hopelessly lost in the unimaginable chaos that by now reigned supreme. It was therefore decided that no action by this column was to be taken during the 7th. Of the other units involved, the 4th Australian Brigade had not moved at all throughout the day; the Indian Brigade had become intermixed and scattered, and the New Army battalions were exhausted after their strenuous climb. Meanwhile, water was becoming ever scarcer. So, as night fell, everyone prepared for what was surely to be the most decisive 48 hours of the campaign.

Below left: The heights of Chunuk Bair seen from a reserve trench at Suvla in September 1915. If the high ground around the Suvla plain had been captured quickly, the Allies would have held a huge area not under observation to stockpile stores. Below right: Hill 971 is the tallest peak just to the right of centre while further to its right is the double peak of Hill Q.

AUGUST 8 — MAJOR-GENERAL COX'S COLUMN

For Major-General Cox's columns, still trying to seize Hill Q and Hill 971, August 8 was to be the calm before the storm. Yet calm is certainly the wrong term to describe the heights of the Sari Bair range that were anything but peaceful during that hot summer of 1915. At 0330 hours, No. 4 Column, commanded by Colonel John Monash, started its advance towards Hill 971 but the time scale made its capture — even if unopposed — an impossible task. And unopposed they were not to be. By mid-morning they were pinned down by Turkish fire which soon escalated into a full infantry attack. Over the next few hours, this column lost over 650 men and almost all its officers. No.1 and No. 3 Columns got hopelessly lost amongst the gullies and, although they were constantly being urged forward, nobody really knew any longer which way forward was. The only column of Cox's forces that made any real progress was No. 2, under Lieutenant-Colonel Thomas Andrus. His men were pushing forward to try and link up with the 1/6th Gurkhas who were still well out in front of everyone else. The 1/6th Gurkhas under Major Cecil Allanson held on for these reinforcements to reach them, but by 1000 hours he realised what few officers had not so far managed to comprehend: that to wait now was to commit suicide later. It was then that Allanson decided to launch an attack on Hill Q and, after rounding up all the stragglers he could find, he started the final ascent. After a good start the men began to come under heavy fire but still they fought on so that by nightfall they had reached a point some 250 feet from the summit. During the night, showing supreme courage, men of the South Lancashires and the Gurkhas managed to get within 100 feet of the top where they dug in, anxiously awaiting daylight.

AUGUST 8 — BRIGADIER-GENERAL JOHNSTON'S ATTACK ON CHUNUK BAIR

The plan to seize Chunuk Bair was now set to commence at 0330 hours on the 8th. The troops to be used were the Wellington Battalion, the 7th Gloucesters and 8th Welsh. The Auckland and Otago Mounted Rifles along with a Maori contingent made up the reserve.

As the troops started their ascent in the half light of the early dawn, the expected fire from the crest did not materialise and as they neared the summit they started to run fearing some kind of terrible ambush. However, as they reached the peak, not a single shot was fired: the Turks had all but gone. The only troops remaining were those manning a single machine gun post and even they were asleep.

Shortly afterwards, the Wellington Battalion under Lieutenant-Colonel William Malone started to dig in. For a brief period the men enjoyed their moment of triumph and, as they looked down onto the shimmering waters of the narrows, they could taste victory. The long awaited break-out from Anzac at last seemed possible and all because some inexplicable panic had overwhelmed the Turkish troops on Chunuk Bair. As the light increased, the Turkish forces holding Hill Q to the left and Battleship Hill to the right, realising what had taken place on Chunuk Bair, started to inflict casualties by firing at this exposed position. The 7th Gloucesters, who had been late in leaving their start point, suffered grievously as they were in the last stages of the final ascent when this murderous fire commenced. Realising that Chunuk Bair must be recaptured quickly, the Turkish forces devoted all their efforts to driving the Allies from it. The Welsh Regiment making their way up behind the Gloucesters, suffered even more heavily with very few men reaching the crest.

The Wellingtons, in the most advanced position, fought grimly against ever growing odds but were wiped out almost to a man as the Turks closed the main Allied line. Lieutenant-Colonel Malone was now in charge of all the forces on the ridge and he fought with exceptional bravery and dash. Somehow, the remnants of the Wellingtons and Welsh Regiment managed to hold their position and inflict massive casualties on the attacking Turks. Trying to get reinforcements to this area proved to be virtually impossible but some did make it. The diary of a young New

Before commencing the final ascent to the top of Chunuk Bair, the New Zealanders were positioned at the Pinnacle, and it was from there that they launched their final assault on August 8 — and from where later New Zealand machine gunners stopped the Turkish advance on August 10. These pictures show the view of the New Zealanders looking up (above) as well as the view the Turks had looking down on them from Chunuk Bair (below).

There is much debate today about the misuse of artillery at Gallipoli. There are many instances where the wrong type of shells were used while in other cases (such as the 1/6th Gurkhas heroic capture of Hill Q), artillery or naval guns are blamed for shelling their own side. Here territorial gunners are in action at Anzac.

This photo is often incorrectly captioned as having been taken at Suvla, but on a modern-day pilgrimage there can be little doubt that this is indeed the site of the gunners' old position. Behind to the north can be seen Walker's Ridge while the gun is firing in the direction of Mortar Ridge and Johnston's Jolly.

Zealand trooper, whose brother was later killed, describes the horrors of this attack:

'8th Roused up at 10 and moved up the gully again, stayed part way up hill until daylight. Some more climbing and then a run over the side of hill with bullets raining around us like hail from machine guns. Sing, Troupe, Bigg, Wither and Melhose hit going over. The whole Reg stopped in a slight hollow for hours while the Turks shelled and sniped us. Men were being killed and wounded all around me. Legs arms and other portions being blown off. (Major Chapman died here) After waiting 7 hours without moving, we went from the jaws of death into the "Valley of Dead" (6 or 700 hundred wounded and dead here) on into the Mouth of Hell we charged up the side of "Chunuk Bair" to relieve the Gloucesters and others. Our men fell like fruit from a tree in a gale. The Turks then rushed us with bombs, only to be mown

down by our men. One came up with a white flag, and a party of bomb throwers. They all fell . . . Again the Turks came on during the night only to be wiped out again. We held the front while reinforcements dug a trench and then came back into it.'

It was during one of these attacks that the gallant Malone — who must take a lot of the credit for holding this position — was killed, many say by a shell fired by his own side. During the night the Turkish attacks slowly lost some of their ferocity allowing a few reinforcements from the Otagos and the Wellington Mounted Rifles to relieve the weary defenders on the crest. Casualties for this action were appalling, the Wellingtons losing 710 out of 760 involved, while the Gloucesters 350 men and every officer and sergeant. The Welsh Regiment also had heavy casualties of 400 men and 17 officers.

AUGUST 8 — SUVLA, CONTINUED INACTION

As August 8 dawned at Suvla, it was still quiet and but for the occasional distant rifle shot, you would not have known there was a war on. On the beach, men were bathing and the feeling was more that of a bank holiday, than of 'pushing vigorously on'. Lieutenant-General Stopford was still aboard the *Jonquil* and was yet to come ashore. Major-General Hammersley, having regained some composure, seems now to have realised the importance of pressing inland to seize the hills. He spent the early part of the morning visiting his brigadiers who all insisted that they needed time to rest and reorganise their troops before pushing on. In the light of this, and in absence of any direct orders calling for an early advance from either Stopford or Sir Ian, Hammersley seems to have become resigned to the fact that nothing could be done until

Looking at the narrows from the heights of Chunuk Bair today. The trees on the right are said to be the place where Mustafa Kemal spent the night before launching the counter-attack to regain positions at Chunuk Bair and the Farm. Kemal had realised much earlier than anyone else that whoever controlled the Sari Bair range of hills controlled the peninsula and, as such, he had been vigorously arguing with his superiors about strengthening the defences there.

the troops had rested, though all the time masses of Turkish reinforcements were approaching. Hammersley did send out some orders for a few limited advances near to the village of Sulajik but this seems to have been more to help clear the hundreds of men milling around the beach than for any tactical reason.

All this time, as if hypnotised, no one paid much attention to the vitally important — and at this time virtually undefended — Tekke Tepe ridge. On the northern flank, around Kiretch Tepe itself, nothing at all was happening. Brigadier-General Lewis Nicol who was commanding the troops on this ridge, sent back a message informing his superior, Lieutenant-General Sir Bryan Mahon, that he was beginning to dig a support line. This was because he had neither received orders to do anything else nor had been informed about the plan or his part in it. However, Mahon took this to mean that the Turkish positions here were too strong to be taken 'without the help of artillery' and this is what he reported back to Lieutenant-General Stopford. Sir Frederick received the message on board the *Jonquil* and paced the deck wondering what to do next. All the while, the sands of time were running out for the Suvla operation as still more Turkish reinforcements moved relentlessly south. Sir Frederick eventually decided to send a message back to Major-General Hammersley congratulating him on 'the results obtained against strenuous opposition and great difficulty' but still not stressing the need to seize the high ground. On informing GHQ of the current situation, which he had not seen for himself, Stopford announced that 'I must now consolidate the position held and endeavour to land stores and supplies which are badly needed.'

This was all too much for Sir Ian who was receiving reports from Anzac that nothing was happening at Suvla even though no Turks stood in the way of a general advance. He therefore decided to send Lieutenant-Colonel Cecil Aspinall and Lieutenant-Colonel Maurice Hankey of the General Staff to Suvla at once to report accurately on the situation. As can probably be imagined, with time now such a critical factor, the task of these two officers was not easy. At the outset, the destroyer that Sir Ian put at their disposal had boiler trouble which forced the two staff officers to hitch a lift on a fishing trawler so they did not get underway until gone 0930 hours.

Men of the Sharpshooters filling up their water utensils from a Turkish well close to the reserve trenches behind Chocolate Hill.

After an intensive search and much sign language, the author finally managed to locate the same well. Once found, an obliging Turkish farmer stood in the picture, making for a perfect comparison. Chocolate Hill lies in the background although somewhat hidden today behind new trees.

Once ashore, hearing no gun-fire, Aspinall and Hankey quickly became aware that all was not well, and they concluded that the front line must be miles inland. One can therefore imagine Aspinall's surprise on meeting a colonel of the artillery to hear that the front line was only a short distance from where they now stood, and that Lieutenant-General Stopford was still on board the *Jonquil*. On asking what the enemy strength was on this part of the line, Aspinall was told that it consisted only of two old men and a young boy.

General view of Lala Baba taken close to Chocolate Hill. Note the small, almost invisible dugout housing two men on the left of the photograph.

Aspinall, justifiably horrified, now rushed off to see Hammersley and find out what his plans were. Hammersley told him that there were no orders to advance until the following day and even that might not be possible if more guns were not landed soon.

Aspinall, now realising how incredibly poorly the operation was going, set off to see Lieutenant-General Stopford on the *Jonquil*. As Stopford greeted Aspinall, the General commented on how well the men had done, Aspinall quickly pointed out that they had not reached the high ground and the opportunity to do so would not last forever. Stopford acknowledged this but insisted that the men (most of whom had not been in action) had to be rested before any advance could be 'resumed'.

Aspinall, quickly realising that nothing was to be gained from continuing this conversation, wired Sir Ian: 'Just been ashore where I found all quiet. No rifle fire, no artillery fire and apparently no Turks. IX Corps resting. Feel confident that golden opportunities are being lost and look upon situation as serious.'

However, this signal never reached Hamilton, who was by this time on his way to Suvla on board the yacht *Triad*. More time was

When the author tracked down the location, in the interest of Anglo-Turkish relations, he decided not to trample over the freshly-planted crops to get a closer view!

lost during this crossing but on seeing his commander Aspinall lost no time in repeating his fears whereupon Sir Ian rushed off to the *Jonquil*. Unfortunately, the conversation that ensued with Stopford appears not to have been recorded but we do know that Stopford declined Hamilton's invitation to come ashore and thought Sir Ian's plan to start an attack that night completely unfeasible. Hamilton was undeterred and headed for the shore to find Hammersley.

On finding the 11th Division's commander, Sir Ian made it quite clear that he wanted an attack now to try and occupy the

Tekke Tepe ridge. However, following the earlier confusion and mix-up of orders, most units were just receiving their instructions to attack the following morning and only the 32nd Brigade were thought to be in a position to resume hostile action at such short notice. Sir Ian instructed Hammersley that even if only one rifle company could be spared, they should be sent at once to occupy the ridge though, even as he spoke, Turkish reinforcements were moving ever nearer.

Major-General Hammersley sent his second-in-command to tell the 32nd Brigade to try and occupy the Tekke Tepe ridge but even this message fell short of actually ordering them to take and hold it. In any case, it was nearly 2200 hours by the time these instructions reached Lieutenant-Colonel John Minogue (who had only recently taken command of the brigade) just as many patrols from the brigade were starting to return. Some of his men had been half way up the Tekke Tepe ridge and only met a few snipers,

The Tekke Tepe ridge runs north to south around the Suvla Plain. As can be seen from this present-day shot, the flat ground that leads up to it is awfully exposed, thus making the high ground strategically all the more important. The peaks could have been taken by the Allies in the first 24 hours had the organisation, planning and operational orders been clearer.

The graves of Lieutenant-Colonel Henry Moore and Major Wilfred Brunner who were the officers sent to lead the desperate attempt to reach the peak of Tekke Tepe before the Turks. Having then been driven off the crest, they were captured and bayoneted. Both officers are now buried in Green Hill Cemetery, although the inscription on the headstone informs the visitor that the precise location of Brunner's grave, right, has now been lost.

The 6 East Yorks were ordered forward to capture the Tekke Tepe Ridge. About 30 men managed to reach the top but were immediately swept off by a larger force of Turks . . . The retirement of this little party was attended by heavy loss. Only the commanding officer, two other officers and two men returned to the foothills and here they were overpowered and taken prisoner. After surrendering, the party was threatened with bayonets and although an Inman [Holy man] tried to stop any killing, Lieutenant-Colonel Moore was bayoneted in cold blood. Lieutenant Still was allowed to tend him, Colonel Moore said that his wound didn't hurt very much and Lieutenant Still began to carry him towards captivity but he died soon afterwards. Lieutenant Still went on to relate a subsequent conversation with a German officer who told him that they were having great difficulty in getting Turkish soldiers to take prisoners, even if they explained to them that captives were required for intelligence.

LIEUTENANT JOHN STILL
6TH EAST YORKS

whilst others had seen trenches near Baka Baba being evacuated and the Turks retreating towards Anafarta Sagir. However, none of this was yet known by Lieutenant-Colonel Minogue who now sent runners out ordering all of his battalions to make their way towards the village of Sulajik and prepare to attack the ridge. Throughout the pitch black night, runners became lost, units got lost and it was over six hours before the 6th East Yorks, under Lieutenant-Colonel Henry Moore, started to advance. They were already dog-tired having marched back to Sulajik and then being forced to dig in. All this time, the Tekke Tepe ridge remained virtually undefended and the race for it was now entering its final stage.

Lieutenant-Colonel Moore and his East Yorkshiremen, along with two sections of engineers under Major Wilfred Brunner, had been making steady progress and now, as daylight started to creep in from the east, they could see their objective ahead. They were not to know, however, that on the other side of the ridge, Turkish reinforcements were also climbing their side of the hill at a similar pace; it was going to be a close-run thing. Sniper fire was desultory as Moore and his men started their ascent but as they reached the peak it started to become heavier. Just as the Colonel and a handful of men made a last sprint to reach the crest, Turkish infantry started to pour over it from the other side. The race had been almost a dead heat but the Turks, with overwhelming numbers, had for all intents and purposes, won comfortably. Moore and his small party were quickly swept off the hill with terrible losses. They were pursued by hundreds of Turkish soldiers as they tried to make their way back towards the rest of their brigade that was by now trying to push up and join them. Reaching the foot of the hill, Moore was forced to surrender with Major Brunner and a small party of men. Both officers were bayoneted in cold blood and only the timely intervention of an Imam (priest) attached to the Turkish unit saved the rest of the men from the same fate. The 9th West Yorks, which had been the closest to Moore's troops, suffered heavily as well and it was not until reinforcements from the 6th Yorks and Lancs arrived that the Turkish advance was halted.

With Moore's death and the failure to capture the Tekke Tepe ridge, the first of three opportunities to seize and hold vitally important high ground during the August offensive was lost.

AUGUST 9-10 — ALLANSON'S HEROES; THE CAPTURE AND LOSS OF HILL Q

Meanwhile, Major-General Cox had sent an order through to Major Allanson of the 1/6th Gurkhas that he was not just to support the attack on Hill Q but that he was now to lead it. Although desperately short of men, Major Allanson was promised that the 39th Brigade would be there in time to give support, and that his attack must start when the bombardment ceased at 0515 hours.

The shelling was heavy and accurate and, as it faded away, Allanson and the Gurkhas and other intermixed units charged forwards. They reached the summit at the same time as the Turks, who had left the position during the barrage, and a bloody hand-to-hand battle began. For the next 10-15 minutes it was absolute mayhem as rifles, shovels, clubs, bayonets, kukri's and any other implement that could be pressed into service was used as a weapon. Faced with this furious onslaught, the Turks fled.

Allanson's small band had achieved their goal, and from their newly-won vantage point they could look down at the narrows and the rear of Achi Baba. If this could now be secured, the Turkish positions to the south would become untenable. Allanson, who was already wounded, decided his best course of action was to press on the heels of the fleeing Turks. He hoped that if they could be driven some way down Chunuk Bair, giving the Allies a buffer zone, this would ensure that any Turkish attack up the slope would be well-nigh impossible and at least a very costly affair. Once again however, the Gallipoli jinx was to strike. Although hotly denied by both the Navy and Army after the war, Allanson, an experienced soldier, had no hesitation in declaring that the shells that now started landing amongst his men were fired by his own side. As a result, Major Allanson was forced to pull his men back to the summit while desperately sending messages of his success; both in the hope of getting reinforced and also to stop a repeat performance of the 'friendly fire' incident. Allanson himself was forced to retire as the bayonet wound he had suffered started to stiffen up and the loss of blood was making him terribly weak.

He was replaced on Hill Q by Major Geoffrey Tomes of the 53rd Sikhs but he was killed after less than 30 minutes on the peak. Captain Selby Phipson, the battalion medical officer, then took charge but wisely left military decision-making to Gambirsing Pun, an experienced Subedar-Major and veteran of many bat-

I had only fifteen minutes left; the roar of the artillery preparation was enormous; the hill was almost leaping underneath one. I recognised that if we flew up the hill the moment it stopped we ought to get to the top. I put three companies into the trenches among my men, and said that the moment they saw me go forward carrying a red flag everyone was to start. I had my watch out — 5.15. I never saw such artillery preparation; the trenches were being torn to pieces; the accuracy was marvellous, as we were only just below. 5.18 it had stopped, and I wondered if my watch was wrong. 5.20 silence. I waited three minutes to be certain, great as the risk was, then off we dashed all hand in hand, a most perfect advance and a wonderful sight. I did not know at the time that the GOC division Godley was on a torpedo-boat destroyer, and every telescope was on us. I left Cornish with 50 men to hold the line in case we were pushed back, and to watch me if I signalled for reinforcements. At the top we met the Turks; Le Marchand went down, a bayonet through the heart. I got one through the leg, and then for about ten minutes we fought hand-to-hand, We bit and fisted and used rifles and pistols as clubs; blood was flying about like spray from a hairwash bottle. And then the Turks turned and fled and I felt a very proud man; the key to the whole peninsula was ours, and our losses had not been so very great for such a result. Below I saw the Straits, motors and wheeled transport on the roads leading to Achi Baba.

MAJOR CECIL ALLANSON
1/6TH GURKHAS

tles on the North-West Frontier. Meanwhile, Phipson set about finding some fresh troops further down the hill. He found some but without orders none would move up to the firing line and help support the beleaguered remnants still clinging to the summit. Empty-handed, Phipson returned to the summit just as night fell and the Turks started to increase their counter-attacks. At times, the Turks got to within 30 yards but still his men clung on. It was in the early hours of the 10th, with the complete failure of the advance on Hill 971 to the north, that orders were received from HQ 29th Brigade to abandon the position and fall back. Under the skilful Gambirsing Pun, with Phipson carefully overseeing but not interfering, the evacuation was carried out successfully. A descent of over 900 feet had to be negotiated carrying all manner of equipment and wounded whilst under fire. The task was not an easy one and was only successful because of the extreme professionalism of the troops.

Thus, after a bloody contest and marvellous victory, because of lack of follow-up support, the second of three near misses for the Allies also ended as a victory for the Turks.

Medical attention at Gallipoli was often only rudimentary; here three Australians give a comrade field dressing up on the heights. Groundwork by the author ascertained that this photo was taken somewhere between the Nek and Walker's Ridge.

AUGUST 9-10 — THE LOSS OF CHUNUK BAIR; MASSACRE AT THE FARM

On the evening of the 9th, shortly before the Gurkhas received their orders to abandon Hill Q, the battle for Chunuk Bair was about to reach its climax. It was apparent that the New Zealanders still holding on were in desperate need of being relieved if there was to be any hope of retaining this valuable position. Since taking it, the Auckland Battalion had lost 12 officers and 308 men, the Otago 17 officers and 300 men, while the Wellington Mounted Rifles, originally a force of nearly 200, could now muster a little over 50.

The units sent up to relieve the New Zealanders were from the 6th Loyal North Lancashires, supported by the 5th Wiltshires. The immediate problem was that there was not enough trench space for all these men but it was optimistically hoped that if they could

Looking from the left flank of Chunuk Bair towards the other two objectives of the attack on the heights. Nearest, surmounted by trees, is Hill Q that was so gallantly taken and held by Cecil Allanson and his 1/6th Gurkhas. Behind can be seen Point 971 or Koja Chemen Tepe which is the highest peak of the Sari Bair range — an objective which was never captured by the Allies.

In this comparison to the picture opposite, the heights of the Kiretch Tepe can be seen in the far distance while in front lie Chocolate and Green Hills. The edge of the Salt Lake is also visible, jutting in from the left.

get in position during the night, they might be able to dig themselves in before daylight on the 10th. As soon as they arrived, the men of the Loyal North Lancashires occupied the trenches being vacated by the New Zealanders and the Wiltshires who, having not slept for over three days, lay down just behind the crestline.

So, as dawn broke, this vitally important position was being held by three companies of the Loyal North Lancashires (38th Brigade) in the front line, with another company at the Pinnacle; to the right and a long way below were two and a half companies of the 5th Wiltshires (40th Brigade); while the 6th Leinsters (29th Brigade), the remnants of the Wellington Battalion and the machine guns of the New Zealand Infantry Brigade were holding the Apex. Thus, Chunuk Bair, one of the most important features captured in the whole of the Dardanelles campaign, was being held by troops belonging to four different brigades from three dif-

ferent divisions. In addition, the various senior commanders had not yet met, and one of them was a complete stranger to Anzac, so the ingredients for yet another Gallipoli fiasco were already in place.

To the north of Rhododendron Spur, around the position known as the Farm, the situation was even more confused. The troops here were so intermixed at all levels that the command structure now relied on individuals, both men and officers, seizing opportunities when they saw them and holding the line when attacked with whatever men were available.

Photograph taken in the soft light of dusk looking back from the farm plateau towards the peak of Chunuk Bair which is surmounted by the New Zealand Memorial, barely visible behind the tall thin tree on the horizon.

Mustafa Kemal, feeling confident that the Suvla front was now relatively secure since his troops had won the race to the crest of Tekke Tepe, now turned his attention to block the attempted break-out from Anzac. His plan was to launch an all-out, make or break attack against Chunuk Bair and the surrounding high ground, and as dawn broke on August 10, the Turkish counter-attack started.

The advanced posts of Loyal North Lancashires were taken out quickly and quietly and at 0445 hours waves of Turks poured over the crest. Little is known of exactly what happened in the

This stunning view of the farm plateau was taken by the author from Chunuk Bair in May 1999. It was from a similar point that the Turks poured down to wipe out the troops many of whom were resting here on August 10. The cemetery that can be seen just in front of the small group of trees in the centre contains hundreds of graves, mostly unidentified. The simple arresting fact demonstrated by this one picture is the complete domination that Chunuk Bair gave those who possessed it over Suvla.

next few minutes as in a short, bloody period the Loyal North Lancs lost 10 officers and over 500 men. The Turks then reached the Wiltshires below, many of whom were still asleep and did not have their kit handy, forcing them to flee. Within the course of five minutes, the Turks inflicted massive casualties and captured the Pinnacle, although further advances were halted by the New Zealand machine-gunners and the men of the Leinsters who grimly held onto their positions at the Apex.

As the Turks now swept down the reverse side of Chunuk Bair, a second major assault was launched, this time from the Turkish right towards the Farm. Nothing is known about this action because virtually no one survived it. The Farm plateau became the scene of just about the bloodiest single action of the entire campaign. A detachment of the Warwickshires was wiped out almost to a man, whilst the 6th Royal Irish Rifles lost all their officers and most of their other ranks. The 29th Brigade HQ was overrun, every officer being either killed or wounded, including Brigadier-General Anthony Baldwin who lost his life somewhere near the front line. Allied troops were forced to retreat to the Cheshire Ridge, and the Farm plateau had to be abandoned until about 1400 hours when men of the 5th Connaught Rangers were ordered to reoccupy it. This they did but the position was now so exposed that it was suicide to try and hold it. So as daylight faded on the 10th, the Farm position was left in the possession of the dead and dying, many of whom remain entombed there to this day.

With the loss of Chunuk Bair, again due to lack of support, the four days of fighting for the heights drew to a close. This most confusing and often impossible-to-follow offensive — which had promised so much yet delivered so little — had cost some 12,000 Allied casualties. As we have seen, on three occasions the Allies came close to achieving that significant breakthrough yet three times the opportunity slipped away. Moore and his men butchered on Tekke Tepe; Allanson and his troops shot to pieces on Hill Q; Malone and his New Zealanders never given the reinforcements they needed on Chunuk Bair.

The chance to win this campaign had now all but been lost and it is probable that most of the senior officers now realised this — at least in their hearts. Nevertheless, it did not stop them ordering a number of costly attacks against positions, particularly at Suvla, that could have been occupied with little or no loss in the first 48 hours following the landing. However, no matter how many men's lives were to be thrown at Turkish positions, the clock could not be turned back; the opportunities had all been missed, condemning the campaign from this point onwards to failure.

The New Zealand National Memorial on Chunuk Bair. Nearby is the Memorial to the Missing that records the names of some 850 New Zealanders, and also Chunuk Bair Cemetery which contains 632 burials, although most are unidentified.

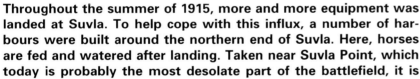

Throughout the summer of 1915, more and more equipment was landed at Suvla. To help cope with this influx, a number of harbours were built around the northern end of Suvla. Here, horses are fed and watered after landing. Taken near Suvla Point, which today is probably the most desolate part of the battlefield, it is

hard to imagine that once this area was teeming with men, equipment, stores and horses. The road running across the foreground comes to an abrupt dead end just to the left of this photo where a stark Turkish monument faces out to sea. Only the distinctive skyline bears witness to the momentous struggles of a bygone age.

AUGUST 11-31

Following a botched attack on what was to become one of the bloodiest features of the Suvla sector, Scimitar Hill on August 9, a new attack was planned to begin on the 12th. The idea originally was to seize the Tekke Tepe ridge in a general attack using many of the fresh troops who were coming ashore. However, it was Stopford's lack of enthusiasm, and his belief that the entire operation was futile, that convinced Sir Ian to postpone the operation until the 13th. However, a limited assault by the 163rd Brigade of the 54th Division did go ahead as planned on the 12th. The attack started at 1600 hours and for the first few hundred yards the troops were unopposed as they made their way through the thick, prickly scrub, but as they left the undergrowth and entered the more open terrain that lay between them and their believed objec-

tives, the casualties started to mount seriously. Soon all units lost their cohesion and were fighting individually, unaware of who or what lay in front or behind them. At the same time, heavy fire from the flanks, particularly from Kidney Hill, intensified as did the casualties.

On the right of this advance were the 1/5th Norfolks who were to become known as Gallipoli's Missing Battalion. This battalion consisted of a company formed from men from the Royal estate at Sandringham and His Majesty King George V, on hearing of their disappearance, asked the military authorities what had become of them. No one really knew and nobody was keen to tell him that they had been sacrificed in yet another wasteful and poorly-planned operation. Thus, the mystery of the missing battalion was born but it turned out that the Norfolks had become entirely cut off near a farm building where they were killed to a man. Even the wounded were not spared but all this remained a well-kept secret for a further 70 years.

The 1/8th Hampshires — known as the Isle of Wight Rifles — also suffered terribly on this day losing eight officers and 300 men. When added to the Norfolk's losses of 22 officers and 350 men — all for no gain whatsoever — one can appreciate what a costly and ill-thought-out daylight attack this had been. It is little wonder that no one wanted to tell His Majesty what had become of his men. Neither of these units, which had only been on the peninsula for some 48 hours, took any further active part in the campaign.

The view (above) from Scimitar Hill looking across the plains to where the men of the 1/5th Norfolk Regiment vanished on August 12. The names of the Norfolks who went missing are recorded on the Helles Memorial (right). Amongst them is Captain Frank Beck who was the estate manager at Sandringham and was a close friend of King George V. The loss of these men led to some serious questions being asked about the running of the Gallipoli campaign. Of the 180-odd bodies recovered from the area in which the 1/5th Norfolks had fought, some 122 were identified by metal shoulder-titles as being from the battalion. However, only two were identifiable by name (Corporal John Barnaby and Private Walter Carter) and they were buried nearby in Azmak Cemetery on October 7, 1919 by Revd Charles Edwards who had been sent to the peninsula by Queen Alexandra to try to discover the fate of her employees. (This episode was portrayed in the 1999 BBC dramatisation *All the King's Men* with David Jason playing Captain Beck.)

Australians with a seemingly captive shrub — actually a Turkish sniper — indicating only too well the latter's skill in concealment.

The rest of the 12th passed quietly on the other sectors. All the time, however, the Turks were strengthening their positions and inflicting casualties amongst the inexperienced troops at Suvla by the use of cleverly-disguised snipers. Lieutenant-General Stopford, who by this stage had been ashore for a number of days, continued to supervise the building of his personal bomb-proof shelter in the belief that they were 'to be here for quite a while'. It was from here that he telegraphed GHQ to inform Sir Ian that the losses from the previous day had been bad and his troops once again needed resting before they could advance. The truth was more that most of the troops who had been involved in the previous day's action were now either dead or wounded.

Sir Ian, now completely exasperated by the constant delays, set off once again for Suvla to see the situation for himself. On arrival, he was informed that the Turks were 'acting aggressively' and that the 53rd and 54th Divisions were not capable of even any defensive duties and were liable to bolt at any time. During the heated debate that followed, it is probable that Sir Ian finally realised that Stopford must be removed although he returned to GHQ outwardly still not having decided what to do next. It was

late that night before he telegraphed Stopford to tell him that he did not expect his corps to make a general advance at present but that he expected them to dig their line as far forward as possible and to prepare and reorganise. Once again Stopford was left to make his own rules. He ordered General Mahon (10th Division) to attack with three battalions along Kiretch Tepe from Jephson's Post, the plan being was to try and seize not only the ridge but also the prominent hillock known as Kidney Hill.

For the past week little more than 500 Turkish gendarmes had held this position but no serious attempt to attack it had been made by the British; now on August 15, the Turks could muster nearly ten battalions within close vicinity to defend it. The attack began at 1300 hours and for once the orders had been issued that ground was to be captured for minimal losses. Progress was so agonisingly slow that by 1800 hours Brigadier-General Nicol called for a more vigorous advance. The Munster Fusiliers duly obliged with a fanatical bayonet charge whereupon the Turks turned and fled. Meanwhile, the Dublin Fusiliers, who were pushing up on the right, took full advantage of this and managed to capture the Turkish strong point on the highest part of the ridge. For once things were going well but, it would not last long.

The distinctive shape of Kidney Hill in front of the Kiretch Tepe ridge. Although the lower slopes of this hill were reached by some men from the Bedfordshire and London Regiments, it was never completely captured. It was also from here that murderous flanking fire helped turn back the assault of part of the 54th Division (which included the 1/5th Norfolks) on August 12.

The 5th Royal Inniskilling Fusiliers, who were attacking slightly to the south, had started well but had come under increasingly heavy fire and by nightfall, having suffered over 350 casualties, they were forced to withdraw. On the far right flank, advancing through the difficult terrain towards Kidney Hill, were men of the Bedfordshire Regiment. Despite the heavy fire, they continued to move slowly forwards but, although reinforced by men of the London Regiment, they were eventually brought to a halt. On hearing that these troops had stopped advancing, Brigadier-General Charles de Winton went up to the front to lead in person. After rallying the troops, the advance commenced again and, although seriously wounded, Brigadier-General de Winton's example seemed to inspire the men. By nightfall, small parties were occupying the south-western shoulder of Kidney Hill. They continued to hold on for most of the night completely unsupported showing just what the New Army units were capable of, despite Stopford's highly critical view of them. However, with the coming of daylight, these troops had to pull back. For a while, all was quiet but there was every reason to expect a fierce Turkish counter-attack at any time.

The counter-attack soon came. In the most advanced positions in the centre of the Kiretch Tepe, the Irishmen came under fierce attack. In this craggy terrain, the bomb was the key weapon and whoever had the most eventually ended up on top. Once again, the Turks had ample supplies so the Irishmen were forced to catch and throw back Turkish grenades. At one stage they were even throwing rocks and stones as nothing more deadly could be found!

By 0900 hours it was clear that without reinforcements the positions captured earlier could not be held. This however was not the time to be asking divisional headquarters for anything. Late on August 15 Stopford was removed from command of IX Corps. His temporary replacement from the Helles sector, Major-General Beauvoir de Lisle, had only just arrived at the Suvla front and was not fully aware of the military situation. Lieutenant-General Mahon, who was senior to de Lisle and who also disliked him, refused to serve under him and promptly resigned. Meanwhile, the men of his division fought and died and all because no one would send them up any support. By 1900 hours on the 16th, with no reinforcements forthcoming, the Irishmen were forced to turn back to their starting positions. British casualties for the last 24 hours numbered some 2,000 and with them went any notion of breaking out from Suvla.

General de Lisle had been brought to Suvla believing that attacks from here would bring to an end the stalemate. This they may well have done if swiftly delivered, but he was probably not aware of how poorly operations had been conducted in the past. After visiting the front lines and speaking to his battalion commanders, he felt confident that he could break the deadlock, and

The desperate shortage of hand-grenades cost the Allies dear on a number of occasions. To help rectify this, men were deployed on the beaches to make a home-made type of grenade called the 'jam-tin bomb'. Their construction was a simple affair, with a small amount of explosive, a fuse and any old bits of metal that could be included to act as shrapnel. In this photo, men surrounded by hundreds of tins collected for just this purpose can be seen producing these bombs on the beach using barbed wire as the shrapnel ingredient.

Left: Major Rome of the Sharpshooters (1/3rd County of London Yeomanry) with brother officers shortly after their landing at Suvla on August 20. Right: In this area, broken rum jars still litter the ground and, whilst the scrub has grown up, it is certainly not impassable. **To the extreme left, barely visible on both pictures, lies a small pier which gives a good reference to pinpoint where Major Rome and his men were once camped. Author, Steve Newman, stands to!**

he sent his plans for regaining the initiative by relaunching attacks to Sir Ian for approval. His proposals were only a little short of an all-out assault across the entire front. However, Sir Ian, realised that, even using the fresh troops of the 2nd Mounted Division soon to arrive, if the venture failed he might not even be able to hold on to what ground he presently held. It was under these constraints that Hamilton scaled down the plans. The objectives were now Scimitar Hill, Hetman Chair, Hill 112 and the W Hills, whilst Hill 60 would be attacked from the Anzac sector. If all these objectives could be accomplished, the exposed Suvla Plain could be abandoned and thus the yardage held by now understrength units could be shortened. The 29th Division were to be brought up from Helles to strengthen the attack; meanwhile, some 3,000 troops — British, Australian, New Zealanders and Gurkhas — were pulled from various understrength units on the Anzac sector to make up the force for the attack on Hill 60.

This was set for August 21. The day dawned baking hot and with it came the flies and smell of death. Many bodies had only been buried in scrapes and the troops regularly trod into these shallow burials. Conditions were appalling and disease was ripe. Some troops, particularly at Anzac and Helles, had to sleep by the latrines even as dysentery spread amongst the ranks. Sickness was now costing the Allies more casualties than enemy action at both Anzac and Helles, a situation that would continue until the first frosts of winter killed off the flies.

That morning life in the trenches was unusually active. The Turks were sniping at anything that moved and many of the men felt sure that the enemy had got wind of the attack that was scheduled to start at 1500 hours following a heavy barrage. The shelling from nearly 90 guns was deemed decisive although, due to a lack of ammunition, the duration had to be cut to last only 30 minutes, rendering it only slightly better than useless.

The W Hills from a reserve trench near Chocolate Hill — a picture from a Sharpshooters' photo album. Note the discarded hat in the foreground.

'Part of an old trench was found amongst the nearby trees on my visit,' says Steve, 'although I'm sorry to say the hat had by this time disappeared so I had to substitute my own!'

By now the weather had become hazy, with visibility further reduced by the dust from the exploding shells. The brief barrage ended all too soon having achieved little and as it finished the first men charged across no man's land. These were troops from the 9th Lancashire Fusiliers and the 5th Dorsets. Both reached the Turkish front line, and succeeded in driving the Turks from it, but at a high cost. The Lancashire Fusiliers had only two officers left, one of whom was wounded, whilst the Dorsets had not only suffered heavy casualties but had also lost contact with one another. Nevertheless, these inexperienced units had behaved very well under the trying conditions. Fighting patrols were sent out to make contact with the Gurkhas but as yet the Anzac assault on Hill 60 had not begun. This in turn forced these patrols to return to their hard won newly-captured positions having learned precious little about the events unfolding around them.

On the left were the men of the 6th Yorkshires and the 6th Yorks and Lancs. Although they continued to advance under heavy fire, they were in fact heading north of their objective. The result was that they came under a cross-fire from a nearby Turkish communication trench and were forced to retire, having gained nothing more than heavy casualties. A similar fate befell the 8th West Riding and the 9th West Yorkshires who were forced back onto the slopes of Green Hill. The 33rd Brigade, who were by this time marching around the Salt Lake to help support these troops, came under increasingly heavy shrapnel fire. Their casualties quickly mounted and, even after getting mixed up with men from the 34th Brigade, they still gamely tried to push on in what was to prove a futile exercise. The Turkish cross-fire became more and more accurate and the attack of the 11th Division had to be halted at around 1700 hours.

In the centre were the veterans of the 29th Division (although very few men now remained active from the April 25 landings). They were attacking Scimitar Hill and Hill 112. The 86th Brigade, who were to assault the latter, had suffered casualties from accurate Turkish shrapnel fire before they had even left their trenches. Their advance across the now-blazing scrub of no man's land had been virtually unsurvivable as hidden machine guns mowed them down in great swathes. Anyone wounded here stood little chance of survival as the burning scrub roasted some while the thick black smoke choked others.

The last of the 2nd Mounted Division crossing the Salt Lake on August 21. Others are already dug in on Chocolate Hill. The lake itself can just be seen in the distance. The original caption to this Middlesex Yeomanry snapshot simply ends: 'Very heavy casualties'.

Eighty years have passed and, with the Salt Lake gradually receding in the early summer sunshine, it is difficult to imagine that a bitter war was ever fought here in the solitude which is now Suvla.

Meanwhile, the 87th Brigade were attacking Scimitar Hill — the same position that had been held by men of the East Yorks before they were recalled to Sulajik to take part in the abortive attempt to seize Tekke Tepe on August 9. Now it was heavily defended but, even so, the attack started well. The 1st Royal Inniskilling Fusiliers managed to secure a foothold at the base having barely lost a man and, after regrouping for about half an hour, they charged up the hill and, despite terrific fire, succeeded in taking the crest. Their success however was short-lived as machine gun fire poured in from the neighbouring hills and artillery shells exploded amongst them, forcing them to retreat. However, as the Inniskillings were trickling back down the hill, the Border Regiment were advancing up it. As a result, many Inniskillings turned about and joined in and once again the crest was taken but it was quickly realised that only the southern slopes of the hill offered any protection from the Turkish fire. It was here that the few survivors huddled while the western slopes were abandoned to the dead and dying who in places lay two or three deep. It was now that the recently-landed 2nd Mounted Division were thrown into the battle to try and make good the attack of the 29th Division

The Mounted Division was largely made up of Yeomanry units, many members being country gentlemen who had to prove their horsemanship to get in. Having left their horses in Egypt, they had arrived at Suvla and been bivouacked behind Lala Baba. Following the hiatus which befell the 29th and 11th Divisions, those units which had been landed from the 2nd Mounted Division were now ordered up to the vicinity of Chocolate Hill. They marched directly across the Salt Lake, all eyes on them as they kept perfect formation under increasingly heavy shrapnel fire. They arrived at Chocolate Hill having suffered surprisingly few casualties and, instead of being ordered as expected to consolidate the gains of the regular troops, they were ordered to attack. They had to try and succeed where the regulars had all but failed, hardly an easy task for troops new to combat. At about 1730 hours these units set off towards Scimitar Hill and Hill 112. No one really knew what their objectives were as indicated by the address given by Lieutenant-Colonel Sir John Milbanke, VC: 'We are to take a redoubt but I don't know where it is and I don't think anyone else does either; but in any case we are to go ahead and attack any Turks we meet.' Milbanke was killed in this attack leading his men and his body was never found.

With daylight slipping away and fierce fires raging; with no one having ever seen the ground before and receiving any direct orders as to where the Turks and the 29th Division were, the whole attack was doomed to failure. Through the dust and smoke the men advanced but, after initially making good progress, they ran into heavy fire. The 2nd Battalion South Wales Borderers (part of the 87th Brigade of the earlier attacking 29th Division) reached the summit of Scimitar Hill to the south but lost all their officers and most of their NCOs in the attempt, being forced to retire half way down the hill where they formed a line. The Yeomanry units then stormed up the northern and central slopes and once again the crest was taken but Turks on the surrounding hills poured fire onto the crest and once again the position had to be relinquished. One small party, led by Brigadier-General Lord Thomas Longford and his Brigade Major, did push on even further but, as nothing was ever heard of them again, it is presumed that they were surrounded and then overwhelmed. . . Their bodies were never found.

As darkness fell, the Turkish fire eased somewhat and the few remaining officers set about reorganising their hopelessly intermixed units and digging in. Brigadier-General William Marshall, (who was commanding 11th Division as Hammersley was ill) set about confirming the reports of success around the W Hills. Having sent officers out to reconnoitre, he quickly learnt that these messages were incorrect. After being briefed on the true situation at the front, it was obvious that even though the Turks had abandoned the summit of Scimitar Hill, they could still control who possessed it by the supporting fire they could pour onto it from Hill 112. So Marshall decided nothing would be gained by ordering a further attack to seize the crest.

It was now apparent to all concerned that Scimitar Hill could not be captured until Hill 112 was taken and that this could not be done until the W Hills were seriously threatened. As the British did not have the resources to consider any such attempt, instead Marshall detailed the men on a humanitarian operation to collect and help the wounded, of whom there were hundreds lying on the battlefield. Meanwhile, the survivors of the Mounted Division marched back to Lala Baba having gained nothing. Thus, at a cost of some 5,300 casualties, the name Scimitar Hill was added to Gallipoli's history in blood.

One of the biggest problems that faced the Allies at Suvla in the sweltering heat that August was fresh water. Some men, having taken up good firing positions, were forced to give them up merely to search for water, whilst others, finding the pipe that was pumping water ashore, cut holes in it to relieve their thirst. Here a fatigue party take a break on the Salt Lake.

'No chance for a rest on my visit!' says Steve. 'The extreme high ground to the left is the Tekke Tepe ridge while to the right, surmounted by a barely discernable small white memorial, is Scimitar Hill. Further round still is Green Hill and the beginning of the slope that forms Chocolate Hill.'

These snapshots from a Middlesex Yeoman's album were taken from the trenches just below Scimitar Hill a few days after the disastrous attack of August 21. Death can almost be smelt in the pictures, even after more than eighty years.

Below: The dip and the scarring on the nearby W Hills allows one to match the scene almost perfectly. It is most eerie standing on a beautifully hot day in the silence at Suvla contrasting the 'then' with the 'now'.

Left: Tints Corner was a small Turkish stronghold that held the Allies at bay. This Sharpshooters' snapshot gives a general view looking back towards Green Hill. **Right:** Recent widening of a small track that leads off the main road between Green and Scimitar Hills led to a photo opportunity that was just too good to be missed — here, a modern-day pilgrim stands in for the old soldier! The trees on the right of the comparison mark Green Hill Cemetery.

The view from just below Scimitar Hill looking across towards the Anzac sector. The sloping ground in the middle distance is that of Hill 60, whilst behind is the distinctive landscape of Anzac.

Soon after the attack on Scimitar Hill had begun, a composite force — made up of British, Australian, New Zealand, Indian and Gurkha troops — started to attack the nearby Hill 60. This position is in fact little more than a knoll but it was hoped that its capture would provide a good view to the north as well as securing the dangerous track that linked Suvla with Anzac. But once again the two main reasons for past failures were about to strike again: lack of artillery support and high quality preparatory reconnaissance. It had proved impossible to obtain up-to-date aerial photographs and those that were available showed little more than what was already known. The artillery bombardment, originally planned to last 45 minutes, had been shortened to only 30 minutes so that the guns could be switched to assist the IX Corps assault on the W Hills and Scimitar Hill. The other unfortunate side affect of this change of plan was that the troops who were about to assault Hill 60 would not begin the advance until after the IX Corps had already started their attack. This raised the possibility that the Turks would be able to halt one attack before turning their attention to repelling the next.

New Zealand officers enjoying a brew-up in May 1915. With his back turned to the camera on the left is Second Lieutenant Desmond Kettle of the Auckland Mounted Rifles who was to be **killed in action on Hill 60 on August 28. His body was never identified and his name is now inscribed on the the New Zealand Memorial which now stands on the hill.**

Shortly after 1530 hours, following the ineffectual barrage, the first wave of troops began to make their way towards Hill 60 only to be met by a storm of fire. In the first few minutes, 110 of the 150 men of the 13th Australian Battalion had become casualties. The second wave (the 14th Battalion), were cut up equally as bad whilst the third wave made no headway at all. The wounded were now lying in the thick scrub which was also camouflaging the true strength of the Turkish positions. This undergrowth was tinder dry and quickly caught fire so that any wounded man who could not extricate himself from the ever-spreading flames was destined to be either burnt alive or killed by his own exploding ammunition.

To the left of this massacre were the men of the New Zealand Mounted Rifles (Otago and Canterbury) who, having also suffered heavy casualties, had at least secured themselves at the foot of Hill 60. To support these virtually isolated troops, the 10th Hampshires were sent forward, only to run directly into a Turkish barrage. Consequently, only one man managed to link up with the New Zealanders.

Covering their left flank were the 5th Connaught Rangers who, after capturing their initial objective at Kabak Kuyu, turned left-handed and took their second objective: the wells around Susak Kuyu. From here, they pushed onto the north-western slopes of Hill 60, where, after a fierce bayonet attack, they succeeded in capturing a portion of the Turkish line. The Gurkhas, who had been so badly mauled in the fighting for the Sari Bair heights less than a fortnight earlier, had made slow progress as they advanced from the plains to the west, and it was nightfall before they were able to link up with the Connaughts and take over the positions so bravely won by the Irishmen.

As night fell, the few Australians surviving from the initial assault were reinforced while the 10th Hampshires, now less than 200 strong, were moved near to Susak Kuyu, a position that it was feared would become untenable if Hill 60 was not taken.

Brigadier-General Andrew Russell (commanding New Zealand Mounted Rifles), after briefly inspecting the situation, realised that the New Zealanders in the centre of the attack were now unable to make any further headway. Fresh troops would

Left: Officers ashore at Anzac — a picture believed to have been taken in September or October 1915. Above: The curve and the terracing are the clue to the location — identified by the author as one of the lower slopes of Plugge's Plateau. However, the original was taken in a trench, i.e. lower down, thus giving the impression of the slopes being a lot steeper. Today the addition of new road, plus the ever-increasing vegetation, has almost disguised it.

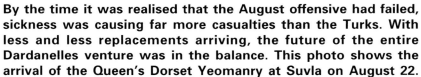

By the time it was realised that the August offensive had failed, sickness was causing far more casualties than the Turks. With less and less replacements arriving, the future of the entire Dardanelles venture was in the balance. This photo shows the arrival of the Queen's Dorset Yeomanry at Suvla on August 22.

The small cove between C Beach and Nibrunesi Point is the exact spot where the men from Dorset landed. This beach was largely sheltered from the critical gaze of Turkish spotters and was thus used to unload a number of men from the 2nd Mounted Division who arrived in mid-August.

have to be used if the little gains of the day were not to be lost at first light. After finally convincing both Brigadier-General Vaughan Cox (GOC 29th Indian Brigade) and Major-General Sir Alexander Godley (GOC NZ&A Division) of the validity of his plan, the recently arrived 18th Battalion were released to take part. They were to attack from a sunken road near Kabuk but once again the problems were numerous. Inexperienced troops were now being ordered to attack a position at night that had not been recon- noitred and without artillery support or even an accurate assess- ment of what positions lay on the summit.

The men were roused and eventually arrived just before dawn at the trench from where the Connaughts had launched their attack a day earlier. None had any idea that their battalion was about to be used in an attack; most thought they were just being sent up to the front to take over part of the line. The officers were then summoned to hear the orders from their Brigade-Major who

emphasised that only the bomb and the bayonet were to be used. On pointing out that they had not been issued with any bombs, one officer was told that 'they must do the best that is possible without them'!

Dawn on the 22nd was now breaking as the first wave charged towards Hill 60. Remarkably, they succeeded in driving many Turks from their trenches but once again follow-up support was not forthcoming. Having gained some ground but not the summit, the assault eventually died away with another 1,300 men added to Gallipoli's ever growing casualty list.

By now the news of the failure to capture Scimitar Hill and the W Hills was general knowledge at Anzac. Many were annoyed and disillusioned by the failure at Suvla as one New Zealand trooper recorded in his diary on the 22nd:

'Battleships started to bombard in earnest. Several thousands of troops advanced across the plain under terrific artillery fire (shrapnel) Turks fired shells which set the scrub and corn on fire. From this blazing mass the wounded could not escape. Dozens fell and many gallant rescues were effected . . . In evening an attack was made on Turkish trenches, an advance on Hill 60 and captured, but was too hot to hold Turks set fire to scrub and Tommies retired to original trenches, came back with the yarn that they had advanced 1,600 yards. Whereas they had not gained anything, only hundreds of killed and wounded . . . Later some of our party went out and were fired on by Turks and Tommies. One had his rifle broken by a bullet. A Royal Irish Fusilier fired 3 shots at a N.Zr 10 yards away and missed him!'

Throughout the next few days both sides licked their wounds and, as the Turks dug and strengthened their positions, the Allied commanders began planning yet another assault on Hill 60. Lieutenant-General Sir William Birdwood (General Officer Commanding Australian and New Zealand Army Corps) was confident that if he could get a thousand fit men for the next attack, it would be successful. However, the Anzac sector was so understrength, from both casualties and sickness, that this number could only be reached by taking men from nine different battalions.

The new attack was scheduled for the afternoon of August 27. On the right were 350 Australians; in the middle a mixture of 400 Australians and New Zealanders, while the left, numbering about 250, was made up of men mainly from the 5th Connaughts. It met with very heavy casualties, the Connaughts losing over 150 whilst the 13th Australian Battalion lost 68 of the 100 men involved. Although a strong position was gained on the slopes of Hill 60, the main defensive works remained firmly in Turkish hands despite the 9th Light Horse being thrown into the battle as well. As the 27th became the 28th, the fighting became even more ferocious as the 10th Light Horse were added to the fray — an action for which they would be awarded a Victoria Cross and five Distinguished Conduct Medals. Slowly, yard by yard, the attackers started to win ground and, shortly before daybreak, the entire network they had been sent to capture had been taken but daylight revealed a disappointing scene. From the trenches they had succeeded in taking, they could now see that a strong Turkish redoubt sat on the summit of the hill blocking the view to the north. For all the bravery and hard fighting, little had been gained except a further 1,100 casualties.

Although the Anzac and Suvla sectors were eventually linked up, it was not the safest journey in the world to travel between the two locations. This is the despatch rider who had the unenviable task of passing messages daily between the two sectors.

The road now runs a few feet further away from the water's edge, and, not surprisingly, no trace could be found of the sunken vessel on the left of the 1915 photo. This small and intimate cemetery, New Zealand No. 2 Outpost, is on the left of the old Anzac line.

To combat the approaching winter storms that lash this part of the world, as well as to ease the landing of stores, numerous improvements were made to the main harbour at West Beach.

However, today, the distinctive rocks are the only clue as to what took place here all those years ago for, almost unbelievably, the entire harbour installation has disappeared!

By now the Australian and New Zealand troops were fast nearing the limit of human endurance. The last few weeks had cost some 12,500 dead and wounded — a third of the entire force. With no more new troops promised, and even replacements becoming fewer and fewer, the chances of the Anzacs being able to take part in any further offensive action was now zero. Nothing more could now be asked of them except to dig in and prepare for a winter campaign.

The grave of Lieutenant-Colonel Carew Reynell (centre) who was killed in the fighting for Hill 60 on August 28. Construction of the permanent cemeteries and memorials could not begin until 1923. Pictures taken in Hill 60 Cemetery in 1915 and 1999.

Human remains collected on Hill 60 by the Imperial War Graves Commission team during 1919. Note that the Turkish lad on the right is carrying a British mess tin and wears a Turkish Army belt buckle. The high ground of the Tekke Tepe ridge is visible in the background.

The cemetery and New Zealand Memorial to the Missing on Hill 60 was built right over the old trenches. Thus it is easy to appreciate the significance of the high ground which lay just beyond which prevented the Allies from having the clear view towards Biyuk Anafarta that they so desperately needed.

POLITICAL UPHEAVAL, MILITARY STALEMATE

Following Sir Ian Hamilton's admission that the August offensive had failed, there was an almost immediate stampede by politicians in London desperate to distance themselves from the entire Gallipoli campaign. Throughout the corridors of Whitehall, stories of the mismanagement of the operation spread. Some of the accounts were reported by journalists who had returned from

Opposite: North Beach, Anzac, shortly after the August offensive had finished. In the foreground can be seen No. 1 Australian Field Hospital whilst in the centre are ordnance and supply depots (along with a solitary YMCA tent). Further away still lie the tents of No. 13 Casualty Clearing Station. The high ground in the background is the Kiretch Tepe ridge. Above: Taken from the northern slopes of Plugge's Plateau, the view 84 years later is stunning — as indeed it was in 1915. Canterbury Cemetery can be seen on the road that runs towards Suvla Bay, as well as the CWGC cottages and workshops. Further round stands No. 2 Outpost Cemetery.

Gallipoli shocked by the appalling waste of human life that they had witnessed. Unable to reveal what they had seen by telegram (as GHQ censored all reports back to London), the reporters waited until they returned and then set about telling anyone who would listen.

Amongst the most vocal was Keith Murdoch (whose son Rupert now owns the vast media empire). He had spent much of the time with the British journalist Ellis Ashmead-Bartlett who represented the press in London and had earlier covered the Balkan Wars for *The Daily Telegraph*. Murdoch agreed to take back for him a detailed report citing the incompetent leadership that he had witnessed. This, however, never reached London as it had to be 'handed in' to the military police on Murdoch's arrival at Marseilles. Nevertheless, it did nothing to deter him and during his time in London he circulated his own report and met amongst others, both Churchill and the Prime Minister Lloyd George. Although his relevations were not the first to reach Whitehall, they did, in many ways, sound the death knell for the Gallipoli adventure. Already His Majesty was said to be furious with Sir Ian after having spoken to Major Guy Dawnay who had been a faithful servant on the General Staff but now felt duty bound to tell of the incompetence of those serving under his Commander-in-Chief.

Although Lieutenant-General Sir Julian Byng, one of the generals requested by Sir Ian in June, had finally arrived, it was doubtful that even competent leadership could now save the campaign. With Byng taking over IX Corps, and Major-General Beauvoir de Lisle returning to command the 29th Division, the way was now clear for Lieutenant-General Sir Bryan Mahon to return. Mahon, who remained popular with his troops had, since his resignation during the August offensive, been twiddling his thumbs on nearby Mudros. Other new appointments included Major-General Stanley Maude who took over the 13th Division and Major-General Edward Fanshawe, who replaced Hammersley commanding the 11th Division. Despite these all-too-late changes, many in Whitehall were also gunning for Sir Ian, and they were in no mood to give in until he was removed.

The Scottish Horse bivouacking on the beach at Lala Baba after landing on September 3, 1915. The area was under shell-fire at the time and casualties quickly mounted. Lala Baba is the hill that can be seen in the background.

Today this part of Gallipoli is almost completely deserted. The beach appears to have eroded little in contrast with other parts of the coastline — even the outcrop of rock that juts out into the sea has barely changed since 1915.

Australian troops stroll along Anzac Cove which quickly became the centre for both headquarters and stores. The dugouts which blanket the hillside have subsequently caused erosion of many of the hills around the peninsula.

Today the scene at Anzac Cove looking towards Ari Burnu is relatively unchanged though the view inland is somewhat restricted by the construction of the coast road which runs on top of the bank to the right of the beach.

During early September, it still seemed that some of the 95,000 replacements Sir Ian had requested might materialise. The French were talking about a new landing on the Asian side of the peninsula and, for a while, Italian troops were also said to be forthcoming. All these promises however were to prove empty. The Italian forces were withdrawn from the equation and the French decided instead to throw any extra troops they could spare into the bloody battlefields on the Western Front. During the September offensive in France, the British and French were to suffer some 250,000 casualties within a few days but whether these men would have been better employed at Gallipoli is an argument with no definitive answer.

As September turned into October, evacuation of the peninsula was contemplated for the first time. On being asked for his opinion, Sir Ian replied that he thought casualties might run as high as 50 per cent. This gloomy report was considered in London on October 14 by the Dardanelles Committee. This committee had been formed from the War Council when the Liberal government had been replaced by a coalition administration and it had met regularly since its first meeting on June 7, making all the key decisions regarding the Gallipoli venture. The important meeting on October 14 was convened following one of the first Zeppelin raids on London which had caused widespread alarm, hardly an ideal time for rational thought. In the end, it was decided that a new commander for the Gallipoli operation was required, and on October 16 Sir Ian received a telegram from Field-Marshal Lord Kitchener, the then Secretary of State for War, recalling him to London.

While all these political developments had been going on in the capital, little had been taking place on the peninsula itself. Total Allied strength was now about 114,000 compared with at least 200,000 at the start of the campaign, and some divisions, such as the hard-pressed Royal Naval Division, were now down to less than 4,000 men. Across the peninsula, sickness was now the main enemy with some 500 cases being evacuated each day. Fresh troops were landing but only in detachments of less than 2,000. Yeomanry and Light Horsemen continued to arrive throughout September and October but they did little more than just replace those sick. At Helles, the French line had been thinned and the British were forced to take over some of their trenches as

The whole scene must have been a very confusing affair to new arrivals at Anzac. This photo, taken by a member of the Bedfordshire Regiment who served there in the autumn, shows the clutter of stores which greeted them on the foreshore.

Taken once again from the road rather than on the beach as the new coast road now obscures the view from the latter. The stillness . . . and the silence . . . is almost oppressive.

Throughout the summer and into the autumn, men and supplies were hurriedly unloaded at Suvla — here horses and mules can be seen being fed and watered after landing between Suvla Point and West Beach harbour.

Today this part of Suvla is one of the most desolate on the entire Gallipoli peninsula. On the right is one of the huge Turkish memorials which mark the various locations where the Allies were halted. In the foreground can be seen West Beach with Little West Beach just visible in the distance. In the background lies Tekke Tepe ridge to the left with the Sari Bair heights on the right.

The food was bully beef and biscuits with apple jam and cheese, and you had dried vegetables which had to be soaked overnight in the dixie to boil next day. It were like eating rubber! The food was almost nil. If we did get any bread, which later on we did perhaps once a month, we got just one loaf between eight men for a day's ration. We'd no fresh water. The water that we drank was brought by boat to W Beach and water-carts collected it and brought it up so far. We were on the west side of Y Ravine and it was a very high cliff. You had to climb a winding path to the top and we had to carry dixies full of water from water-carts up to this gun position.

I was put on as latrine orderly and we had to dig a trench for the latrine and you had to stand astride to do your business, and then you had to cover it with soil because the flies were dreadful! The latrine was like a hole in the ground. I had to cover it with a ground sheet pegged above the hole and at night if I struck a match to light a candle in the dark, the ground sheet was just black with big flies, and when you were eating jam or biscuits you had to knock flies off to get them to your mouth. Most of us got dysentery. That was the biggest scourge we had on Gallipoli, dysentery and ill-health from lack of fresh water and lack of proper food. I got dysentery very badly. I hadn't the strength to go up and down the cliff across the ravine and up the hill to get to the Medical Officer (he was on the other side) and in the end I lost two or three stones.

SERGEANT H. KEIGHLEY
29TH DIVISION, ROYAL ARTILLERY

well. Consequently, any new commander would have to decide quickly what to do with an ever-decreasing force if he were to have any army left to command.

As far as the troops were concerned, the good thing about this static period was that as the weather cooled the flies died. The Turks, too, were exhausted and desperately short of good artillery ammunition; by this stage one in three of their shells was failing to explode. This situation changed with Bulgaria's attack on Serbia on October 10 as their entry into the war on the side of the Central Powers opened the direct rail link from Germany to Constantinople. This facilitated the provision of high-quality German shells.

There was great anxiety at Gallipoli as to what the winter storms would do to the landing points for the resupply of the troops. It was feared that a prolonged period of bad weather could lead to a critical shortage of food, water and ammunition — any one of which would alone be able to determine the outcome of the entire campaign.

These pictures show Gully Beach — then and now — a contrast from the day when a storm hit the beach. Eighty years later, the erosion continues apace, a little more of the beach being washed into the sea every year. This photo, showing the edge of what was once part of the road, is taken approximately ten feet closer to the high ground than the contemporary shot of 1915.

In October the weather started to deteriorate. Violent storms on at least three occasions suspended the landing of supplies and even washed away the landing piers at Anzac. It was into this land of confusion that the new Commander-in-Chief, Lieutenant-General Sir Charles Monro, arrived. He finally set foot on Imbros on October 28 and immediately set about his task with a gusto. He had been given clear and concise instructions from Kitchener (more than Sir Ian ever received) as he had insisted on being fully briefed on all matters before his departure. His first task was to put together a report, not only of the military situation but how to extract the Allies from it. What London wanted to know was whether this would be by taking the peninsula or by evacuating it. To a large extent, though, this had already been decided by

Whitehall's agreement with the French to help support the Serbs in their struggle against Austria. This was to be achieved by landing troops at the Greek port of Salonika as by this stage the French were all for abandoning Gallipoli. Thus, at the end of October, what remained of the 10th (Irish) Division under Mahon left the peninsula destined for Salonika.

Lieutenant-General Monro did not suffer fools or incompetence, and those officers left from Sir Ian's era soon appreciated that he was a much tougher commander. On October 30 he crossed over to the peninsula itself where he visited all three sectors in the one day: not an easy task in itself. On arrival at W Beach, he was met by the usual Gallipoli clutter: men unloading pitching lighters by hand, mules kicking up, boxes of supplies crazily stacked all over

W Beach on October 8, 1915 — note the men having either just arrived or in the process of unloading supplies on the furthest pier. It must be remembered that all supplies brought ashore at Gallipoli had to be manhandled, thus giving some idea of the logistics problem that faced the Allies.

The remains of the furthest pier are still quite visible unlike the dugouts which used to line the hills above W Beach. In many places on Gallipoli, the hillsides have collapsed where the dugouts used to stand. The small pillbox at the base of the hill is a much more recent structure and is now derelict.

the beach, and the all-pervading, revolting stench of death. Having just come from the Western Front, all this must have come as a terrible shock. While Suvla was not quite as bad, at Anzac it was even worse. Monro, being the no nonsense man that he was, did not waste time on niceties. After briefly touring each sector, he returned to each divisional HQ and posed the corps commanders the same questions: 'Were the troops physically fit enough to capture the enemy's positions?' and 'If no drafts were to arrive, but the Turks received more ammunition and fresh troops, could they hold on?'

On hearing the truthful replies from his corps commanders, the following day Monro sent this telegram to Kitchener.

'After inspecting the Gallipoli peninsula I have arrived at the following conclusions: The troops on the peninsula — with the exception of the Australian and New Zealand Army Corps — are not equal to a sustained effort owing to the inexperience of their officers, the want of training of the men, and the depleted condition of many of the units.

'We merely hold the fringe of the shore, and are confronted by the Turks in very formidable entrenchments with all the advantages of position and power of observation of our movements. The beaches are exposed to observed artillery fire, and in the restricted area all stores are equally exposed. Action by surprise can no longer be counted on, as the Turks are in considerably stronger force than they were and have had ample time to provide against surprise landings.

'Since the flanks of the Turks cannot be attacked, only a frontal attack is possible, and no room is afforded on any of these beaches for the distribution of additional divisions should they be sent. Nor is there sufficient space for the deployment of an adequate force of artillery, the action would be impaired by poverty of observation and of good positions for searching or counter-battery effect. Naval guns could only assist to a partial degree. In fact, an attack could only be prosecuted under the disadvantages of a serious lack of depth and of absence of surprise, seeing that the Turkish position dominates our line throughout. The uncertainty

The question as to whether the Allies were to evacuate or hold on dominated strategy from October onwards. The key problem was that if the troops were to stay, winter supplies had to be landed quickly . . . but, if they were to go, then everything that had already been landed would have to be taken off again, thus delaying the whole operation. V Beach is seen here awash with supplies giving some idea of the quandary.

Whilst lining up this photo, numerous fragments of broken wine bottles were found giving a possible clue as to what some of these crates contained! In the distance on the hilltop we can see the Helles Memorial which records the names of nearly 21,000 British and Commonwealth soldiers and sailors who were either missing in action or whose graves could not be identified after the war.

of the weather might also seriously hinder the landing of reinforcements and regularity in providing the artillery ammunition to the amount which might be required.

'I am therefore of opinion that another attempt to carry the Turkish lines would not offer any hope of success. The Turkish positions are being actively strengthened daily. Our information leads to the belief that heavy guns and ammunition are being sent to the peninsula from Constantinople. Consequently, by the time fresh divisions, if available, could arrive, the task of breaking the Turkish lines would be considerably more formidable than even it is at present.

'On purely military grounds, therefore, in consequence of the grave daily wastage of officers and men which occurs, and owing to the lack of prospect of being able to drive the Turks from their entrenched lines, I recommend the evacuation of the peninsula.

'As to the estimate of loss which would be involved, I am not at present able to make a definite statement. So much would depend on the degree to which the Turks attacked us during our withdrawal, on how far the re-embarkation could be conducted unobserved, and on the weather conditions which prevailed at the time. Admiral de Robeck has been asked to give me an estimate, but does not feel able at present to make a precise statement.

'I have no information as to the influence on the situation which would be caused by a complete German communication with Constantinople. We are told that the Germans have taken over the Turkish submarine and air services, and that Turkish machine guns and artillery are being manned by German experts. It would appear certain that even if no German troops are sent to this theatre, ammunition and materials of war will be despatched in quantities which will greatly add to our present difficulties.

On the right of the Allied flank, behind the Lone Pine position, lay Bolton's Ridge which has a number of valleys running off it. One of them is Poppy Valley which looks down towards Gaba Tepe. This position was enfiladed by the Turkish guns at Olive Grove, thus illustrating one of Sir Charles Monro's concerns. In the foreground is Lieutenant Bert Lowring of the 6th Australian Light Horse.

With incredibly thick scrub in this area — in places well over seven feet high — it is not the easiest place in which to get your bearings. In the background can be seen Gaba Tepe with the rear slopes of the Achi Baba ridge in the distance. To the left is Bolton's Ridge while straight ahead is the Valley of Despair and Holly Ridge.

'I have endeavoured in the expression of my opinion to give full weight to the effect which will be created in the East by our evacuation, and I consider that the force now in the peninsula, or such portions of it as may be able to evacuate, would be more favourably placed in Egypt. This force, before it can be usefully employed, stands much in need of rest, reorganisation and training. The corps and divisional commanders have done splendid work in the peninsula, but they do not possess the opportunity or time, as they now stand, to create this force into a reliable fighting machine. Hence I think that the loss of prestige caused by withdrawal would be compensated in a few months by increased fighting efficiency.

'I propose leaving here to visit Maxwell in Egypt on Tuesday (2nd November) and will report further on the situation in the Near East after consultation with him. I shall then proceed to Salonika.'

With this report of little more than a page, the fate of the Gallipoli venture was sealed. Lieutenant-General Monro, who had

Fresh from France with its peaceful harbours and docks and with trains and motors awaiting the arriving steamer, Monro was not prepared for the scenes which met his gaze as he landed at W Beach. The local conditions to which the Gallipoli army had long since grown accustomed — the open beach, the crazy piers, the landing of stores by hand from bumping lighters, the strings of kicking mules, the heavy dust, the cramped spaces, the jostling crowds on the narrow beach within range of the enemy's guns — filled him with blank amazement. Arriving later at Anzac Cove, where conditions were still more difficult his wonder only grew. To the staff officer beside him he remarked with a whimsical smile: 'It's just like Alice in Wonderland, 'curiouser and curiouser'.

BRIGADIER-GENERAL ASPINALL-OGLANDER
MILITARY OPERATIONS, GALLIPOLI, VOLUME II, 1932

Having backed the Gallipoli plan from its outset, Kitchener was desperate to see it through to a successful climax and he perceived evacuation as a disaster in the making. This view forced him to back any scheme that offered success: from a new landing at either Bulair on the Asian side, to a renewal of the naval assault. At this stage, renewing the bombardment of the forts may well have been the only option with any hope of success but, one by one, these plans all fell by the wayside.

Kitchener arrived at Mudros on November 9, and immediately began reporting back his findings to the Prime Minister. However, the question that everybody wanted answering — whether to stay or go — still remained unanswered. From the tone of Kitchener's telegrams, it is obvious that he finally began to realise the difficulties that Sir Ian had faced back in April. Also, by not sending out the additional troops and more ammunition that the generals had requested, he could now see that the failure of the August offensive was partly his fault. But still no final decision was made.

With still no final decision made about evacuation, Lord Kitchener came to Gallipoli to see the problems for himself. In this photo he can be seen (second left) studying the lie of the land from Walker's Ridge, looking towards the heights of Anzac and the more distant Suvla plain. It is at one of these vantage points that, with his hand on General Birdwood's arm, Kitchener said: 'Thank God, Birdie, I came to see this for myself. You were quite right. I had no idea of the difficulties you were up against.'

been on the peninsula for less than 24 hours and was destined never to return, had nonetheless played a major role in the future of the campaign. After reaching Cairo, he was given command of the Salonika operation and Lieutenant-General William Birdwood was placed in charge at Gallipoli. Later Winston Churchill, who as one of the key architects of the campaign still believed fully in it, was to say, (unfairly as most of Monro's observations were correct): 'He came, he saw, he capitulated'.

However, it was not all over yet. Kitchener had meanwhile decided to visit the peninsula himself as the government were loath to make such a far-reaching decision until they had heard his views. Even so, contingency evacuation plans were now drawn up for approval.

Today on Walker's Ridge it is not hard to imagine Kitchener glowering over the landscape. In the foreground, largely hidden by trees, are the CWGC workshops. Following the beach further round leads us to Lala Baba and the Salt Lake. The high ground of the Kiretch Tepe ridge can be seen climbing in the far distance.

Despite Kitchener's slowly fading political status, he still remained to most soldiers an almost legendary figure. Whilst at Gallipoli he took the time to address the troops, in this case on North Beach in the Anzac sector.

With the slope of Plugge's Plateau a distinctive Anzac landmark, finding the exact location of this shot was not difficult. Less easy was to imagine the men being assembled on this spot to hear from someone who was already a legend in his own lifetime.

By November 16 the situation in Salonika was not only dangerous but was verging on the embarrassing. It was now feared that the Greeks might join the Central Powers in which case the troops already ashore would stand little chance of survival. Kitchener, having met King Constantine of Greece on November 19, succeeded in persuading him to remain neutral but by now Kitchener was convinced that to keep Greece out of the war, Salonika needed reinforcing; thus the writing was firmly on the wall for Gallipoli.

Kitchener returned to Mudros on November 21, the same day that the Turks launched an attack against the 52nd Division's section of the line at Helles. This action had followed a far heavier bombardment than was normal for the Turks but, even so, it had been easily repulsed, adding weight to General Birdwood's school of thought that unless German infantry were sent to Gallipoli, his troops could hold on and that evacuation was unnecessary.

However, later that night, after meeting with Monro on Mudros, Kitchener decided that evacuation was the only course of

action left. The following morning, the 22nd, he despatched a message to London stating that he advised that both Anzac and Suvla should be evacuated but Helles should continue to be held. In addition, he all but admitted that if the troops Sir Ian had requested in the first place had been released, the whole situation would have been vastly different.

After considering Kitchener's reports, London could still not make up its mind, the War Committee voting for an entire evacuation yet the Cabinet was undecided. However, with Monro's opinion having been validated by Kitchener personally, the General was appointed Commander-in-Chief of all Mediterranean Forces (less those stationed in Egypt), whilst Birdwood became the Commander of the Dardanelles Army.

Kitchener left the theatre on November 24 and, pre-empting the Cabinet's final decision, issued orders for the thinning of stores under the pretext that they were needed in Salonika. Troops were also withdrawn to Mudros, Imbros and Mitylene under the impression that they were going for a rest whereas in reality they were being used to start preparing transit camps.

Gully Beach was used for the headquarters of various units throughout the campaign. In this case, the caption states that we are viewing the HQ of the 42nd East Lancs, the division having started to arrive during the Second Battle of Krithia in early May.

By now operations on the peninsula were restricted to limited local actions. At Suvla, attempts had been made to seize some ground along Kiretch Tepe but, after brief yet fierce fighting, the positions had remained unchanged. At Anzac, mining was the order of the day with deep underground tunnels being constructed, filled with explosive and then detonated under the enemy lines. Occasionally, two groups of miners from opposing sides would come across one another below ground resulting in grim hand-to-hand combat in the dark in which shovels were the main weapons used. How many of these unrecorded brutal fights took place is something we shall never know. One local action at Helles, which involved three mines exploding in quick succession under the Turkish positions near the Vineyard, resulted in some success although it was not possible to follow this up as most of the units were so under strength.

All these minor skirmishes were nothing compared to what Mother Nature now had in store when a violent south-westerly gale hit a little area on November 26. The landing of supplies had to be suspended and all ships were ordered to either stand off or return to the protection of Imbros. Piers at Anzac and Helles were swept away and the man-made harbour at Imbros breached and a number of ships sunk. As the day wore on, torrential rain started to fall across the peninsula which started to flood the trenches, particularly in the Suvla sector. The deluge — which continued for 24 hours — brought walls of water into the British trenches and with it decomposing bodies, dead animals and all manner of equipment and debris. Some British trenches filled to the parapet which forced the men to abandon them and either make their way back to the beach or to lie in the quagmire behind the trench line. One of the worst hit areas was that held by the 86th Brigade of the long suffering 29th Division where the trenches all but collapsed.

The barren hillside is now covered in greenery but erosion has narrowed the beach and wiped away the memorial that stands in the right foreground of the 1915 picture.

An ambulance struggles through the mud of Gully Ravine in mid-November — more typical of the Western Front than Gallipoli.

As nature heals the scars, only the shallow bank remains to mark out this corner today.

The Turks were suffering equally as badly and they too could be seen climbing from their trenches in a struggle for survival. Throughout this period, an almost unofficial truce broke out at Suvla as both sides fought against nature. As the rain eased on the night of November 27, the wind turned to an icy northerly gale. Quickly, the rain turned to snow and before long one of the worst blizzards to hit this region was underway. With the almost complete collapse of many trenches, parts of the front were only held by snipers but they took little action against their equally-suffering adversaries.

At Anzac, the position was marginally more bearable. Engineers had constructed caves as shelters from the shelling, and these were now used to escape the worst of the storm. Also the rougher terrain gave more shelter from the biting wind. Likewise, at Helles, the sloping ground saved the trenches from the degree of flooding that was being experienced at Suvla.

As the snow eventually petered out and skies cleared, the temperature plummeted still further. For many men, already weakened by dysentery, poor health and constant front line conditions, this was the final agony. Many froze to death where they stood or lay whilst others, desperate to reach the shore, died in the attempt. The winter clothing that would have so alleviated the situation, due to an unfortunate course of events, being the most

The threat of winter storms and the destruction that they could cause, were without doubt a relevant factor to the decision makers as to whether to stay or go. It was following scenes like this one at Anzac, after the first of the November storms, that made people realise that whatever the decision was to be, it had to be made soon.

Left: Scene on West Beach at Suvla around the end of November or beginning of December. Note the particularly large curved rock in the centre of the photo, which still remains completely unchanged from how it appeared in 1915 (right). Where once Red Cross wagons once waited, now stands the author's four-wheel-drive and a motorcycle belonging to a local fisherman.

Our officer, Captain Newton Phillips, seeing the state of the men, said it was a case of every man for himself and God for us all. So we made for this dugout which was more than half full of boxes of these bombs. There was about two feet of water in the dugout but we piled some of the boxes at one end to get above it, then we settled down to sleep. About midnight there was a short lull in the storm and another officer, Buck Adams, came round to inspect if the bombs were all right and he shone a torch into the dugout and ordered us out of there, so we both decided that we should go down to the beach and walk along the sand which would be better than stamping around in the mud and freezing. On our way we came across a big galvanised tank that had been put up on sandbags to hold paraffin oil supplies. The storm had washed away the sandbags under the tank, the tank had then fallen down and all the oil had run out to sea. We thought the empty tank would be a grand shelter from the storm and would be dry inside and a shelter from the wind and the cold. I started to crawl inside when my head came into contact with hobnailed boots. I shouted to the man to shift up and make room for two more men, but there was no response. Then we realised something was wrong and we found that there were seven men in the tank and they'd all been suffocated with the fumes.

They were all dead! We had a real fright at finding this and intended reporting it when we got to our camp. Then we made our way towards our camp and rounding a corner we saw what seemed to be a number of men sitting and sprawling in the mud. We found on getting nearer to them there were 23 men all frozen to death. They'd left the front line trench after being there for 36 hours and were making their way to the beach to a boat which was waiting to take them out to a Red Cross boat to give them food and a night's rest and more food supplies before they returned to the front line again, as supplies could not reach them owing to the floods. They had had a ration of rum before leaving the trench — that was all they had there — and the effects of the rum on their way down to the boat had worn off. They had slumped down where they were and had been frozen to death. You see, when the rain stopped a bitter frost set in, and men who'd been soaking wet the previous day had the clothes frozen to their bodies, and if you took off your overcoats they could be put to stand upright frozen stiff. For a couple of days after the storm died down we were on duty digging graves.

SAPPER J. JOHNSTON
44TH (WELSH) FIELD COMPANY, R.E.

Left: The areas most badly affected by the storm on November 26 were at Suvla where the water running off the high ground flooded the trenches lower down, after which an icy wind blew in across the open plain. However, at Anzac, the same awful terrain that had so hindered attacks in the past, now saved the troops from the worst effects of the storm by facilitating drainage.

At Helles, the sloping ground also removed a lot of the water before it froze but, even so, the dugouts — seen here of the West Kent Yeomanry — look less than hospitable. Right: Today, like the rest of the area, it is vastly overgrown and barely recognisable as the same place. Our author says that on a sweltering June day, imagining blizzard conditions made the contrast even more difficult!

recently-landed stores, was one of the first to be taken off in preparation for the as-yet-unconfirmed evacuation. The men had no dry clothes to change into and by the morning of the 28th frost-bite cases were pouring onto the beach.

The 86th Brigade was all but out of action. The Munsters, who had landed in April over a 1,000 strong, were now down to less than a 100 men. On the beach the medical facilities were not

prepared for anything like this scale of casualties. Doctors struggled night and day but with boats still being unable to land and evacuate the sick and wounded, space undercover was fast running out and it was November 30 before the weather conditions allowed the first of the sick to be taken off. Some 5,000 troops had suffered from varying degrees of frostbite while a further 200 had died or drowned during the storm.

There were many small cemeteries scattered across the peninsula in 1915 that were often the result of individual battles or dedicated to particular units, but when the Allies left, many were lost. Here, Sergeant Smith of the West Kent Yeomanry looks at a grave in the South-East Mounted Brigade Cemetery near Y Ravine. Many of the small cemeteries, so lovingly tended during the campaign, could not be maintained after the war, so the remains were exhumed for reburial in one of the 31 permanent cemeteries. Yet many graves were either never found or not identified, becoming just another name to be added to the 21,000 missing on the Helles Memorial.

With the damage to the piers, evacuation at speed was once again impossible and in London new doubts had surfaced over the wisdom of the whole plan. Lieutenant-General Monro, now pressured Kitchener for a positive decision. If they were to stay, winter supplies needed to be landed quickly to prevent a repeat performance of the past few days. If they were to go, however, he was loath to land more stores that would, in most cases, have to be removed again before the troops could leave, as the stores cluttered up the assembly areas on the beaches. On December 7, the Cabinet met, realising that any more delays would seriously jeopardise the chance of a successful evacuation. It was also perceived that the landing of the extra troops necessary to support a winter campaign would upset the French who were keen that any more men sent to the Mediterranean should go instead to Salonika. It was under these conditions, that finally, the decision was taken to evacuate Suvla and Anzac, whilst retaining a foothold at Helles.

THE EVACUATION

SUVLA AND ANZAC

The plans for the evacuation of Suvla and Helles were both well thought out and superbly executed. The operation was full of risk as ashore on the Suvla — Anzac front were some 90,000 men, 5,000 animals, 2,000 vehicles, 200 guns and tons of stores.

In places the Turkish trenches were less than ten yards from the Allied lines and it was essential that the enemy should have no idea as to what was going on if a disaster was to be avoided. In some places the Turks would have to advance less than 300 yards to be able to fire directly into Anzac Cove which would lead to a massacre of any remaining troops. At Suvla, with the winter weather having now reflooded the Salt Lake, other than the front line trenches, the sector was now cut in two, the two areas being known as 'A' and 'B' linked only by a bridge across the Cut. Three lines of reserve trenches had also been dug at Suvla in case the enemy discovered the plan before its completion although the chances of any rearguard party surviving in this event were virtually nil.

It was a blessing that Helles was not to be evacuated at the same time as to lift the last remaining men from all three sectors would, the Navy reckoned, take three nights but from just the Suvla-Anzac sector only two. It was thought the chances of three consecutive nights of calm weather remote and with every passing day the chance of discovery by the Turks increased.

At Anzac, orders were issued for long periods of no shooting but that any Turkish incursions were to be met by a hail of fire. By this tactic, it was hoped, that the Turks would get used to the inactivity so as the line was thinned out, they would not notice any difference. The troops in the front line were also starting to see

Top right: Photograph taken on December 14, 1915 of Williams Pier on North Beach with the Sphinx behind. Note the terraces on the right excavated into the hills. Right: Today nothing visible remains of Williams Pier whilst the new road almost completely hides the Sphinx from the beach. This photograph was taken from the road, where the amount of erosion is obvious, especially where many of the former dugouts lay.

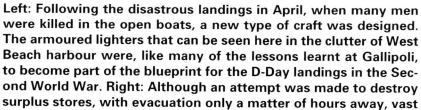

Left: Following the disastrous landings in April, when many men were killed in the open boats, a new type of craft was designed. The armoured lighters that can be seen here in the clutter of West Beach harbour were, like many of the lessons learnt at Gallipoli, to become part of the blueprint for the D-Day landings in the Second World War. Right: Although an attempt was made to destroy surplus stores, with evacuation only a matter of hours away, vast quantities had to be abandoned to the Turks. This photograph shows the final preparations being made for the last of the men to escape. Below: In recent years, one or two small fishing boats have started to re-use the old West Beach harbour at Suvla, even though it is now completely denuded of its wartime quayside. On showing this picture to local fishermen, they took quite some convincing that it was indeed the same place!

changes with men suffering from minor ailments not returning to their units. Whilst most thought the excuse of thinning the lines for winter not to be true, the majority were expecting another new landing rather than a full scale evacuation.

Throughout the first week of December, both men and supplies were re-embarked and by the 8th the garrison was down to 83,000 men. All the time, however, the Turks had to be convinced that nothing was changing. Dummy batteries replaced the real ones and these were moved to new positions every night. Supply dumps were kept looking full and during the day more 'supplies' — often boxes full with sand — would be landed. The more the plan evolved, the more likely it seemed that the whole sector

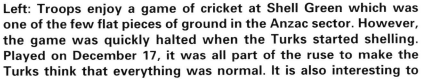

Left: Troops enjoy a game of cricket at Shell Green which was one of the few flat pieces of ground in the Anzac sector. However, the game was quickly halted when the Turks started shelling. Played on December 17, it was all part of the ruse to make the Turks think that everything was normal. It is also interesting to note the well-maintained grave in the outfield. **Right:** Today, with the wall of the immaculate Shell Green Cemetery in the foreground and scrub now taking over the old wicket, other than the hot June day it is hard to imagine a more unlikely place for a cricket pitch.

could be evacuated without arousing Turkish suspicions, a proposition no one had seriously believed would be possible when the order for evacuation had been given.

It was, as we have seen, imperative that the front line trenches at Anzac were held to the last. Also both Suvla and Anzac had to be abandoned on the same night. The Navy reckoned that they could remove a maximum of 10,000 men per night from each sector but, as the final stage was to be carried out over two nights, this meant that a total of 20,000 men on each sector had to be reached as quickly as possible. This intermediate stage was completed on the night of December 17/18; now came the critical period.

Nerves were jangling throughout both sectors as any serious Turkish attack at this stage would have disastrous affects on the strict timetable of evacuation. Men were detached to wander around the rear areas lighting fires in deserted tents whilst fatigue parties continued to clear rubbish and unload 'supplies'. All was still quiet.

The men who remained in the front line trenches had also got into the spirit of deception. Apart from sprinting around the trenches, firing from different positions to make out that they were still manned, a new invention was born: the self-firing rifle. The idea was basic but very efficient. A piece of string was tied to the trigger of a rifle and the other end attached to an empty container. Into this, water dripped from another vessel that was suspended above. As the weight of water increased, so it pulled the trigger. The length of time before the rifle fired was determined by the rate of drips, various intervals being set to simulate sniper action. As more men departed so more timed rifles were set up and still the Turks suspected nothing.

Left: During the last few days before the evacuation, Anzac Cove was virtually deserted but those men left were employed on fatigue parties to light fires in unoccupied tents, particularly at meal times, and make themselves obvious in other ways at places that were known to be under observation. Fortunately for the Allies, the German and Turkish airmen flew too high to notice the disappearance of thousands of men. This picture was taken on December 17, 1915. Right: The road which now cuts through Anzac Cove has greatly changed the appearance since then. In this shot, both the line of the new road as well as the constant erosion that keeps pulling parts of the cove into the sea can clearly be seen. In the background lies part of the coastline in the Suvla sector which leads to Nibrunesi Point. In the far distance stands the Kiretch Tepe ridge.

At dusk on the 18th, the beaches became a hive of activity as the first men to leave in the final stage began their trek towards the shore. Throughout the night, from both Anzac and Suvla, the boats, many ex-Channel steamers, took off the men and by morning, some 10,000 men had been embarked from both Anzac and

An Australian photograph illustrating the delayed-action rifle mechanism invented by Lance-Corporal William Scurry (later Captain MC, DCM) of the 7th Battalion, AIF. The rifle was fired by means of weights operated through water escaping from one container into another, until the lower can was heavy enough to pull the trigger. Obviously only one shot could be fired from each weapon as there would be no way of loading a fresh round in the breach. A rifle could be left like this to operate up to 20 minutes after being set and six were employed by the 3rd Brigade following the departure of the last party.

Suvla. The weather had assisted the operation and a calm sea, a full moon hidden by clouds, and a morning mist helped enormously. Meanwhile, the Turks could be seen strengthening their positions yet still oblivious to the full scale evacuation that was going on right under their noses. So far not one casualty had been sustained; if the secrecy could be maintained for a further 24 hours, everyone would get away safely

The 19th saw the last few men making every effort to simulate normal activity. Incinerators and fires were kept burning, men made themselves obvious at positions that were known to be under observation, mule carts were driven around loaded with empty boxes, and fatigue parties continued to work 'normally'. Even as night fell, the customary sound of ration convoys jingling towards the front was simulated to ensure the Turks suspected nothing.

They did, however, cause great anxiety at Suvla where they started to shell not only the main pier but also the forming up area selected for that night's re-embarkation. The shells the Turks were now using were of Austrian or German origin and, as such, they were far more reliable and powerful than the ammunition they had previously been using. Fortunately for the Allies, the area was so sparsely occupied that from the 50 shells or so that landed, there was only one casualty. The few remaining British guns near Lala Baba immediately responded and the Turkish shelling soon ceased. The embarkation staff breathed a collective sigh of relief. The damage to the pier was quickly repaired and the troops went back to simulating normality while all prayed for nightfall.

At Helles, two limited attacks had gone ahead. One was fairly successful whilst the other gained nothing but at least these actions helped in turning attention away from the northern sector where the critical moment was now only hours away. As darkness fell, a destroyer turned on its searchlight, blinding the Turkish position on the flank at Gaba Tepe. This seemingly small action, allowed the men holding the position to be picked up directly from the beach rather than having to make their way to the main embarkation point.

The main body of troops at Anzac were to be embarked in three waves, 'A', 'B' and 'C'. The troops of 'A' contingent were to depart at dusk, 'B' at 2300 hours, and 'C' at 0100 hours. There was

Chatham's Post, named after Lieutenant William Chatham of the 5th Light Horse (who commanded the covering party whilst this position was constructed), was situated on the extreme right of the Anzac position — seen here from Wilson's Lookout in November 1915. The men are from the 2nd Australian Light Horse.

Taken in the early light of dawn, the scene here has changed little with only the scrub and a more recent Turkish pillbox to mark the passing of 85 years.

With the removal of Sir Ian Hamilton, his replacement, Lieu-tenant-General Charles Monro, had his command widened to cover all troops in the Mediterranean (less those in Egypt) where-upon General Birdwood became the commander of the Gallipoli operation. Here he is seen on his last day at Anzac, perhaps con-templating what might have been.

The beach here has changed a lot less than many places on the peninsula, probably because it is a little harder to reach than the more popular Anzac Cove. In the far distance can be seen the Kiretch Tepe ridge, whilst in front of that stands the small No. 2 Outpost Cemetery where 152 lie buried of whom 66 are of unidentified remains.

great competition to be in the final groups as the few survivors of April felt it was their right to be last off, whilst the new replace-ments equally wanted a chance to show their courage.

In the catalogue of errors which mark the Gallipoli campaign, for once — albeit far too late — every detail had been taken care of. To dull the sound of the men leaving the floors of the trenches had been pulled up and boots were wrapped in sand-bags or socks. At places where confusion was likely, marker trails had been laid using flour or salt while others were lit up with candles shielded in biscuit tins. In addition, special traffic-officers had been appointed to supervise the smoothness and silence of the operation. As the men gradually trickled away they left not only the self-firing rifles but also a large number of booby traps to slow down the occupation by the Turks.

At 0130 hours the last of the 'B' party left the shore. It only now remained to get off the final 2,000 men from the 'C' group who were holding the most crucial front line trenches. So well had the evacuation gone that it was even running slightly ahead of schedule. At 0240 Lone Pine was abandoned; 0255 saw Quinn's Post and Pope's Hill deserted; 0315 Russell's Top and at 0324 the last man left Walker's Ridge. By 0330 hours all the men were clear of the heights and the order was given to fire the mine at Russell's Top. The explosion bought a storm of Turkish fire upon the deserted Anzac trenches but no shelling upon the beaches, and at 0400 hours the last lighter headed out to sea. A few officers still remained to round up stragglers but none arrived. So at 0410 hours on December 20, perhaps the most famous of all the Gal-lipoli sectors — Anzac — was finally abandoned.

With the sea out of photo to the left, this picture was taken at an area known as Hell Spit. The barbed wire entanglements are the Australian's last line of defence, presumably erected shortly after the order for evacuation was given.

The same view today. The track leads to Beach Cemetery (which is just out of view to the left) whilst the cemetery in the centre is Shrapnel Valley. There are 391 burials in the former while 683 lie in the latter.

At Suvla things were also going well and there, too, the Turks remained oblivious to what was taking place. In places they continued firing at deserted trenches hours after the last man had left. The evacuation at Suvla was carried out in a slightly different way to that at Anzac. As the men left the front line, they passed through a series of newly-dug trenches, each protected by barbed wire, with the only exit via specially prepared gates. An officer stationed at each gate counted the men through and, when all on his list had passed, he would phone through to the next gate, before closing his behind him.

By 0315 hours, the last gates around Lala Baba were closed and at 0400 General Maude and his officers departed the sector to the south of the Salt Lake. An hour later the northern sector was abandoned, the last act being to set fire to the petrol-soaked supplies that littered the beach. Commander Edward Unwin, VC, the same officer who had been awarded the Victoria Cross for his actions on the *River Clyde* at V Beach back in April, was amongst the small party on the last boat to leave Suvla Bay.

The evacuation from Suvla-Anzac had seen some 83,000 escape with only one man wounded and this was from a spent bullet. Although vast amounts of stores had not been completely destroyed, hundreds of tons had been reloaded as well as almost all the artillery.

For many hours the Turks failed to appreciate what was happening. After the explosion at Russell's Top, some seized the crater and reported that the Anzac trenches appeared empty but these messages were not immediately acted upon though, as the day progressed, the Turks became ever braver in venturing forwards. The fear of an ambush and the risk of booby traps further slowed their advance, and it was not until nightfall, as the destroyers that had remained offshore shelling the piles of supplies on the beach departed, that the Turks took possession of Anzac and Suvla. That night, some 16 hours after the last boat had left, a fierce storm arose sweeping away the flimsy piers; it had been that close. As a German war correspondent wrote, and is quoted in the official history of the campaign: 'As long as wars last, the

Above: Suvla, on the afternoon of evacuation, with stores stacked ready for destruction. Right: A tranquil scene today.

evacuation of Suvla and Anzac will stand before the eyes of all strategists as a hitherto unattained masterpiece'.

The success of the evacuation no doubt went some way to repairing the damage done to Britain's military prowess in the region. There was, still the question of Helles and it seemed unlikely the Turks would be hoodwinked for a second time.

After the evacuation was complete, mines and explosives on time-fuzes exploded amongst the remainder of the stores that had to be abandoned. Meanwhile, British ships stood off the coast shelling the beaches to try and complete the destruction.

Left: In this picture, taken on the morning of December 20 from the foredeck of HMS *Cornwallis,* the stores on the beach at Suvla can be seen burning fiercely while, later in the morning (right), a parting shot falls short as the fires die down.

HELLES

With the successful evacuation of both Suvla and Anzac, all eyes now turned to Helles but no word had yet been given as to whether this sector was to be retained or evacuated. The problem was a vital one for if it was to be held more supplies would have to be landed, but if it was to be evacuated, then this had to start soon or the winter storms would make the operation impossible. Lieutenant-General Monro was in favour of total evacuation and the Navy now saw little point in retaining its force to help blockade the narrows. With London receiving these same views, most people thought evacuation was virtually certain. It had already been decided to put the whole front under one command and, as such, the French started to leave on December 12. By December 22, all but one colonial unit had left. They had been persuaded to leave their artillery behind, not only to support the remaining British but also to convince the Turks that nothing strange was afoot. However, the gap being left by the French had to be filled and it was the misfortune of the long suffering 29th Division, recently evacuated from Suvla, to come back to take over this section of the line. What a blow this must have been to these men who, having been through so much, were once again returned to the front just when they thought they had shaken the dust of Gallipoli from their boots for ever. On Christmas Eve they re-entered the front lines unsure of what the future was to bring.

Having seen IX Corps and the Anzacs escape, General Otto Liman von Sanders, was desperate not to repeat this mistake at Helles. Orders were issued to keep the pressure on the British lines to test if they were being weakened, and men and artillery freed by the Allied evacuation of the northern sectors were moved to Helles. Special bridges were built so that if the British lines were weakened, artillery could be rushed forward over the trenches to shell any departing shipping. Von Sanders also saw to it that special teams were set up to assault the beaches and set fire to any boats they could find. Meanwhile, observation was also stepped up.

The British, keen to give the impression that they were going nowhere, ordered limited offensive action while all the time stores were being thinned in readiness for the final order from London. VIII Corps response was magnificent. Four divisions of these tired and worn-out British troops now faced 21 Turkish divisions.

Anything that could not be evacuated was literally broken up by hand or burned on the beaches in the final hours leading up to the evacuation. Here men on X Beach smash up surplus barges.

Eighty-odd years later, much of the beach and almost all of the road has been reclaimed by the sea. Otherwise little has changed and one can still just make out the top of the path carved into the rock face which used to run down to the beach.

With the Anzac-Suvla evacuation having been completed so successfully, few believed that the same plan would work again at Helles. Nevertheless, preparations for evacuation went ahead at full speed while all the time the Turks probed the front lines and shelled the beaches. Left: Here a round from one of the Asiatic guns can be seen falling short off W Beach on January 7, 1916.

Many of the supplies that can be seen here were eventually destroyed as time for the final evacuation ran out. Right: In June 1999, the remains of the piers could clearly still be seen beneath the azure waters of the Aegean yet on desolate W Beach itself, the clutter and excitement of 1915 has made way for an era of peace and tranquility.

Here and there they straightened the line or captured a feature; raided trenches or carried out mining and sapping. Doubtlessly, though, there was the general feeling of not wanting to 'cop it' at this late stage.

On Christmas Day, Lieutenant-General Birdwood made a visit to the peninsula. He had still not received any definite orders about evacuation but all the signs were that it was imminent. Having conferred with his French counterpart, it was decided to get the last remaining French unit off as soon as possible. He also asked his local commanders to start drawing up their own plans for evacuation. The 42nd Division, desperately in need of a rest, was withdrawn and replaced by the 13th Division from Mudros, although plans for the 29th Division to be relieved were cancelled

as it was felt that, despite its losses, this division could still be relied upon to be both calm and professional if the plan started to go wrong.

Stores that were not required, even if the decision was to stay, were constantly being loaded during the hours of darkness. The piers at W and V Beaches were strengthened in readiness for the order which finally arrived on December 28. A short telegram announced that the government had agreed to evacuation at the earliest possible time. It was now that the real work began.

The plan was to be similar to that which had been so successful at Anzac. To start with there would be a first stage in which all troops surplus to those needed to hold the front lines would be evacuated. The figure needed to hold the front for seven days was estimated to be around 22,000 but the Navy reckoned the most they could evacuate in one night would be 15,000 men. This caused somewhat of a problem. Birdwood and Lieutenant-General Sir Francis Davies, (General Officer Commanding VIII Corps) were both adamant that the final stage at Helles must be carried out in one night. The Turks were being extremely vigilant and the chance of keeping the exodus secret for two nights, as at Suvla and Anzac, were unlikely to work a second time. Following a joint meeting of Naval and Army officers, it was believed that if certain improvements could be carried out on the piers, it would be possible to take off 17,000 men on the last night. This figure, although some 5,000 short of what was originally deemed to be necessary to hold the front lines, was agreed. Risks had to be taken.

Important lessons had been learned from the Anzac-Suvla evacuation and many officers who had done such a splendid job there were bought back to help with the detailed planning. By January 1, 1916, the last French troops began leaving their positions to be replaced by the Royal Naval Division. Other than the French gunners left manning the artillery, that nation's involvement in the Gallipoli campaign was now at an end.

Throughout this intermediate stage, the weather continued to play havoc with the loading of stores and it was apparent by the 4th that either a lot of matériel would have to be abandoned or the final night would have to be postponed. In the end, it was decided that the supplies would have to be left behind to lessen the chance of discovery. By the morning of January 7 the garrison was down to around 19,000. The front line trenches were still held in force while at the same time all the tricks from Anzac and Suvla were being used to deceive the enemy that it was business as usual.

Coincidentally General von Sanders also chose the 7th as the day to launch his attack against the Helles sector. A massive barrage opened up on the British front line and support trenches although by now these were largely empty. The barrage was one of the heaviest of the campaign and it continued for some four hours, many of the guns and shells used being new arrivals from Germany. The 13th Division were particularly heavily hit and just after 1600 hours two large mines were exploded near Gully Spur. The Turkish lines bristled with bayonets and it seemed that they were about to attack in force to try and drive the British back into the sea. An assault was launched but it was met with heavy rifle and machine gun fire, the Turks being cut down before they even neared the British front line. In many places, the Turkish soldiers, as if they sensed that the campaign was already over, refused to attack and stayed firmly in their trenches. Near Fusilier Bluff, however, a more organised assault developed. The 7th North Staffords succeeded in repulsing this attempt but at a cost of over 150 men, including their commanding officer Lieutenant-Colonel Hercules Walker. The Navy too had helped in blunting this attack when the destroyers *Wolverine* and the *Edgar* fired almost their entire stock of ammunition to help make up for the shortage of artillery pieces ashore.

The failure of this assault convinced the Turks that, even if evacuation was to happen at Helles, it was not imminent; as a result a relatively peaceful night followed. The quiet night allowed some 2,300 men to be evacuated, plus a lot of stores and animals that would otherwise have been abandoned. On the morning of

General Francis Davies standing outside his headquarters on the stone terraces along the cliff overlooking W Beach shortly before the evacuation. Sadly, although these structures look so permanent, the terraces on which they stood have eroded so much that it was difficult to pinpoint the precise location today.

Left: Throughout the days preceding the final evacuation at Helles, men were busy helping to fool the enemy into believing nothing was afoot. Stores, usually boxes filled with nothing more than sand, were unloaded from lighters that continued to arrive at the normal frequency. In this picture, men can be seen pushing trailers less than 24 hours before the final departure. Right: Without the pier to enable the photograph to be taken further out to sea, an exact comparison is difficult but, by comparing the rocks, all the evidence points to this being the same location even though the hillside shows few traces of its former military construction.

the 8th, Davies reported that his garrison now stood at some 17,000 and he was ready, when ordered, for the final withdrawal.

This decision lay with the Navy as it was now purely a question of weather. An early decision was essential as many of the ships would have to leave from Mudros and could not put to sea any later than midday if they were to arrive at Helles at dusk. On January 8 the weather was calm and bright with only a gentle breeze and Admiral de Robeck was advised that no change was anticipated for at least 24 hours. With such a forecast, the final withdrawal was ordered to go ahead that night.

The men were to leave in three waves, most from W and V Beaches but some 400 men would leave from Gully Beach and X Beach. The first batch was to leave after dark and would consist of around 7,000 troops; the second of 6,000 men would embark between 2230-2330, whilst the third of just short of 4,000 would leave between 0200-0300.

As night fell the men who had suffered an anxious day started to make their way towards their embarkation points. By 1900 hours, however, the weather was taking a turn for the worse with a gale picking up and by 2100 hours the wind was nearing 40 miles an hour. On two occasions, one of the flimsy piers was struck by drifting lighters but a team led by Lieutenant George Taylor, working in freezing waters and pitch black, managed to repair the damage which allowed a further 3,000 men — the last of the second wave — to get away before the pier was hit again and this time put out of service.

One of the men from the Royal Naval Division recorded this day in his diary and his entries reflect the strain of the occasion:

'Leaving trenches tonight, how will it all go . . . Everything will be well if the artillery doesn't play on the beach, everybody too excited to speak. Have left trenches and all is going well . . . My God have they discovered our move shells rain down on V Beach.

Not a bloody soul in sight. It was obvious my mates had anticipated zero-hour and, instead of waiting for one another, had hot-footed it for the beach individually. Not that I blame them, I was often tempted to do so myself these last two hours and now real panic set in and I followed their example. It was an eerie experience. I guess the first man who lands on the moon will feel like I felt that night. The loneliest man in all the world. And the most frightened. As I tore panic-stricken along the lines of trenches leading towards the gully and thence to the beach, it was like as if I was on a dead world.

Stumbling over valises thrown away, piles of blankets left in all sorts of odd places, tripping over rifles left sprawled across the trench — to my fevered imagination it seemed to take me hours to negotiate even a few traverses. But the strangest, the most eerie and the most frightening element was the absence of all human life. The trenches — normally full of men and now deserted. I felt as if I were picking my way panic-stricken through the deserted catacombs of a dead and long-gone civilisation. Eerie! My God! I've never been so scared. The drifting heavy clouds over the moon's face alternate the night into an ever-changing pattern of light and dark — an unnerving night of sinister forebodings, where every little sound I made seemed like the clatter of Doom. Not even a rifle shot anywhere — to remind me that somewhere, even if only in the Turkish lines, there is still some human life left on this earth.

Seawards, too, the absence of all life. Not even the comforting view of the lighted hospital ship. I guess she's made her last trip here and is now on the way to Alex.

Round the traverse of the trench I come across a soldier fast asleep on the firing step, head lolling on one side. Thank God at last for some company, another human being besides myself on this nightmare planet. But it's the wrong sort of sleep. I shake him gently and he rolls flat on the trench floor, still and grotesque. There'll be no comforting chat with this chap. There's a bullet wound in his temple. He must have been killed very, very recently to have been left like that, probably in the mass press forward to the beach — probably killed through some silly sod not having adjusted the safety catch on his rifle properly. They'd no time even to pretend to bury him — he'd been left where he was.

At last I leave the trenches and attain the open deep gully. Run soldier run — you might still make it — you might still catch the last boat leaving the shore. Panting, swearing falling flat on my face in the mud, sometimes in my urgent haste I stumble along the gully and eventually reach the beach and join a few others stood on the edge of the shore and hollering seawards.

From out of the void of the night is a faint reply and now — God be praised — we espy a little pontoon-type raft being towed towards us. The raft already contains about a dozen men and we wade out and scramble aboard with them and the naval pinnace tows us slowly to the ship out at sea. The sea's a bit choppy and the raft alongside the ship bobs up and down dangerously. In the fitful darkness I discern with difficulty a little hatchway in the side of the ship and, one by one, we wait until the heaving raft is level with the hatchway of the ship, then jump the intervening few feet separating us. It's a tricky job, and the naval bloke keeps bawling out hoarsely the need for extreme care. The chap who jumped before I did was real unlucky. His iron-studded army boots slipped on the wet raft as he jumped and he slipped into the water and as the raft bobbed up and down he got his skull crushed between the raft and the ship's side. My turn now — a panic-stricken long jump. I land stunned but safe on the iron footplates in the bowels of the ship.

I sat at the stern of the rescue ship with my platoon sergeant. After a long silence the sergeant chuckled, 'Old Abdul'll get the surprise of his life in the morning. Not a bloody British soldier there . . . except for the bloody thousands we've left there. An' they won't be giving' Abdul much trouble, Ah'm thinking.'

I guess it was the reaction of the last few hours, but I found myself wracked with unmanly sobbing. I'm not sure why. I don't think it was so much the thought of all the chaps I'd known as kids and now left there — all the thousands of the other blokes who'd never breathe the air again. I don't know what it was — it could have been grief. But most, I think, was the dreadful feeling of the shame of it all — the British Army having to evacuate the peninsula like this, and after all this gigantic wasted effort. Such things hurt a soldier more than you'd think — even an amateur soldier like myself.

PRIVATE CHARLES WATKINS
6 LANCASHIRE FUSILIERS

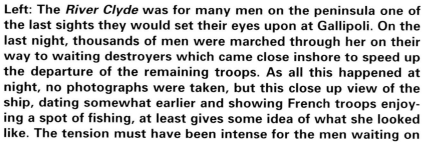

Left: The *River Clyde* was for many men on the peninsula one of the last sights they would set their eyes upon at Gallipoli. On the last night, thousands of men were marched through her on their way to waiting destroyers which came close inshore to speed up the departure of the remaining troops. As all this happened at night, no photographs were taken, but this close up view of the ship, dating somewhat earlier and showing French troops enjoying a spot of fishing, at least gives some idea of what she looked like. The tension must have been intense for the men waiting on

this open pier, knowing that the Turks might discover the plan at any time and then rain down shells upon the beach. The sally ports from where the men emerged on April 25 are clearly visible, as are the sand-bagged positions on the bow which housed machine guns to help suppress Turkish fire on the approach to V Beach during the initial invasion. **Right:** Steve says that the distinctive cliffs were the only clue for this location: 'The local fishermen sitting in a nearby cafe were curious as to what I was doing and they voted this picture their favourite!'

Happily only a march of less than a 100 yards from beach to *River Clyde* seems like miles. . . . "Move quickly!" orders the skipper of the destroyer, no need to tell us that! The bugle on the beach sounds, we have about 30 seconds to take cover and we are right in the centre of the pier. Here she comes. A giant shower is sent up as she falls short. . . We are aboard without a casualty, Thank God, but what a strain on us all. No sooner on board *Prince George* than she is shaken from end to end. Torpedoed but no explosion. Arrive Imbros at Dawn. Am one of 54 left of the originals. Now time to reflect all 6 of my pals who joined up with me are gone forever. . . . What a price to pay. Nerves shattered friends gone . . . will that smell of death ever leave us?'

The 'torpedoing' of the *Prince George* was felt by most of the men aboard. She fired white rockets to signal an attack from a submarine and two destroyers rushed to her aid in an attempt to engage the enemy although no submarine was located. After the war captured records showed that no submarines had been present so it is assumed that the *Prince George* must have run into some underwater wreckage.

By now there were growing fears for the last wave who were still to depart. The gale was growing stronger and much credit must go to the Navy personnel who, continually and in the ever worsening conditions, managed to get their ships alongside the piers both quickly and quietly.

This view of Gully Beach was taken from the path that leads down to it from the West Krithia Road. One of the lighters that was meant to leave here on the last night became grounded in the appalling weather that prevailed during the final hours of the evacuation. With no other vessel being available the men had the stark choice of either marching around to W Beach at the double or risk being abandoned.

In some places the steep sides to Gully Ravine have eroded, considerably changing many of the views beyond recognition, but fortunately the entrance from Gully Beach has stood the test of time. In this shot, other than the scrub and the almost complete destruction of the pier, the lie of the land would still be familiar to many of the soldiers of 1915. The remains of the lighter still lies alongside the pier.

At Gully Beach the weather had bought about another problem: one of the two lighters had become grounded. The remaining vessel was loaded to the hilt and sent off but General Maude with 160 men remained ashore. Maude was convinced that no other lighter would be able to get ashore at Gully Beach in the conditions then prevailing so he set off with his men for W Beach. However, by now (0220 hours), W Beach was starting to close down its operations and the Maude party still had over two miles to cover. At 0240, a messenger arrived at W Beach explaining the problem and informing the embarkation officers that Maude would arrive at W Beach within the next 15 minutes. The embarkation staff were becoming more and more concerned by the deteriorating weather, having only just managed to get off the remaining troops. However, Maude's party was being delayed by the numer-

ous obstructions that had been put across the road to stop any rapid Turkish advance and it was 0315 before they arrived at W Beach. There was still no sign of Maude himself and it later transpired that on discovering he had left his baggage on the stranded lighter at Gully Beach, he insisted on returning to retrieve it. At 0330, the loaded lighters were still waiting for the General although the front line trenches had by this time been empty for over three hours and any moment the Turkish artillery might open up and take a terrible toll amongst the tightly-packed vessels. Added to this, the sea was almost running at the point where further embarkation was impossible. Under these conditions, the skipper of the lighter decided to give Maude just five more minutes. Luckily, just before he was about to cast off, Maude and his staff officer appeared, pushing his baggage along on a wheeled stretcher.

These unique German/Turkish postcards, produced to publicise the amounts of matériel captured, pictures (clockwise) bridging pontoons at Kemikli; ambulances at Teke Burnu; machine gun carts at Sigin Dere; and a howitzer and limbers at Ari Burnu . . .

The fuses to detonate all the remaining supplies were lit and the last British troops to leave the peninsula did so at 0345 hours on January 9, 1916. The Helles evacuation had gone amazingly well and 35,268 officers and men, nearly 4,000 animals, 127 guns, 328 vehicles and 1,600 tons of supplies, had been saved. Once again not a single casualty had been sustained although hundreds of tons of supplies had had to be abandoned. As the last boats pulled away from the shore, the sky took on a red glow as the supplies on the beach began

. . . together with ammunition wagons; mortars at Sigin Dere; a general view of the chaos left behind at Teke Burnu and, finally,

water distillation towers (for turning salt water into drinking water) at Ari Burnu.

to burn followed by a huge roar as the main magazine blew up. This time the Turks did not hesitate as they had done at Anzac and Suvla and red rockets fired from both the peninsula and the Asian side lit up the sky over the narrows. Almost in a fit of rage, as if sensing they

had been tricked again, Turkish artillery pounded the beaches to no avail as they only succeeded in shelling some of the supplies that the British had been trying to destroy anyway! Turkish troops poured out of their trenches, but too late . . . the enemy had gone.

7

EPILOGUE

There can be few more controversial episodes in British military history than that of Gallipoli. Such was the feeling of failure that for years afterwards Churchill would be greeted whenever he spoke at public meetings by cat-calls of 'what about the Dardanelles'.

However, in a world war that was completely bereft of any strategic plan other than killing more men than you lost, Gallipoli was not necessarily the strategic blunder that many claimed. The idea of knocking Turkey out of the war and helping the Russians into the bargain was a sound one. On March 18, the naval assault had, by their own admission, all but beaten the Turks into submission. On two further occasions, the limited forces available to Sir Ian Hamilton came very close to achieving the breakthrough which could have led to the ultimate victory. Getting so close to success surely assuages — at least in part — the belief that the plan was an impossible one from the start.

Without doubt, much of the blame for failure lies in the lack of planning and quality of the generalship. Other observers sight bad luck at key moments but, as with most things, one tends to make one's own luck.

The 'Westerners', who were convinced throughout that the war could only be won in France, believed in 1918 that they had been vindicated. The 'Easterners' however, quoted the massive

> *The drama of the Dardanelles campaign by reason of the beauty of its setting, the grandeur of its theme and the unhappiness of its ending, will always rank amongst the world's classic tragedies. The story is a record of lost opportunities and eventual failure; yet it is a story which men of British race may ponder if not without pain yet certainly not without pride; for amidst circumstances of unsurpassed difficulty and strain the bravery, fortitude and stoical endurance of the invading troops upheld most worthily the high traditions of the fighting services of the Crown.*
>
> BRIGADIER-GENERAL C. F. ASPINALL-OGLANDER
> *MILITARY OPERATIONS, GALLIPOLI, VOLUME II, 1932*

The Helles Memorial is both the overall Allied memorial to the Gallipoli campaign and also to the missing who have no known graves. It does not include the Australians and New Zealanders who lost their lives at Anzac and have their names recorded on their own memorials. Also inscribed at Helles are the names of all the ships and army units that took part. It stands over 30 metres high and is visible to all the ships passing in and out of the Dardanelles. In all, there are some 21,000 names commemorated on the walls.

loss of life in Europe as proof that looking for a 'cheaper' way of winning the war was surely the right thing to do. Many historians today still fall into one of these categories but, whatever school of thought one favours, there can be no doubt that the men who served and died there all deserve our respect.

As to how many died on the Gallipoli peninsula, there are various figures and it is now impossible to give a definitive figure. The official history states 43,000 British and Commonwealth dead, while other published sources put the figure as high as 46,000. The totals that I have used emanate from the Australian War Memorial in Canberra and are the only figures that break down the casualties into individual countries. The assesment is that of the 410,000 British, French and Commonwealth soldiers involved, 252,000 became casualties and of this number just over 50,000 were killed as follows:

A collection of relics recently picked up at Gallipoli (not all found by the author). Many of the bullets were retrieved from the waters around Anzac while the water bottle came from Little Table Top. One of the shells was found at Lone Pine the others at Lala Baba.

KILLED IN ACTION OR DIED OF WOUNDS

British	21,255
France	9,874
Australia	8,709
India	7,594
New Zealand	2,701
Total	**50,133**

The Turkish figures are somewhat looser. Around 500,000 troops were engaged and it is estimated that about 55,000 men were killed out of a total of 251,000 casualties. The closeness of these figures with the Allied losses once again demonstrates how narrow a margin there was between the victor and the vanquished.

Of the five major battles that Turkey was to be involved in during the Great War, Gallipoli was to be its only victory.

Many men of the Australian Light Horse and also the British 2nd Mounted Division were to fight again against the Turks in Palestine where they gained their revenge. Other units involved at Gallipoli served in Salonika or Egypt whilst most of the Anzacs and the Royal Naval Division went on to fight on the Western Front. The 29th Division, which perhaps had the hardest time of all, left Gallipoli some 4,000 strong — all that was left out of a force that in August was over 17,000 strong. They, too, were destined for the muddy fields of France.

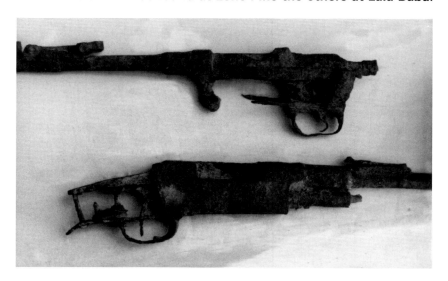

The remains of this British SMLE and French Lebel were found at Helles.

The original architect of the Dardanelles scheme, Winston Churchill, was cast into the political wilderness for many years before his finest hour arrived in 1940. Another future Minister, Clement Attlee, who later served as Deputy Prime Minister during the Second World War, would also draw from his experiences at Gallipoli where he had served as a young captain.

Lord Kitchener, whose political power was already diminishing, did not live to see out 1916 as he was drowned when the cruiser HMS *Hampshire* struck a mine en route for Russia.

Sir Ian Hamilton was never asked to command in the field again In retirement he remained an upright figure surrounded by his military trophies and souvenirs in his house near Hyde Park in London. He maintained strong links with his former subordinates and never once became involved with the 'mud-slinging' that followed the failure of the campaign. He died in 1947 aged 94, a large congregation of contemporaries and comrades attending his memorial service in Westminster Abbey.

His opposite number, Otto Liman von Sanders, remained with the Turkish army until defeated in Syria in 1918. From there he returned to Constantinople where he surrendered to the occupying Allies. He spent most of 1919 interned on Malta after which he returned to Germany where he died a few years before Hitler's rise to power. To the end, he adopted a dignified stance and constantly denied rumours that German soldiers had been involved in Turkish massacres of Armenians. His foresight and fortitude is a major and, perhaps, largely underestimated part of the Turkish victory at Gallipoli. Mustafa Kemal — Turkey's 'Man of Destiny' — is worthy of a book all of his own and indeed many have been written about him. Perhaps more famously known as Atatürk, as well as being the saviour of Gallipoli, he is also seen as the father of modern Turkey.

Of the ships involved, the *Goeben* and *Breslau* were renamed and in 1918 they attempted to break out of the straits. Both struck mines and the *Breslau* went to the bottom, whilst the *Goeben* was beached. She ended her days years later as a training ship of the Turkish Navy.

Perhaps one of the saddest and most short-sighted fates was that of the *River Clyde*. She remained firmly beached at Sedd-el-Bahr until 1919 when she was refloated and towed to Malta by a Spanish salvage company. From there she was repaired before

A member of the Imperial War Graves Commission surveys Anzac Cove which, even in 1919, was still littered with the debris of war. The IWGC team were given the daunting task of gathering together the many scattered burials and concentrating them in 31 cemeteries, as well as identifying as many of the individual remains as possible.

The area is little changed with the exception of the new road which runs slightly higher than the original track of 1919. In the background stands the Gaba Tepe headland.

Above left: A graphic illustration of the problems faced by the IWGC and the methods used to overcome them. To transport the necessary blocks of stone uphill over rough terrain for the construction of the new cemeteries, an overhead cable run was erected. This unnamed cemetery was under construction in June 1923.

Above right: Shrapnel Valley Cemetery pictured the same month, with the concrete retaining wall at the front having been completed together with the memorial stone at the rear. The permanent stone-faced pedestal grave markers, used at Gallipoli instead of headstones because of the risk of subsidence, are not yet in place.

A panoramic view taken on June 9, 1923 of the country around Green Hill Cemetery (centre left), looking towards Scimitar Hill, from Chocolate Hill. This cemetery is the second largest on the peninsula with 2,971 burials.

Left: Another view of Green Hill Cemetery where work is about to commence installing the permanent headstones. To the right in the middle-distance can be seen the slope of Scimitar Hill, whilst beyond rise the foothills of the Tekke Tepe ridge. Right: The cemetery has now become a lush sanctuary in the desolate Suvla Plain.

being sold onto a shipping company based on the Mediterranean. First she was renamed the *Angela* and then the *Maruja y Aurora*. She spent the next 40 years plying the Mediterranean and in 1966, when the old lady was due to be scrapped, the owners offered her to the British Government and any other interested parties. Unfortunately no one was interested in preserving her and a unique piece of First World War history was sentenced to the scrapman's torch.

The 'beetles', or landing craft as they became known, were used between the wars for carrying sand and gravel and even refuse from the big cities. It is somewhat ironic that whilst many see Gallipoli as having gained nothing, so many lessons were learned from this first true amphibious assault. The specialist landing craft produced in later years that would be used in future amphibious attacks, including D-Day, were developed from these vessels. Kitchener's wish 'that next time they'd get it right', with hindsight, seems strangely prophetic.

At the end of hostilities in 1918, an Allied occupation force sailed up the Straits under the watchful eyes of the Turkish gunners, and was landed at Constantinople. Later, Commodore Roger Keyes, a keen exponent of renewing the naval assault, even during the latter stages of the campaign, made the same journey. Stunned into almost complete silence, his only words were: 'It would have been easier than I thought'.

Two teams of Commonwealth War Graves Commission gardeners work continually on the cemeteries to keep them immaculate, one based at Helles, whilst the other works at Anzac and Suvla. Here, on a hot summer's day, the grave markers at Quinn's Post Cemetery are re-engraved.

Chunuk Bair Cemetery with the bones of the fallen awaiting interrment . . . and as it appears today (see also page 194).

By the end of the war, many of the graves that had been so carefully tended before the evacuation had fallen into disrepair and others were no longer marked or possible to identify. Throughout 1919, the Imperial War Graves Commission tirelessly worked on the peninsula and it was agreed that where possible the dead should lie in permanent cemeteries near to where they fell. Of the 36,000 British and Commonwealth dead, only 9,000 were ever identified. A further 13,000 lie in unnamed graves, their names being recorded on the Helles Memorial along with the 14,000 who have no known grave. Today, the 31 cemeteries that were built are all kept in immaculate condition by the Commonwealth War Graves Commission and many retain names that have long since disappeared from any map. The cemeteries have all been landscaped with fragrant flowering bushes and plants that attract the migrating wildlife. As you move between the headstones, your footsteps cushioned by pine needles, it is virtually impossible to imagine the horrors that took place on this, the most beautiful of all battlefields.

The Turkish dead were not accorded the same honours and, although some memorials to the fallen have been erected, at the time many bodies were just rolled into one of the numerous gullies and buried. Today, scattered sunbleached bones are all that remain.

Returning veterans have always commented on the solitude and on a pleasant spring afternoon on the heights of Sari Bair, or at the desolate Suvla Bay, it is easy to see why. Across the battlefield, it is still fairly easy to pick up debris from the campaign. Shrapnel balls, spent bullets, buckles and buttons are all uncovered regularly by the farmers working their fields. Other than that only the ghosts remain.

Ari Burnu Cemetery at the north end of Anzac Cove. Today, it is one of the most visited cemeteries — a stark contrast to how it appeared in 1919 (opposite). The sunken wreck is the steamer *Milo*.

Those English, French, Australian, New Zealand and Indian heroes
who shed blood on the soil of this country
Here you are in the soil of a friendly country
Rest in peace.
You are side by side and lying together with the Mehmetcik's.
You the mothers who sent their sons to war from far away countries!

Wipe away your tears. Your sons are lying on our bosom.
They are at peace and they will rest in peace
After having lost their lives on this land.
They have become our sons as well!

KEMAL ATATÜRK, 1934

201

GALLIPOLI'S GALLANTRY

There can be few places in the world that have seen quite as much suffering and heroism in such a small area as Gallipoli. In the 259 days of land occupation (including the early hours of January 9, 1916), 38 Victoria Crosses were won, and to this can be added one further VC awarded to a Royal Marine, Eric Robinson in February 1915, for an incursion on the Asiatic side of the Dardanelles. The Gallipoli campaign was second only to the Western Front for the number of VCs awarded during the Great War. And there must be countless other deeds which we will never know about, that surely would have qualified for this award 'For Valour'.

Gallipoli's VCs are spread throughout the Services, being awarded to just about all branches of the armed forces of the time. Of the 39 awarded, 28 went to the Army (18 British, nine Australian and one New Zealand) the other 11 being given to naval units: eight to the Royal Navy itself, (including two to submariners); two to the Royal Naval Division and one to the Royal Naval Air Service. Of these are included the first VC to be awarded in the First World War to the Royal Naval Reservist; the first to an Australian; the first to a New Zealander, and the first to a Royal Marine.

Of Gallipoli's VC awardees, 11 would later perish, either on the peninsula or from wounds received there, and another three would not see the end of the war.

Many other firsts are also attributable to Victoria Crosses given for unique exploits at Gallipoli. The 'six before breakfast' won by the Lancashire Fusiliers on the first morning of the landings lies second only to the defence of Rorke's Drift in 1879 for numbers issued to a single unit for a single action, and throughout the remainder of the war, no other unit would receive six VCs for one action. Another record was set by the crew of the *River Clyde*, four of whom were decorated, the highest number to one ship for one action.

Of the ranks and ages of the men who won this prestigious award, once again it could not be more diverse and 22 officers, 10 NCOs and 7 privates, from the age of 18 to 51 could, at the end of the campaign, put the immortal letters 'VC' after their name.

LIEUTENANT COMMANDER ERIC ROBINSON
FEBRUARY 26, 1915

Following the bad weather that had put a brief halt to the naval effort to storm the Dardanelles, a new attack went ahead on February 25, 1915. Although partially successful in destroying some guns, it was decided that on the following day a party of Marines should be landed ashore to blow up whatever remained and Lieutenant Commander Eric Robinson, the torpedo officer on HMS *Vengeance,* was chosen to lead this mission. His orders were vague, as little was known about Turkish strength in the area. At 1430 hours, all eyes aboard the *Vengeance* turned to watch the unfolding drama ashore near Kum Kale. Robinson, who wore his conspicuous white naval uniform was easily spotted leading his men under heavy fire towards their objective. Having destroyed two Turkish anti-aircraft guns he then pushed on alone, even further inland to destroy a large calibre Turkish gun, under heavy fire the whole time. As the *London Gazette* of his award states:

'*Lieut Commander Robinson on the 26th February adavanced alone, under heavy fire, into an enemy's gun position, which might well have been occupied and, destroying a four-inch gun, returned to his party for another charge in which a second gun was destroyed. Lieut Robinson would not allow mem-*

bers of his demolition party to accompany him, as their white uniforms rendered them very conspicuous. . .'

He received his award from His Majesty King George V on October 5, 1915. Although recalled to the navy in 1939, ill health forced him to retire in 1941. He passed away in 1965 and his Victoria Cross is not publicly held.

Artist's impressions by Edgar A. Holloway of the VC actions of Midshipman George Drewry (*above*, in water wearing the head-scarf helping the wounded man) and *below*, Commander Edward Unwin and Able Seaman William Williams towing the barge. Both pictures from the contemporary *Deeds that Thrill the Empire*.

THE SIX V BEACH VCs

The gallantry at both V and W beaches make the VCs won here amongst the most famous ever awarded. As has already been described, on April 25, 1915, V Beach was the scene of the beaching of the converted collier the *River Clyde* in a modern day re-run of the woodern horse of Troy. Its crew was made up of 24 volunteers, screened and hand-picked by the ship's captain, Commander Edward Unwin.

Following the failure of the *River Clyde* to beach as near to the shore as possible, and that of the lighters that were supposed to link together to allow the troops to disembark quickly, something needed to be done quickly to kick start the landing. Midshipmen George Drewry and Seaman George Samson started connecting the lighters together and then tied them to the stern of the steam hopper that Drewry commanded. Commander Edward Unwin decided to secure the lighters to some rocks and did so under a hail of fire assisted by Able Seaman William Williams and another small steam boat. The steam boat was unable to get right into the shore so both Unwin and Williams dived into the water to start manhandling the boats. Drewry had also entered the water and after a foray ashore he joined Unwin and Williams. Drewry braved Hell again as he went aboard to get more rope but when he returned the unfortunate Williams was dead. However, he and Unwin had succeeded in lashing the lighters together and pulling them ashore. Still holding the vessels together, waist deep in water and under heavy fire, Unwin ordered the disembarkation to begin. Even after the first of the troops had left the *River Clyde* in such futile circumstances, Drewry continued to try and secure the lighters. Unwin had by this stage had become so exhausted by the continual immersion in the cold water that he was once again hauled aboard the *River Clyde*.

The other member of Unwin's team to gain the VC on this day was Samson. After Drewry had left him on a lighter he worked furiously in both removing the wounded and repairing the pier that had been constructed from the remaining lighters. For the next 30 hours, Samson risked his life time and time again going to the beach to pick up more of the injured. He was seriously wounded on April 26 and was given no chance of survival; later it transpired that he had been hit more than a dozen times. Samson's bravery and fortitude thus epitomises all that the Victoria Cross stands for.

Commander Edward Unwin   **Midshipman George Drewry**   **Seaman George Samson**   **Midshipman Wilfred Malleson**   **Sub-Lieutenant Arthur Tisdall**

COMMANDER EDWARD UNWIN
V BEACH, APRIL 25, 1915

Commander Unwin remained at Gallipoli for the rest of the campaign. Following the *River Clyde* débâcle, he later became the beachmaster at Suvla Bay during the landing there in August. During the evacuation of Suvla on December 20, he was among the last men to leave on the last boat. After the war, Unwin continued to enjoy the sea and was a keen yachtsman,. He died in 1950 and was buried, ironically, on April 25. His Victoria Cross is not on public display.

MIDSHIPMAN GEORGE DREWRY
V BEACH, APRIL 25, 1915

Midshipman Drewry received the first VC of the war to be given to a member of the Royal Naval Volunteer Reserve. He remained with Commander Unwin through the Suvla landings but shortly afterwards was returned to HMS *Hussar*. He applied for and received promotion and then commanded the HMT *William Jackson* and it was on this ship that he was killed in an accident at Scapa Flow on August 2, 1918. Today, a stained glass window at All Saints Church in Forest Gate in East London commemorates his memory. His Victoria Cross is presently on display at the Imperial War Museum, London.

ABLE SEAMAN WILLIAM WILLIAMS
V BEACH, APRIL 25, 1915

Able Seaman Williams was the first man serving with the Royal Navy to receive the VC posthumously, and his award was received on his behalf by his father from King George V in August 1915. His home town of Chepstow also paid their respects in the unveiling of a memorial and also a painting of the *River Clyde* action, which can be seen at St Mary's Parish Church.

Williams has no known grave and is thus commemorated on the Portsmouth Naval Memorial. His Victoria Cross was sold by London auctioneers Dix Noonan and Webb for £46,000 in June 1997.

SEAMAN GEORGE SAMSON
V BEACH, APRIL 25, 1915

Seaman Samson survived his wounds although he still had 13 pieces of shrapnel in his body when news of his VC was announced. He received his medal on October 5, 1915 from King George V. Although unable to return to active service because of his wounds, which continued to give him pain throughout his life, he played an active part in recruiting and at the end of the war he rejoined the Merchant Navy. He died on Bermuda following a bout of pneumonia in February 1923 and was buried in the island's military cemetery. His Victoria Cross is at present held in a private collection.

MIDSHIPMAN WILFRID MALLESON
V BEACH, APRIL 25, 1915

Eighteen-years-old, Midshipman Malleson, serving on HMS *Cornwallis*, was on the second of four boats as they approached the shore. However, having reached dry land with surprisingly few losses, casualties quickly started to mount as Turkish fire relentlessly poured down onto them.

As he tried to manoeuvre one of the lighters into place, Malleson saw Drewry wounded in the head. Having had his head dressed, Drewry recommenced work again and started to swim for the shore but in a weakened state against a strong tide with a rope that was too short. Malleson decided he must try to help so, having recovered a rope that was directly in line with the worst of the Turkish fire, he set about swim-

ming out to make the connection that the unfortunate Drewry had been unable to make. Despite the rope breaking, he made a further two attempts, all the time under heavy fire, to complete this most difficult task.

Malleson was the youngest recipient of the VC during the Gallipoli operation and the only one who remained unhurt out of those awarded on V Beach. He received his VC from King George V in 1918 before going on to command submarines.

During the Second World War, Malleson was assistant captain of the Malta Dockyard. He retired from the Navy in 1948 and died in 1975. His Victoria Cross is now held by Edgeborough School.

SUB-LIEUTENANT ARTHUR TISDALL
V BEACH, APRIL 25, 1915

Sub-Lieutenant Arthur Tisdall's VC is interesting in that it was not awarded until nearly a year after the relevant action due to the extensive investigation into identifying the man who so many had seen saving wounded on V Beach on April 25. His citation states that *'during the landing from the River Clyde at V Beach . . . Sub Lieut Tisdall, hearing wounded men on the beach calling for assistance jumped into the water and, pushing a boat in front of him, went to their rescue . . . Sub Lieut Tisdall made four or five trips between the ships and the shore, and was thus responsible for rescuing several wounded men under heavy and accurate fire. . .'*

Tisdall's VC was the first awarded to a man serving with the Royal Naval Division in the Great War. He was killed in action on May 6, 1915 during the Second Battle of Krithia and, although originally buried close to where he died, his grave was subsequently lost and he is now commemorated on the Helles Memorial. His VC is now held by the Royal Naval Volunteer Reserve Museum in London.

Captain Richard Willis was destined to live a charmed life throughout the Great War. He survived both the First and Second Battles of Krithia before being seriously wounded during the Third. He was invalided back to England and he received his VC from the King at Buckingham Palace in September 1915. It was also around this time that the famous picture in the *Illustrated London News* (see page 202) showing the W Beach landing was published, Willis being the central figure leading his men with a walking stick. He returned to active service and saw action at both Ypres and the Somme as well as during the Allied breakthrough in 1918.

In 1920 he retired from the Army and went into education and spent the next 37 years teaching. He died in 1966. His VC was sold by Dix Noonan and Webb for £54,000 in November 1996 and is presently on loan to the Lancashire Fusiliers Museum.

Captain Willis (above) and his medals (left)

THE 'SIX BEFORE BREAKFAST' — THE VC'S OF W BEACH.

The Victoria Crosses won on W Beach are perhaps amongst the most famous ever awarded. The action on this day, by one unit — the 1st Battalion, Lancashire Fusiliers — set a record for the Great War and is indeed only surpassed by the heroic defence of Rorke's Drift over 60 years before. The actions of the six men concerned were so closely matched that one citation was given for all.

Initially, only Captain Richard Willis, Sergeant Alfred Richards and Private William Keneally were awarded the Cross. However, after much campaigning by Brigadier Owen Wolley-Dod, himself a Lancashire Fusilier and at the time serving on Hunter-Weston's staff, the awards of the Distinguished Conduct Medal to Sergeant Frank Stubbs and Corporal John Grimshaw were amended and replaced with the VC. The *London Gazette* ran the same citation twice: once in August 1915 for the first three VCs and again in March 1917 when the second three were announced. It read as follows:

'On the 25th April 1915, three companies and the headquarters of the 1st Battalion Lancashire Fusiliers in effecting a landing on the Gallipoli peninsula to the west of Cape Helles were met by a very deadly fire from hidden machine guns, which caused a great number of casualties. The survivors however, rushed up to and cut the wire entanglements, notwithstanding a terrific fire from the enemy, and, after overcoming supreme difficulties, the cliffs were gained and the position maintained. Amongst many very gallant officers and men engaged in this most hazardous enterprise Captain Willis, Sergeant Richards and Private Keneally have been selected by their comrades as having performed most single acts of bravery and devotion to duty.'

CAPTAIN CUTHBERT BROMLEY
W BEACH, APRIL 25, 1915

Despite being wounded during the W Beach action, Captain Cuthbert Bromley refused to leave his unit and remained with them until wounded again during the First Battle of Krithia. After having been hospitalised for three weeks, he returned to his unit in mid-May only to be wounded again on June 28 during the Battle of Gully Ravine. He was evacuated to Egypt where he made a full recovery but on returning to the peninsula on board the troopship *Royal Edward,* he was drowned when the vessel was sunk by a torpedo. He is commemorated on the Helles Memorial. His VC came up for auction in 1985 but was unsold.

PRIVATE WILLIAM KENEALLY
W BEACH, APRIL 25, 1915

Although Private William Keneally survived the horrors of W Beach, and the First, Second and Third Battles of Krithia, he was still set to perish on the peninsula. After being wounded on June 28 during the Gully Ravine action, he died of his injuries the following day and was laid to rest in the Lancashire Landing Cemetery at W Beach, the scene of his most famous action. He was not only a veteran of France, but had already served six years in India with the 1st Battalion before the war. Born in Wexford, Ireland, he was a native of Wigan. His VC is not publicly held.

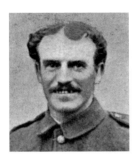

SERGEANT ALFRED RICHARDS
W BEACH, APRIL 25, 1915

Following terrible wounds that he received on W Beach, Sergeant Alfred Richards had to have his right leg amputated in Egypt. Yet, despite being unfit for further military service, he maintained strong links with his old regiment and received his VC from King George V in 1915. He married soon after. During the Second World War Richards served in the Home Guard. He passed away in 1953, his VC now being held in a private collection.

CORPORAL JOHN GRIMSHAW
W BEACH, APRIL 25, 1915

Corporal John Grimshaw was another serviceman who lived a charmed life at Gallipoli. Having come through the landing at W Beach unscathed, he went on to survive all the other notable engagements that claimed the lives of so many men from his regiment, and was eventually evacuated from the peninsula with frostbite following the storms in late 1915. Back in England, he was presented with the Distinguished Conduct Medal; only the following year would the award of his Victoria Cross become known to him.

After receiving his VC from the King, in 1918 he returned to active service in France. After holding a number of posts he eventually retired from the army in 1953. He was the last survivor of the 'six before breakfast' and died in 1980. His award is now in a private collection.

SERGEANT FRANK STUBBS
W BEACH, APRIL 25, 1915

Frank Stubbs is the only one of the six to be killed in the action that won him his award and today he is commemorated on the Helles Memorial as he has no known grave. His VC was presented to his mother in 1917 and today it can be seen at the Lancashire Fusiliers Regimental Museum in Bury, Lancashire.

LIEUTENANT COLONEL CHARLES DOUGHTY-WYLIE
CAPTAIN GARTH WALFORD
V BEACH, APRIL 26, 1915

Following the gallantry on the beaches during April 25, we only have to move on 24 hours to find the next award of a Victoria Cross at Gallipoli. After the disaster at V Beach, two officers in particular realised that something had to be done quickly to save the landing. Those two — Lieutenant Colonel Charles Doughty-Wylie and Captain Garth Walford — were both to win the ultimate award as well as give the ultimate sacrifice. In death they shared the same citation for the award of the VC which was published in June 1915 making them the first VCs of the campaign to be officially acknowledged. The citation reads as follows:

'On the morning of the 26th April, 1915, subsequent to a landing having been effected on the beach at a point on the Gallipoli peninsula, during which both the Brigadier-General and Brigade-Major had been killed, Lieutenant-Colonel Doughty-Wylie and Captain Walford organised and led an attack through and on both sides of the village of Sedd-el-Bahr on the old castle at the top of the hill inland. The enemy's position was very strongly held and entrenched, and defended with concealed machine guns and pom-poms. It was mainly due to the initiative, skill and great gallantry of these two officers that the attack was a complete success. Both were killed in the moment of victory.'

Captain Garth Walford.

It was said that Lieutenant-Colonel Doughty-Wylie charged forwards holding only a small cane as he did not wish to actually kill Turks as he had lived there before the war and had many friends in the country. Indeed, he had been decorated by the Turks for helping stave off a massacre in Adana in 1912-13.

Doughty-Wylie was buried where he fell in an isoloated grave on the summit of Hill 141 to the north of Sedd-el-Bahr. His VC was sent to his wife Lillian towards the end of 1915 and today is in the care of the Royal Welch Fusiliers Museum, Doughty-Wylies former regiment.

Although Captain Walford is most famous for his heroics at V Beach, he had already served in France and Belgium prior to going to the Mediterranean. He had escaped from Mons as well as being involved in the Battle of the Aisne. Walford now lies buried close to where he fell in V Beach Cemetery. His VC is not publicly held.

Contemporary view of Walford's grave.

CORPORAL WILLIAM COSGROVE
NEAR V BEACH, APRIL 26, 1915

Whilst Doughty-Wylie and Walford were winning their far-more-publicised VCs, Corporal William Cosgrove, a six foot six Irishman, was also about to be awarded one for his heroics directly in front of the Turkish front line. As the citation for his VC states:

'For most conspicuous bravery in the leading of his section with great dash during the attack from the beach to the east of Cape Helles, on the Turkish positions, on the 26th April 1915. Corporal Cosgrove on this occasion pulled down the posts of the enemy's high wire entanglements single-handed, notwithstanding a terrific fire from both front and flanks, thereby greatly contributing to the successful clearing of the heights.'

There is no doubt that whilst some acts of bravery are spur-of-the-moment exploits, Cosgrove's was definately not. He was one of 50 men picked to go out into no man's land to tackle the Turkish barbed wire defences and, having been on V Beach for 24 hours, he could have been under no doubt of the dangers he faced. To not only act as cooly as he did but also to survive was truly a miraculous act. He was, however, wounded during the action and was invalided first to Malta before returning to his native home near Cork.

With the creation of the Irish Free State in 1922, Cosgrove transferred to the British Army and served until 1934. Two years later he died in London, his death due in no small part to the shrapnel that remained in his body. He was returned to Ireland where he was laid to rest in Upper Aghada. His Victoria Cross has been sold a number of times and is currently owned by a private collector.

LANCE CORPORAL WALTER PARKER
ANZAC SECTOR, APRIL 30-MAY 2, 1915

Lance Corporal Walter Parker was a member of the Portsmouth Battalion of the Royal Marine Light Infantry when he won his VC in action at the Anzac sector near 400 Plateau. His was the last VC of the Gallipoli campaign to be gazetted and it was not until June 1917 that the citation was released:

'On the night of 30 April-1 May, 1915, a message asking for ammunition, water, and medical supplies was received from an isolated fire trench at Gaba Tepe. A party of non-commissioned officers and men were detailed to carry water and ammunition, and, in response to a call for a volunteer from among the stretcher-bearers, Parker at once came forward; he had during the previous three days displayed conspicuous bravery and energy under fire whilst in charge of the battalion stretcher-bearers. Several men had already been killed in a previous attempt to bring assistance to the men holding the fire trench. To reach this trench it was necessary to traverse an area at least four hundered yards wide, which was completely exposed and swept by rifle fire. It was already daylight when the party emerged from shelter and at once one of the men was wounded; Parker organised a stretcher party, and then going on alone succeeded in reaching the fire trench, all the water and ammunition carriers being either killed or wounded. After his arrival he rendered assistance to the wounded in the trench, displaying extreme courage and remaining cool and collected in very trying circumstances. The trench had finally to be evacuated, and Parker helped to remove and attend the wounded, although he himself was seriously wounded during this operation.'

Parker's wounds were very serious and on returning to England he was invalided out of the Army. He commenced work in a munitions factory but by the time he received his VC from King George V in 1917 he was a very sick man and he died in 1936 having spoken very little of his exploits. His VC is now on display at the Royal Marines Museum in Southsea.

LIEUTENANT COMMANDER EDWARD BOYLE
SUBMARINE *E14* APRIL 27-MAY 18, 1915

Lieutenant Commander Edward Boyle's VC was not awarded for a single act of bravery but for a continued spell of sustained courage. *E14* was the first submarine to pass in and out of the Dardanelles, sinking at least three ships in the process, including a Turkish transport ship that was carrying 6,000 reinforcements. If it had not been for faulty torpedoes he would doubtlessly have sunk more vessels but the boost in morale which resulted from the victories achieved by this brave crew in relatively untried technology was the real gain for the Allies. Although Boyle did not return from his mission until May 18, news of his award reached the Fleet the next day. The citation followed shortly afterwards:

'For most conspicuous bravery in command of Submarine E14, when he dived his vessel under the enemy's minefields and entered the Sea of Marmora on the 27th April 1915. In spite of great navigational difficulties from strong currents, of the continual neighbourhood of hostile patrols, and of the hourly danger of attack from the enemy, he continued to operate in the narrow waters of the Straits and succeeded in sinking two Turkish gunboats and one large military transport.'

It is also only right to note that the rest of the crew of *E14* were all decorated, the officers being awared two DSCs and the crew DSMs.

Edward Boyle remainded on submarines and by the end of the Gallipoli campaign had made three more trips up the Straits. He remained closely attached to the Navy for the rest of his life and it was a tragic end when this pioneer of submarine warfare was run over by a lorry in 1967. His VC is now on display at the Submarine Museum in Gosport.

The submarine *E14* was eventually sunk in the narrows in 1918 whilst attempting to finish off the cruiser *Goeben*. Its commander, Lieutenant Commander Geoffrey White, went down with his vessel. At the end of hostilities, with the release of the few survivors from POW camps, it was decided that White should be awarded the VC.

Above: **E11** returns to base from its epic battle in the Sea of Marmara where the whole crew were pictured (*below*).

LIEUTENANT COMMANDER MARTIN NASMITH
SUBMARINE *E11*, MAY 19-JUNE 7, 1915

Following the success of Boyle in the Sea of Marmora, Lieutenant Commander Martin Nasmith set out in *E11* to equal the daring deeds of *E14*. Already a well respected submariner, his voyage was if anything even more exciting than that of the *E14*. His VC which was gazetted some three weeks after his return tells the story.

'For most conspicuous bravery, in command of one of His Majesty's submarines, while operating in the Sea of Marmara. In the face of great danger, he succeeded in destroying one large Turkish gunboat, two transports, one ammunition ship, and three store-ships, in addition to driving one store-ship ashore. When he had safely passed the most difficult part of his homeward journey he returned again to torpedo a Turkish transport.'

What the citation does not mention is the fact that Nasmith had entered the harbour at Constantinople where he sank the ammunition ship. The panic this caused can not be underestimated. He also attempted to land some men ashore to blow up a section of the Baghdad to Berlin railway, a daring mission that would be fulfilled on his next venture up the Straits. Once again the entire crew was decorated with DSCs and DSMs for one of the most daring acts of submarine warfare carried out during the entire war.

Nasmith received his VC from King George V in January 1916 before going on to become the youngest captain in the Royal Navy. Honours and awards followed him throughout his life and when Admiral Sir Martin Nasmith, VC, died in 1965, his VC remained with the family.

LANCE CORPORAL ALBERT JACKA
COURTNEY'S POST, MAY 19, 1915

Lance Corporal Albert Jacka was to become the first Australian of the war to win a VC and a more deserving case is hard to imagine. Jacka was part of the 14th Battalion which were holding the important position known as Courtney's Post on the morning of May 19 when the Turks launched a ferocious attack. The citation really does not do justice to the full hero-ism of Jacka's exploit. The brief account in the *London Gazette* published in July 1915 reads as follows:.

'For most conspicuous bravery on the night of 19-20 May [the action actually took place entirely during the day of May 19] *at Courtney's Post, Gallipoli Peninsula. Lance-Corporal Jacka, while holding a por-tion of our trench with four other men, was heavily attacked. When all except himself were killed or wounded, the trench was rushed and occupied by seven Turks. Lance-Corporal Jacka at once most gal-lantly attacked them single handed, and killed the whole party, five by rifle fire and two with the bayo-net.'*

Jacka was commisioned in April 1916 and went on to distinguish himself in the fighting on the Somme and many say he should have earned at least a bar to his VC for his countless brave actions. He was awarded a Military Cross and Bar before being gassed in 1918. Slowly recovering from the injuries he sus-tained, he returned to Australia in 1919 and was demobilised the following year. However he never fully recovered his health and he passed away in 1932 at the age of 39. His VC is now held by the Australian War Memorial, Canberra.

Artists impression of Lance-Corporal Jacka holding Courtney's Post. *Inset:* Jacka after he was commissioned.

SECOND LIEUTENANT GEORGE MOOR
KRITHIA, JUNE 6, 1915

Second Lieutenant George Moor was second only to Midshipman Malleson in terms of youth for winning the VC at Gallipoli. There is no doubt that his bravery helped secure the British line from being 'rolled up' by the Turks during a fierce attack but the manner in which he stemmed the retreat is far less clear. Some say that he shot four British soldiers who were fleeing whilst others refute the allegation. The fact is that however he halted the Turks advance, it

was a price worth paying for the hundreds of lives saved by preventing them exploiting a breakthrough. Moor's VC was announced in the *London Gazette* at the end of July 1915:

'For most conspicuous bravery and resource on the 5th June [the action was in fact on June 6], *during operations south of Krithia, Dardanelles. When a detachment of a battalion on his left, which had lost all its officers, was rapidly retiring before a heavy Turkish attack, Second Lieutenant Moor, immediately grasping the danger to the remainder of the line, dashed back some 200 yards, stemmed the retire-ment, led back the men and recaptured the lost trench. This young officer, who only joined the Army in October, 1914, by his personal bravery and pres-ence of mind saved a dangerous situation.'*

In September 1915, Moor was invalided back to England suffering from severe dysentery and, after a period of recuperation, he received his VC from King George V at Buckingham Palace on October 18, 1915.

Moor next saw action on the Somme in 1916 and he remained on the Western Front until he was sev-erly wounded in the arm in December 1917. He returned to the front, this time serving as an acting General Staff Officer throughout the German 'Spring Offensive' of 1918. He received a Military Cross and

Bar for his exploits before succumbing to influenza on November 3, 1918, aged 22. His VC was presented to the Hampshire Regiment Museum in Winchester by his brother where it can be seen today.

SECOND LIEUTENANT HERBERT JAMES
GULLY RAVINE, JUNE 28-JULY 2, 1915

Second Lieutenant Herbert James' VC is in many ways epitomises all the qualities that the Victoria Cross stands for. In his case, he rallied troops from another unit into an attack and, later, when under a fierce counter-attack, he held the trench single-handed until a barricade had been erected behind him to secure the position. The citation for his award was published on September 1, 1915:

'For most conspicuous bravery during the operations in the Southern Zone of the Gallipoli Peninsula. On 28th June, when a portion of the regiment had been checked, owing to all the officers being put out of action, Second Liutenant James, who belonged to a neighbouring unit, entirely on hi own initiative, gathered together a body of men and led them forward under heavy shell and rifle fire. He then returned, organised a second party and again advanced. His gallant example put fresh life into the attack. On 3rd July, in the same locality, Second Lieutenant James headed a party of bomb throwers up a Turkish communications trench and after nearly all his bomb throwers had been killed or wounded, he remained alone at the head of the trench and kept back the enemy single-handed until a barrier had been built behind him and the trench secured. He was throughout exposed to murderous fire.'

When he came to win his VC, James had already been wounded at Gallipoli on April 26. Following his eventual departure from the peninsula in September, he went on to be awarded the Military Cross, the French Croix de Guerre and the Panamanian Medal de la Solidaridad. He was wounded again in 1916.

James eventually retired from the Army in 1930 with the rank of major. He died in August 1958 and his VC, the first to be awarded to a member of the Worcestershire Regiment, is now in a private collection.

CAPTAIN GERALD O'SULLIVAN
GULLY RAVINE, JULY 1-2, 1915.

'For most conspicuous bravery during operations south-west of Krithia, on the Gallipoli Peninsula. On the night of 1st-2nd July, 1915,when it was essential that a portion of a trench which had been lost should be regained, Capt O'Sullivan, although not belonging to the troops at this point volunteered to lead a party of the bomb-throwers to effect the recapture. He advanced in the open under a very heavy fire, and in order to throw his bombs with great effect, got up on the parapet, where he was completely exposed to the fire of the enemy occupying the trench. He was finally wounded, but not before his inspiring example had led on his party to make further efforts, which resulted in the capture of the trench. On the night of 18-19th June 1915, Captain O'Sullivan saved a critical situation in the sane locality by his great personal gallantry and good leading.'

Despite being wounded, Captain Gerald O'Sullivan returned to his unit — the Inniskilling Fusiliers — just before the ill-fated attack on Scimitar Hill in August. He was last seen entering a trench where it was believed that he was wounded. He was posted missing in action but it transpired that he had in fact been killed outright during this attack. O'Sullivan is now recorded as being killed on August 21, 1915. As he has no known grave, his name is inscribed on the Helles Memorial. His VC was sent posthumously to his mother and now believed to be in a private collection.

SERGEANT JAMES SOMERS
GULLY RAVINE, JULY 1-2, 1915.

Sergeant James Somers won his VC in the same action as O'Sullivan, and the citation was published in the *London Gazette* on September 1, 1915:

'For most conspicuous gallantry on the night of 1-2 July 1915, in the southern zone of the Gallipoli Peninsula, when owing to hostile bombing, some of our troops had retired from a sap. Sergeant Somers remained alone on the spot until a party brought up bombs. He then climbed over into the Turkish trench, and bombed the Turks with the great effect. Later on, he advanced into the open under heavy fire, and held back the enemy by throwing bombs into their flank until a barricade had been established. During this period he frequently ran to and from our trenches to obtain fresh supplies of bombs. By his great gallantry and coolness Sergeant Somers was largely instrumental in effecting the recapture of a portion of our trench which had been lost.'

Somers had an eventful war. Having already been seriously wounded in the retreat from Mons, he spent some months recuperating at home in Ireland before going on to Gallipoli where he won his VC. He received his award from King George V at Buckingham Palace in October 1915. He was subsequently gassed on the Western Front when serving with the Army Service Corps, although some accounts indicate that he was accidentally gassed while handling the substance. He died on May 7, 1918 at home in Ireland. His VC is not publicly held.

PRIVATE LEONARD MAURICE KEYSOR
LONE PINE, AUGUST 7, 1915

Throughout the heavy fighting that followed the attack at Lone Pine some of the most heroic yet bloody fighting of the campaign took place. This can be gauged by the fact that no less than seven VCs were won during this attack and subsequent defence of the position. Private Leonard Keysor was a 29-year-old Londoner who had answered the call to arms whilst in Australia and had ended up as a member of the 1st Battalion, AIF. Following the capture of the Lone Pine position, men of this battalion were moved forward to help in opposing the fierce Turkish counter-attacks that were expected. Keysor was known already on the peninsula for his expertise in bombing, a skill that was to earn him the Victoria Cross, as the citation, that was gazetted on October 15, explains.

'For most conspicuous bravery and devotion to duty at Lone Pine trenches, in the Gallipoli peninsula. On August 7th, 1915, he was in a trench which was being heavily bombed by the enemy. He picked up two live bombs and threw them back at the enemy at great risk to his own life, and continued throwing bombs, although wounded, by himself, thereby saving a portion of the trench that it was most important to hold. On August 8th, at the same place, Private Keysor successfully bombed the enemy out of a position from which a temporary mastery over his own trench had been obtained, and was again wounded. Although marked for hospital, he declined to leave, and volunteered to throw bombs for another company which had lost its bomb-throwers. He continued to bomb the enemy until the situation was relieved.'

Keysor received his award from King George V at Buckingham Palace on January 15, 1916. He later served in France where he was wounded again before reaching the rank of lieutenant. He died of cancer in October 1951 aged 65 and was cremated in St John's Wood, London. His VC is now at the Australian War Memorial in Canberra.

Corporal Dunstan

Corporal Burton

LIEUTENANT WILLIAM SYMONS
LONE PINE, AUGUST 8-9, 1915

Lieutenant William Symons was in command of D Company of the 7th Battalion, AIF, who were moved forward to help fend off the expected Turkish counter-attacks on August 8, 1915. His citation was gazetted on October 15 that year:

'For most conspicuous bravery on the night of August 8-9th, 1915, at Lone Pine trenches, in the Gallipoli peninsula. He was in command of the right section of the newly-captured trenches held by his battalion, and repelled several counter-attacks with great coolness. At about 5 a.m. on the 9th August a series of determined attacks were made by the enemy on an isolated sap, and six officers were in succession killed or severely wounded, a portion of the sap was lost. Lieutenant Symons then led a charge and retook the lost sap, shooting two Turks with his revolver. The sap was under hostile fire from three sides, and Lieutenant Symons withdrew some 15 yards to a spot where some overhead cover could be obtained and in the face of heavy fire built up a sand barricade. The enemy succeeded in setting fire to the fascines and woodwork of the head cover, but Lieutenant Symons extinguished the fire and rebuilt the barricade. His coolness and determination finally compelled the enemy to discontinue the attacks.'

Symons was evacuated from the peninsula with enteric fever but was sufficiently well to receive his VC from King George V at Buckingham Palace on December 4. He later served in France where he was wounded once and then gassed in 1917.

After marrying he moved to Australia before returning to England in 1922. During the Second World War he commanded a battalion of the Local Defence Volunteers. After his death in June 1948, his VC was sold by his widow and is now in the possession of the Australian War Memorial.

LIEUTENANT FREDERICK TUBB
LONE PINE, AUGUST 9, 1915

Lieutenant Tubb commanding B Company of the 7th Battalion, also known as the Victoria Battalion, had been in reserve in Brown's Dip behind the Lone Pine position awaiting the order to move up to the front line. The order finally came at 8 p.m. on August 8 when he and his men were ordered to the area of the front from which Symons and his men were just being withdrawn. His citation for the Victoria Cross was announced in the *London Gazette* on October 15, 1915:

'For most conspicuous bravery and devotion to duty at Lone Pine trenches, in the Gallipoli peninsula, on 9th August 1915. In the early morning the enemy made a determined counter-attack on the centre of the newly-captured trench held by Lt Tubb. They advanced up a sap and blew in a sandbag barricade, leaving only one foot of it standing, but Lieutenant Tubb led his men back, repulsed the enemy, and rebuilt the barricade. Supported by strong bombing parties the enemy succeeded in twice blowing in the barricades, but on each occasion Lieutenant Tubb, although wounded in the head and arm, held his ground with the greatest coolness and rebuilt it, and finally succeeded in maintaining his position under very heavy bomb fire.'

Tubb's injuries kept him from his unit and front line service until December 1916 when he went to France where he was quickly promoted to the rank of major. During the Third Battle of Ypres, he was wounded by a sniper whilst leading his men in an attack near Polygon Wood, and mortally wounded when caught in a British barrage on the way to a dressing station. He died later that day and now lies in Lijssenthoek Military Cemetery in Belgium. His VC is now held by the Australian War Memorial in Canberra.

CORPORAL WILLIAM DUNSTAN
CORPORAL ALEXANDER STEWART BURTON
LONE PINE, AUGUST 9, 1915

Both these corporals were with Lieutenant Tubb during his action to regain the lost sap at Lone Pine. They received a joint citation that was published on October 15, 1915:

'For most conspicuous bravery at Lone Pine trenches, in the Gallipoli peninsula on August 9th 1915. In the early morning the enemy made a determined counter-attack on the centre of the newly-captured trench held by Lieutenant Tubb, Corporals Burton and Dunstan and a few men. They advanced up a sap and blew in a sandbag barricade, leaving only one foot standing, but Lieutenant Tubb, with the two corporals, repulsed the enemy and rebuilt the barricade, although Lieutenant Tubb was wounded in the head and arm and Corporal Burton was killed by a bomb while most gallantly building up the parapet under a hail of bombs.'

Alexander Burton was only 22 at the time of his death. Like many of the casualties of Lone Pine he has no known grave and is commemorated on the Lone Pine Memorial. His VC was worn by his father at special events and was finally donated to the Australian War Memorial in 1967.

With the announcement of the award of his Victoria Cross, William Dunstan at once became a local celebrity, much against his wishes. He received his award from the Governor-General at Parliament House, Melbourne, in June 1916. Following the end of hostilities, he married his long-time sweetheart before becoming successful in the newspaper business. He passed away in March 1957 following a heart attack. His VC is also held by the Australian War Memorial in Canberra.

PRIVATE JOHN HAMILTON
LONE PINE, AUGUST 9, 1915

Private John Hamilton was to become the only member of the 3rd Battalion, AIF, to win a VC in the Great War. The courage he showed lasted throughout the battle at Lone Pine where he first went over the top. Hamilton was only 19 and had played a key role in the fierce bombing duels that had taken place since the outbreak of fighting around the Lone Pine positions. Following his expertise with the bomb, he then proved to be equally deadly and courageous with the rifle in an action which resulted in the highest award for courage. His citation that was posted in the *London Gazette* on October 15:

'For most conspicuous bravery on the 9th August, 1915, in the Gallipoli peninsula. During a heavy bombing attack by the enemy on the newly-captured position at Lone Pine, Private Hamilton, with utter disregard of personal safety, exposed himself under heavy fire on the parados, in order to secure a better fire position against the enemy's bomb-throwers. His coolness and daring example had an immediate effect. The defence was encouraged, and the enemy driven off with heavy loss.'

Following evacuation from Gallipoli, Hamilton spent a short time in England where he received his VC. He then rejoined his unit in France where he served throughout the Somme battles. He was made an officer shortly after the end of hostilities before returning to Australia in 1919. During the Second World War he again saw service this time with a Pioneer Battalion in Papua New Guinea and the Army Labour Service with whom he was promoted to captain. He died in Sydney on February 27, 1961 and was buried at Woronora Cemetery. He is also commemorated at the Australian War Memorial in Canberra which now holds his Victoria Cross.

CAPTAIN ALFRED JOHN SHOUT
LONE PINE, AUGUST 9, 1915

Although revered as an Australian hero, Captain Alfred Shout was born in New Zealand in 1882. After fighting the Boers in South Africa, where he gained a Mentioned in Dispatches, he emigrated to Australia in 1907. He landed in Gallipoli on April 25 and immediately found himself in the thick of the action fighting an almost invisible enemy with both skill and bravery. On April 27 Shout was wounded at least twice yet he refused to go to the rear and persisted in both helping other wounded and holding back the Turks. For this action he received the Military Cross.

Shout returned to his unit shortly afterwards and was wounded again on May 11 and was this time mentioned in Sir Ian Hamilton's dispatches. Shortly afterwards he was promoted to captain. He led his men into action at Lone Pine and is recorded by many of his men as having accomplished all manner of brave feats, yet his citation for the Victoria Cross singles out an action at Sasse's Sap on August 9. It was published on October 15, 1915:

'For conspicuous bravery at Lone Pine trenches, in the Gallipoli peninsula. On the morning of 9th August, 1915, with a very small party, Captain Shout charged down the trenches strongly occupied by the enemy and personally threw four bombs amongst them, killing eight and routing the remainder. In the afternoon of the same day, from the position gained in the morning, he captured a further length of trench under similar conditions, and continued personally to bomb the enemy at close range, under very heavy fire, until he was severely wounded, losing his right hand and left eye. This most gallant officer has since succumbed to his injuries.'

Shout was evacuated but died of wounds on board ship and was buried at sea. He is commemorated on the Lone Pine Memorial. Shout's VC is held in a private collection.

CORPORAL CYRIL BASSETT
CHUNUK BAIR, AUGUST 8-10, 1915

Continuous work on repairing telephone lines on the exposed ground around Chunuk Bair earned Corporal Cyril Bassett the honour of being the first New Zealander to win a Victoria Cross in the Great War, and the only New Zealander to win the highest award for gallantry at Gallipoli. This in itself is unusual because New Zealand troops were considered by many to be the best soldiers on the peninsula, possessing both the discipline of the British with the initiative of the Australians. Bassett's citation was gazetted on October 15:

'For most conspicuous bravery and devotion to duty on the Chunuk Bair ridge, in the Gallipoli peninsula, on 7th August 1915. After the New Zealand Infantry Brigade had attacked and established itself on the ridge, Corporal Bassett, in full daylight and under a continuous heavy fire, succeeded in laying a telephone wire from the old position to the new one on Chunuk Bair. He has subsequently been bought to notice for further excellent and most gallant work connected with the repair of telephone lines by day and night under heavy fire.'

He received one bullet through his boot that missed his foot; another through his right-hand pocket whilst a third pierced his tunic collar, all without causing him an injury. Later in April he was repatriated sick to England. He eventually rejoined his unit in June 1916 in France. Bassett was commissioned in 1917 and received a recommendation for the Military Cross which for some reason was not granted. He was wounded in late 1917 and again in March 1918. Bassett was back in uniform in the Second World War in which he reached the rank of lieutenant colonel.

When he died in 1983 aged 91, Bassett was the last Gallipoli VC holder then still living. His Cross is now held by the Queen Elizabeth II Army Memorial Museum, New Zealand.

CAPTAIN PERCY HANSEN
SCIMITAR HILL, AUGUST 9, 1915

Captain Percy Hansen was a member of the 6th (Service) Battalion of the Lincolnshire Regiment. His action in rescuing wounded from the area around Scimitar Hill marks the first VC to be awarded for the landings at Suvla. It was in the ill-fated attempt on August 8 to recapture Scimitar Hill that Captain Hansen was awarded the VC. Having gained some ground, the Lincolns were forced to retire when Turkish fire from two sides threatened to annihilate them but, in so doing, many of the wounded had to be abandoned in no man's land. Hansen's citation for the award that was gazetted on October 1, 1915 takes up the story:

'For conspicuous bravery on 9th August 1915 at Yilghin Burnu, Gallipoli peninsula. After the second capture of the 'Green Knoll' his battalion was forced to retire, leaving some wounded behind, owing to the intense heat from the scrub which had been set on fire. When retirement was effected, Captain Hansen, with three or four volunteers, on his own initiative, dashed forward several times some 300 or 400 yards over open ground into the scrub under a terrific fire, and succeeded in rescuing from inevitable death by burning no less than six wounded men.'

Hansen received his VC (along with a Military Cross also awarded for bravery on the peninsula) from King George V at Buckingham Palace in December 1915. He continued to gain regular promotions and whilst serving with the General Staff in France he added a Distinguished Service Order to his impressive list of decorations.

He stayed in uniform between the wars and by 1941 had reached the rank of brigadier. At the end of hostilities, he was put in charge of Civil Affairs in Norway and he retired from the army in 1946. Brigadier Hanson died in 1951 following a bout of pneumonia. His VC is held privately.

LIEUTENANT WILLIAM FORSHAW
THE VINEYARD, AUGUST 7-9, 1915

Lieutenant Forshaw's VC was the fist to be awarded to the 42nd Division which had suffered so hideously in the Helles sector. The award was made for the attack near the Vineyard. Having gained this position at a great cost, Forshaw was part of the 9th Manchesters who were sent to hold it. His citation in the *London Gazette* on September 9, explains:

'For most conspicuous bravery and determination on the Gallipoli peninsula from 7th to 9th August, 1915. When holding the north-west corner of the 'Vineyard' he was attacked and heavily bombed by Turks, who advanced time after time by three trenches which converged at this point; but he held his own, not only directing his men and encouraging them by means of exposing himself with the utmost disregard to danger, but personally throwing bombs continuously for 41 hours. When his detachment was relieved after 24 hours he volunteered to continue the direction of operations.

Three times during the night of 8th-9th August he was again heavily attacked, and once the Turks got over the barricade, but after shooting three with his revolver he led his men forward, and captured it. When he rejoined his battalion he was choked and sickened by bomb fuses, badly bruised by a fragment of shrapnel, and could hardly lift his arm from continuous bomb throwing. It was due to his personal example, magnificent courage and endurance that his very important corner was held.'

Forshaw was invalided home and received his VC from the King in October 1915. He served with an Indian Regiment through the latter stages of the war before retiring from the Army in 1922.

During the early part of the Second World War he served in the Home Guard but died in 1943 apparently of a heart attack. His VC is now held by the Manchester Regiment Museum.

PRIVATE DAVID LAUDER
THE VINEYARD, AUGUST 13, 1915

Following the gallant and successful defence of the newly-captured trenches around the Vineyard, further reserves were sent up to help rebuild positions and to ensure the Turks were not able to recapture this position. One of these units was the 1/4th Royal Scots Fusiliers of whom Private Lauder was one. Having already helped fight off one Turkish attack, Lauder and a few men were keeping up a constant barrage of jam-tin bombs onto the Turkish front line to dissuade them from further offensive action. One of these bombs thrown by Lauder hit the parapet and fell back into his own trench that was packed with men. He had less than three seconds to act, yet he saved many lives.

'For most conspicuous bravery when with a bombing party retaking a sap. Private Lauder threw a bomb which failed to clear the parapet and fell amongst the bombing party. There was no time to smother the bomb and Private Lauder at once put his foot on it, thereby localising the explosion. His foot was blown off but the remainder of the party through this act of sacrifice escaped unhurt.

For some unexplained reason, Lauder's award was not announced until 1917, by which time he had had an artificial leg fitted and was able to receive the award from King George V. Lauder's injuries obviously exempted him from any further active service but in the Second World War he enlisted as an air raid warden.

David Lauder, who was born in East Glentire, Airdrie, Scotland, on January 21 1894, died at his home in Glasgow on June 4, 1972. His medals have been on the market twice: firstly at Sotherbys in November 1979 when they sold for £10,000 and more recently in July 1994 when at auction at Spinks they went for £17,000.

PRIVATE FREDERICK POTTS
SCIMITAR HILL, AUGUST 21-23, 1915

The attack against Scimitar Hill on August 21 signalled in many ways the end of the line for the Gallipoli adventure. The operation, which was the largest in numbers of men involved, achieved nothing except thousands of casualties, many from the 2nd Mounted Division that comprised mostly Yeomanry units. Amongst the men who charged up the slopes of Scimitar Hill (also known as Hill 70) was a Private Frederick Potts of the Berkshire Yeomanry. He was wounded near the crest just below the Turkish trenches on August 21; his citation published on October 1, 1915 describes his action:

'For most conspicuous bravery and devotion to a wounded comrade in the Gallipoli peninsula. Although himself severely wounded in the thigh in the attack on Hill 70, on the 21st August, 1915 he remained out over forty-eight hours under the Turkish trenches with a private of his regiment who was severely wounded and unable to move, although he could himself have returned to safety. Finally, he fixed a shovel to the equipment of his wounded comrade, and using this as a sledge, he dragged him back over 600 yards to our line, though fired at by the Turks on the way. He reached our trenches at about 9.30 p.m. on the 23rd August.'

Potts was recovering in England when news reached him of the award of the VC and he received it later that year from King George V at Buckingham Palace. Due to the nature of his wounds, he did not return to active service and was released from the Army. He carried out Home Guard duties during the Second World War but died November 1943. In attendance at his funeral was Arthur Andrews the man whose life he had saved on the slopes of Scimitar Hill. Potts was the only member of the Berkshire Yeomanry to win the VC; it is now in a private collection.

SECOND LIEUTENANT HUGO THROSSELL
HILL 60, AUGUST 29, 1915

The story of the struggle to capture Hill 60 is one of raw courage and desperate fighting that so nearly ended in success. Since the joint attack with the British at Suvla on August 21, various small-scale attacks had been going on against the Turkish trenches on Hill 60. Australians, New Zealanders, British and Gurkhas had all attacked and in places gained a little ground. On August 29, following a successful seizure of a Turkish trench by the New Zealanders, a further assault was ordered to exploit this success using men of the Australian 10th Light Horse. This unit had suffered hideously in its attack against the Nek on August 7 and was still not yet back to full strength.

One of the men about to take place in this attack was Second Lieutenant Hugo Throssell. Having succeeded in wrestling the trench from the Turks, the Light Horsemen now had to defend it against unenviable odds as Turkish counter-attacks started in earnest. It was during these attacks that Second Lieutenant Throssell, who had taken command on the death of his captain, won his award:

'For most conspicuous bravery and devotion to duty during operations on the Kaiakij Aghda (Hill 60), in the Gallipoli peninsula on the 29th-30th August. Although severely wounded in several places during a counter-attack, he refused to leave his post or to obtain medical assistance till all danger was passed, when he had his wounds dressed and returned to the firing line until ordered out of action by the medical oficer. By his personal courage and example he kept up the spirits of his party, and was largely instrumental in saving the situation at a critical period.'

Hugo Throssell returned to England to recover from his wounds but contracted meningitis which very nearly killed him. However, he recovered sufficiently to receive his VC from King George V at Buckingham Palace later that year. He then returned to Australia and took part in the recruiting drive before returning to the 10th Light Horse in 1917. He was severely wounded during the Battle of Gaza in which his brother (who had been badly wounded during the charge at the Nek) was killed. Following the recovery from his wounds, he returned to Australia and was eventually demobbed in February 1919.

Throssell claimed that the war had made him a socialist and he campaigned actively with his wife for the Australian Communist Party before making a move into property. However, with the recession that hit world markets in the 1920s, his debts mounted and he committed suicide in 1933, reportedly to help his family gain a war pension. He was the only Light Horseman to win the ultimate award for bravery in the Great War and his medals were donated to the People for Nuclear Disarmament before being sold and later donated to the Australian War Memorial in Canberra.

Hugo Throssell and an impression of his VC action.

SQUADRON-COMMANDER RICHARD DAVIES
FEREJIK JUNCTION, BULGARIA,
NOVEMBER 19, 1915

Although the VC awarded to Squadron-Commander Davies was not won on the peninsula itself, it is nevertheless classed as a Gallipoli VC for a number of reasons. Firstly, it was in an action that was directly supporting the campaign and secondly it took place between the dates of the landing and the evacuation (unlike, for example, Lieutenant Norman Holbrook, who won a VC for torpedoing a Turkish battleship in the Dardanelles in December 1914).

Richard Davies was an airman with the Royal Naval Air Service based on Imbros under the enigmatic Commander Charles Sampson. With Bulgaria's entry into the war, it was decided that an attack should be made on the Ferejik Junction through which most of the supplies would have to travel from Germany to Turkey. Having already attacked the junction a few days earlier, the operation on November 19 was not expected to be any more difficult. The aircraft all arrived over the target safely and commenced their attack. The citation for Davies' VC (and also a DSC for the same action to the other pilot involved, Flight Sub-Lieutenant Gilbert Smylie) was gazetted in January 1916:

'On the 19th November, these two officers carried out an air attack on Ferejik Junction. Flight Lieutenant Smylie's machine was received by very heavy fire and brought down. The pilot planed down over the station releasing all his bombs except one, which failed to drop, simultaneously at the station from a very low altitude. Then he continued his descent into the marsh. On alighting he saw the one unexploded bomb, and set fire to his machine, knowing that the bomb would ensure its destruction. He then proceeded towards Turkish territory. At this moment he perceived Squadron-Commander Davies descending and fearing that he would come down near the burning machine and thus risk destruction from the bomb Flight Sub-Lieutenant Smylie ran back and from a short distance exploded the bomb by means of a pistol bullet. Squadron-Commander Davies descended at a safe distance from the burning machine, took up Flight Sub-Lieutenant Smylie, in spite of the near approach of a party of the enemy, and returned to the aerodrome, a feat of airmanship that can seldom have been equalled for skill and gallantry.'

Davies returned to England after the evacuation of the peninsula and received his award from King George V at Buckingham Palace in April 1916. Later that year he served with an operational squadron in France that was involved in the fledgling science of strategic bombing. By 1918 Davies was heavily involved in the development of aircraft carriers and continued to work his way up through the ranks. He eventually retired in 1944 as a Vice-Admiral having served on various vessels during the Second World War. He died in February 1966, and his Victoria Cross is now on display at the Fleet Air Museum at Yeovilton.

Second Lieutenant Alfred Smith's selfless sacrifice at Fusilier Bluff, as depicted in Deeds that Thrill the Empire though the men have been incorrectly shown wearing steel helmets.

SECOND LIEUTENANT ALFRED SMITH
FUSILIER BLUFF, DECEMBER 22, 1915

With the successful abandonment of both Anzac and Suvla, all attention now turned to the British garrison at Helles. As Christmas approached, one unit which had the job of convincing the Turks that the British were determined to stay at Helles was the 1/5th East Lancashires, who were positioned in the most northern positions around Fusilier Bluff. On the night of December 22, men from this unit were involved in a bombing with a group of Turks and one of these Lancastrians was Second Lieutenant Smith. He was in the act of throwing a bomb when he slipped and released it by accident in his own trench. The citation for his VC tells the remainder of the story.

'For most conspicuous bravery. He was in the act of throwing a bomb when it slipped from his hand and fell to the bottom of the trench, close to several of our officers and men. He immediately shouted a warning and himself jumped clear into safety; but seeing that the officers and men were unable to get into cover, and knowing well that the bomb was due to explode, he returned without hesitation and flung himself on it. He was instantly killed by the explosion. His magnificent act of self sacrifice undoubtedly saved many lives.'

Smith's act of self-sacrifice so close to the end of the campaign, left a profound mark on those serving on the peninsula. In many ways it sums up the bravery of all the troops in the Gallipoli campaign who were often asked to virtually commit suicide in poorly-planned attacks and did so without question or hesitation. His parents received his VC at Buckingham Palace in December 1916 and today it can be seen at the Towneley Hall Museum in Burnley, Lancashire. Smith was the son of the Chief Constable of Burnley, William Henry Smith.

FOOTNOTE TO HISTORY

For more than 40 years, Sir Martin Gilbert has studied and researched the life and times of Winston Churchill. After the death of Winston's son, Randolph in 1968, Martin (knighted in 1995) took over the mantle of official biographer, writing six volumes of narrative and editing ten volumes of Churchill documents.

In 1966, Randolph had published the first set of two companion volumes covering Churchill's life from 1874 to 1900 and when he died the years 1901 to 1914 had already been compiled and assembled. In the two years before Randolph's death, Martin worked as his research assistant preparing a chronology of the Dardanelles campaign — a campaign which was to bring about Churchill's downfall — but it was not until 1969 that Martin discovered the real reason for his dismissal by Prime Minister Asquith.

In his book *In Search of Churchill,* published by HarperCollins in 1994, Martin explained that 'within a year after taking over from Randolph, I completed the first, rather tentative, draft of Volume 3. With it I flew to Istanbul where I was an official guest of a foreign government. . . . On the following day I was taken to the naval museum in which I saw charts of the Dardanelles minefields, in which it was clear just how close the Anglo-French naval force had come to penetrating them in the assault of March 18, 1915. There was also a note about the desperate shortage of ammunition of the Turkish mobile shore batteries: by a bizarre quirk of historical irony, the Imperial Russian intelligence service had reported this very fact to the Tsar. And in the Second World War, trying to show Churchill some goodwill during a stormy Moscow meeting, Stalin had repeated this to Churchill.

'Somehow Stalin had understood that Churchill's Achilles' heel was the Dardanelles, and felt that a kindly reference to that campaign would be a means to win him over. In March 1915 Churchill, then only forty, but at the height of his powers and popularity, had pinned his hopes on the swift and relatively bloodless defeat of Turkey. As First Lord of the Admiralty he had been in charge of the Royal Navy for the previous four years of peace, bringing it to a peak of war preparedness. It was clear from the records of the War Council (Prime Minister Asquith's War Cabinet) that Churchill had confidence in the ability of British and French

'As a general rule historians should do their own research and Gilbert is a paragon amongst researchers. This zeal in pursuit of every scrap of evidence on Churchill's life is an example to all biographers.' So ran one review of Martin Gilbert's book *In Search of Churchill*, a fascinating account of his voyage of discovery in completing the biography of unquestionably Britain's greatest statesman of the 20th century. But, unexplained until Martin came along, was the true reason behind the sudden dismissal of Winston Churchill as First Lord of the Admiralty. Above left: Sir Martin contemplates his subject on the spot where Churchill (right) found solace at Chartwell.

warships to push past the Turkish minefields and forts at the Dardanelles. . . . With Turkey knocked out of the war, Britain and France would, as they believed, be able to strike at the German and Austro-Hungarian monolith from the south, drawing onto the side of Britain, France and Russia three hitherto neutral states, Italy, Greece and Bulgaria. For the Greeks, the prospect of the fall of Turkey would make Constantinople a prize worth fighting for. The annexation of Eastern Thrace would be the spur for the Bulgarians to fight. Italy, once she committed herself, would be able to control, and even to annex, the Adriatic coast of Austria-Hungary.

Bombarding the Turkish forts. Probably one of the greatest ironies of the campaign was that the Allies abandoned their naval attack at the very moment when the Turks had exhausted their ammunition. The *Queen Elizabeth*, seen firing a broadside (right).

'Not only the War Council records, but the Foreign Office papers, and Lord Kitchener's War Office files — all at the Public Record Office — showed the precise evolution of the British naval attack at the Dardanelles. The British Ambassador in St Petersburg, in a telegram that reached London in the early hours of January 2, 1915, stressed, as a matter of urgency, that such British action would give the Russians a means of countering the Turkish advance into the Caucasian provinces of the Tsarist Empire. This point, as the records showed, had been taken up at once by Kitchener, who wrote to Churchill that morning: 'Do you think any naval action would be possible to prevent Turks sending more men into the Caucasus and thus denuding Constantinople?' Kitchener's letter was a catalyst in the concept that Russia might be helped on its Turkish Front by some British action at the Dardanelles, and that Constantinople might be the prize of victory.

'The Admiralty archives provided the next piece of the jigsaw puzzle. They showed that Admiral Fisher, the First Sea Lord whom Churchill had just brought back to the Admiralty, had suggested a substantial naval and military assault against Turkey, including a naval attack at the Dardanelles and a military landing at Gallipoli peninsula. Fisher's papers at Lennoxlove — the ones that Randolph had sent me to see in 1964 — made clear that Churchill was at first hesitant about the new Turkish strategy. He wrote to Fisher in reply to the Admiral's plan to land troops at Gallipoli: 'I would not grudge 100,000 men because of the great political effects in the Balkan peninsula: but Germany is the foe, and it is bad war to seek cheap victories and easier antagonists.'

'That same week, as the Admiralty telegrams showed, Churchill asked the Admiral on the spot if something might be done by ships alone. In reply, the Admiral expressed his willingness to try some form of naval assault. Churchill became convinced that something decisive for the outcome of the war could be done. As the naval plans progressed and the planning obstacles were overcome, Churchill's keenness grew. Even the volatile Fisher had moments of dramatic enthusiasm, going so far as the urge that the most modern British battleship of all, the *Queen Elizabeth*, instead of 'uselessly' test-firing her as yet untested 15-inch guns into the ocean at Gibraltar, should test them against the Turkish forts at the Dardanelles.

'By the end of February Churchill was borne futher along the path of the swift defeat of Turkey by the incredible enthusiasm of every member of Asquith's War Council . . . but Kitchener was emphatic that troops were not needed: the naval attack would do the trick.

One of the *Queen Elizabeth*'s claimed successes at the time was scoring a direct hit with one of her 15-inch shells on this Krupp 10-inch piece.

Uneasy at this, and asking for his dissent to be recorded by the Cabinet Secretary, Churchill agreed to go ahead with ships alone. When, a few days later, Kitchener showed no interest in providing air support in the shape of the army's fledgling Flying Corps, Churchill stepped in with the even smaller, but keen, Naval Air Service, which he had helped to establish as an independent air fighting force four years earlier. One of the young pilots, Richard Bell Davies, was to win the Victoria Cross for rescuing a downed airman from the clutches of a Turkish Army patrol. Davies, when I found him in retirement on the south coast during my Randolph days, was as indignantly sure as many other survivors of the campaign that if only Churchill had been allowed to continue, victory might have come. Instead, the naval attack had been called off by the Admiral on the spot after several ships hit mines, and 650 men drowned, 600 of them on the French warship, the *Bouvet*. The naval attack on the Narrows was never renewed, even though minesweeping continued, and, in Churchill's view, a second naval attack could have been mounted with the still considerable naval forces gathered there. But the Admiral, after first agreeing to try again, decided not to take what he regarded as too big a risk. Churchill sent several telegrams urging renewed action, but did not have the authority to overrule the man on the spot. . . .

'Churchill was never to shake off the charge of recklessness with regard to the planning and execution of the Dardanelles attack, even though the main charges almost always concerned the military atttack, not the naval one. . . .

'All these factors, some already a part of history since 1923 through Churchill's own second volume of *The World Crisis,* some new, were in my manila folders as I flew from Istanbul to Ankara. I had been told that I could meet Ismet Inönü, who had been Atatürk's lieutenant at the Dardanelles and was later his successor as President. At the time of my visit in 1969 Inönü was under house arrest. I waited in my hotel for three days, while various Foreign Ministry emissaries told me how difficult it would be to see the former leader. On the fourth day a diplomat and a soldier came to escort me to Inönü's house. . . .

'Inönü told me that Atatürk had always insisted on speaking the language of the visitor, and that he, Inönü, would therefore speak to me in English. I was flattered, though he quickly lapsed into French. He had two points that he wanted to make about Churchill: that the naval attack at the Dardanelles had come to within an ace of success, and that he, Inönü, had thought at the time that the Turkish naval forces would have been decimated in

The failure to press home the naval operation, and the disaster of the subsequent military campaign, was laid squarely at Churchill's door and long after the war was won he would be greeted at meetings with heckler's crying: 'What about the Dardanelles?'

the Sea of Marmara, exposing Constantinople itself to the vastly superior naval forces of the Entente. Inönü made the point which Churchill had made at the time, in vain, that in the immediate aftermath of the set back of March 18, had the Admiral John de Robeck tried again, he would have had a good chance of success.

'I made one more call while still in Ankara, to Atatürk's house. His former secretary, Afet Inan, whom I was told by my diplomat escort had been his last and favourite mistress, showed me his library. I opened the drawer in which he had kept his maps. There was his working map of the Dardanelles, a 1911 British military map, printed in Cairo. So it was not the British alone who had to rely on other people's efforts: Lord Kitchener's nominee to lead the military forces in April 1915, General Sir Ian Hamilton, had taken out with him the 1908 Baedeker guide book to Constantinople and Asia Minor. This worthy Leipzig volume was hardly the most useful guide to a military campaign which had to start on a coastline disfigured (from an invading soldier's point of view) by cliffs and gullies constantly altered by tides and erosion.

'I browsed about Atatürk's bookshelves. Shortly before his death he had hoped to welcome Churchill to Turkey, and his Private Secretaries, two of whom I met on this visit, had collected Churchill's books for him to read. There on the shelf was the Dardanelles volume of *The World Crisis,* which Churchill had published in 1923. At the point where de Robeck had refused Churchill's request to make a second attack on the minefields, Atatürk had written in the margin a Turkish phrase, "History is ruthless to him who is without ruthlessness." But Churchill did not have the authority to order the Admiral to make the second attack. He could urge and cajole, but he could not impose action. . . .

'Together with Norman Pemberton, the Commonwealth War Graves custodian, we visited the beaches at which the military landings had taken place in April, and again in August 1915. We climbed the heights, at Cape Helles and at Anzac, which those landings had failed to capture. At Cape Helles we stood in silence by the naval monument, looking out on an absolutely placid sea, beneath which still lies the detritus of the great warships that had been sunk. We stopped at almost every cemetery, read the names on so many of the gravestones, and marvelled at the work of maintaining trees and flowers and shrubs in such a hostile landscape. At Y Beach I found wild irises, and put a few in the relevant

In Memory of

THOMAS HUGH COLVILLE BT MAJ FRANKLAND

Captain
Royal Dublin Fusiliers
who died on
Sunday, 25th April 1915. Age 35.

Son of the late Col. Colville Frankland and Mary Jay Frankland.

Commemorative Information

HELLES MEMORIAL, Turkey
Panel 190 to 196

Then a Lieutenant, Thomas Frankland was captured with Churchill on November 15, 1899 when the armoured train sent to support a cavalry reconnaissance to Colenso, Natal, was ambushed by the Boers.

pages of the British official history. At Cape Helles I saw the grave of one of Churchill's army friends from the turn of the century, Major Thomas Frankland, a fellow prisoner of the Boers captured during the armoured train ambush, and one of the first to be killed in the W Beach landings.

'It was easy to understand, at that place, Churchill's terrible sense of frustration and of anger, that if only the naval attack had been tried a second time, if necessary a third time, then the terrible slaughter on the beaches and in the trenches of the peninsula could have been avoided. It was all the more understandable when, on opening my manila folders on the peninsula itself, I re-read Churchill's reasoning for attacking Turkey at the Dardanelles: that it would end the slaughter and the stalemate that had begun to be the curse of the Western Front. "Are there not other alternatives", he had written to Asquith on December 29, 1914, "than sending our armies to chew barbed wire in Flanders?"

At the Lord Mayor's Banquet on November 9, 1914, Prime Minister Asquith, with a united cabinet behind him, gave one of the most inspired speeches of his career: 'We shall not sheathe the sword, which we have not lightly drawn, until France and Belgium have regained all, and more, than all that they have lost'.

'In May 1915, Asquith gave way to the Conservative pressure to create an all-party government. The Conservative ministers had been in the political wilderness for ten years. They did not want to remain there any longer. A serious shortage of shells on the Western Front and the threat of a controversial parliamentary debate on the Dardanelles, caused Asquith to lose his nerve, and to agree to a coalition. The Conservatives had very few conditions: the first and most emphatic was that Churchill, their foe from the day that he crossed over to the Liberal benches in 1904, must go. Asquith gave way.

'I did not know why Asquith had succumbed to Conservative pressure. The Churchill letters that I had found in his personal archive revealed only Churchill's anguish, at his imminent fall from high office.

'Shortly after my return to Britain, with the image of the Dardanelles still vivid in my mind I received a visitor. She was a tall, attractive, amusing and voluble woman, who had witten to me out of the blue, introducing herself as a friend of Randolph's and a cousin of Clementine's. Her name was Judy Montagu. I took her out to dinner at one of my favourite Oxford restaurants. Hardly had we sat down when she bent down and opened a basket, bringing up to the table a folder full of letters.

'The letters were handwritten, in an elegant hand that I recognized at once as Asquith's. They had been written to her mother, Venetia Stanley, Clementine's first cousin. The letters covered the whole period of the planning and execution of the Dardanelles. They were incredibly detailed, often telling far more about the course of the discussion in the War Council than the official record had done. There was a letter for virtually every day, sometimes two and even three letters in any one day. Not only had Asquith revealed to Venetia, at the time, the evolution of the Dardanelles, but he was particularly fascinated by Churchill, recounting to her

Herbert Henry Asquith, 1852-1928. He was Prime Minister and First Lord of the Treasury from 1908 to 1916, and in 1925 was raised to the peerage as Earl of Oxford and Asquith.

Asquith's mistress was the beautiful Venetia Stanley. He fell in love with her one Sunday morning in the spring of 1912 and, when he could not see her, he wrote sometimes three times a day.

Churchill's conversations, moods, plans, interventions, all in detail and with great colour. Then, in the week that the Conservatives demanded Churchill's head on a plate, there was a terrible change in the correspondence, hitherto caressing its tone and seductive in its intention. Venetia, tired of Asquith's unrelenting attentions, had taken the one decisive step open to her to shake them off and to turn her back on them once and for all. She had informed him that she intended to marry. Her husband would be none other than the man they had both often laughed about and even mocked, Edwin Montagu, a member of Asquith's Government. . . .

'Now Venetia would marry the mocked-at Montagu, she did not want Asquith to write to her again, and wanted no more to do with him. He was devastated. Whatever dreams he had harboured of intimacy with her (he was 62 and she was 27) were shattered. Their drives together in his car along the Embankment were over. His tempting confidence of daily war policy-making would have to stop. He did not know which way to turn. Hitherto he had sought her advice about every political crisis. He had bombarded her each day with the most secret war news, and with his most detailed thoughts on war policy and politics. Now he could confide in her no longer. When Lloyd George, the Chancellor of the Exchequer and the second most powerful member of the Liberal team, went to 10 Downing Street to insist that the only way forward was to accept the Conservative demands, bring them in, and sacrifice Churchill, Asquith had no strength left but to acquiesce. No sooner had Lloyd George left than Asquith wrote to Venetia:

"Never since the war began had I such an accumulation (no longer shared!) of anxieties . . . one of the most hellish bits of these most hellish days was that you alone of all the world — to whom I have always gone in every moment of trial & trouble, & from whom I have always come back solaced and healed & inspired — were the one person who could do nothing, & from whom I could ask nothing. To my dying day, that will be the most bitter memory of my life . . .

"I am on the eve of the most astounding & world-shaking decisions — as I would never have taken without your counsel & consent. It seems so strange & empty & unnatural: yet there is nowhere else that I can go, nor would I, if I could."

She worked as a nurse at the London Hospital in the Mile End Road and Asquith would go there whenever wounded were admitted (left) as an excuse to see her. Right: Today, this is the rear entrance fronting Stepney Way.

'Shortly after Asquith wrote this letter, Churchill appeared in his room full of confidence that he could deal effectively with any House of Commons debate on the Dardanelles, that he could set out the documents that would show that his actions had not been irresponsible, that he could rout the Conservative critics, and, even though he had been deserted at that very moment by Admiral Fisher, could not only defend what had already been done, but find a replacement for Fisher and see the naval attack through to success at the Dardanelles. Asquith heard him out, then said, as if he had heard nothing, "No, this will not do. I have decided to form a national government with a coalition with the Unionists, and a very much larger reconstruction will be required." Before Churchill could plead with Asquith to let him stay in charge of the navy, the Prime Minister turned to him with the words "What are we to do for you?"

'With these seven words, Churchill knew that his days at the Admiralty, perhaps even his days in public life, were over. He never knew that Venetia, whose company he always enjoyed, and

was to go on enjoying for many years, had broken Asquith's heart and destroyed his will to fight.

'Churchill left the Admiralty under a black cloud of Conservative hostility, abandoned by his Liberal leader's unexpected and sudden "What are we to do for you?" which he was never to forgive. Clementine, outraged, sent Asquith a long, handwritten letter.

"The Dardanelles haunted him for the rest of his life," Clementine told me. "He always believed in it. When he left the Admiralty he thought he was finished. He didn't believe he would ever be asked back into government. I thought he'd never get over the Dardanelles. I thought he'd die of grief."

'Appointed in June 1915 to the sinecure of Chancellor of the Duchy of Lancaster, Churchill was unable to exert any further influence on the continuing battles at Gallipoli. The shadow of the Dardanelles haunted him, as did Asquith's behaviour in throwing him over, as he saw it, without giving him the chance to defend his policies in Parliament.'

NOW THEY LISTEN TO CHURCHILL

Kept out of Conservative Cabinets for years, Winston Churchill comes back as a political power because his warnings proved true.

Venetia's letter ending the affair was received by Asquith on May 17, 1915. The Prime Minister was devastated, losing all stomach to fight to save Churchill and to preserve the Liberal government intact in the House of Commons. So Churchill was dismissed . . . and he almost certainly went to his grave never knowing the real reason. That was only discovered by Martin Gilbert in the revelation given to him by Venetia's daughter Judy Montagu in the comfort of the Sorbonne restaurant in Oxford in 1969. Thus are determined the fates of men and mice . . . but the loss of a woman's love can never have had such a fateful outcome.

On August 6, 1929, while Churchill was crossing the Atlantic from Southampton to Quebec on board the *Empress of Australia,* a fellow politician who was with him noted in his diary: 'My usual evening talk with Winston turned mainly on the Dardanelles. Talking of the series of mischances which just prevented our getting through, he said jestingly that his only consolation was that God wished things to be prolonged in order to sicken mankind of war, and that He had interfered with a project which would have brought the war to a speedier conclusion.' Right: Almost back in the saddle . . . a *PIcture Post* illustration of February 25, 1939.

ALLIED CEMETERIES

Includes Australia, Canada, India, New Zealand, South Africa and the United Kingdom

CEMETERY	NAVY		ARMY		AIR FORCE		MERCHANT NAVY		MISC.		TOTALS	
	Known	Unk	Known	Unk	Known	Unk	Known	Unk	Known	Unk	Known	Unk
Ari Burnu Cemetery, Anzac	3	—	208	—	—	—	—	—	—	42	211	42
Azmak Cemetery, Suvla	—	—	390	—	—	—	—	—	—	684	390	684
Baby 700 Cemetery, Anzac	1	—	42	—	—	—	—	—	—	450	43	450
Beach Cemetery, Anzac	26	—	343	—	—	—	—	—	—	22	369	22
Canterbury Cemetery, Anzac	—	—	22	—	—	—	—	—	—	5	22	5
Chunuk Bair Cemetery, Anzac	—	—	10	—	—	—	—	—	—	622	10	622
Courtney's and Steel's Post Cemetery	4	—	61	—	—	—	—	—	—	160	65	160
Embarkation Pier Cemetery	—	—	282	—	—	—	—	—	—	662	282	662
The Farm Cemetery, Anzac	—	—	7	—	—	—	—	—	—	645	7	645
4th Battalion Parade Ground Cemetery	3	—	106	—	—	—	—	—	—	7	109	7
Green Hill Cemetery	—	—	499	—	—	—	—	—	—	2472	499	2472
Hill 10 Cemetery	4	—	545	—	—	—	—	—	—	150	549	150
Hill 60 Cemetery	—	—	76	—	—	—	—	—	—	712	76	712
Johnston's Jolly Cemetery	—	—	37	—	—	—	—	—	—	144	37	144
Lala Baba Cemetery	2	—	161	—	—	—	—	—	—	53	163	53
Lancashire Landing Cemetery	249	—	855	5	5	—	3	—	—	135	1112	140
Lone Pine Cemetery	9	—	654	—	—	—	—	—	—	504	663	504
The Nek Cemetery, Anzac	—	—	10	—	—	—	—	—	—	316	10	316
New Zealand No. 2 Outpost Cemetery	—	—	33	—	—	—	—	—	—	150	33	150
No. 2 Outpost Cemetery	—	—	86	—	—	—	—	—	—	66	86	66
Pink Farm Cemetery, Helles	27	—	325	—	—	—	—	—	—	250	352	250
Plugge's Plateau Cemetery, Anzac	—	—	17	—	—	—	—	—	—	4	17	4
Quinn's Post Cemetery, Anzac	1	—	178	—	—	—	—	—	—	294	179	294
Redoubt Cemetery, Helles	176	—	458	—	—	—	—	—	—	1393	634	1393
7th Field Ambulance Cemetery	—	—	364	—	—	—	—	—	—	276	364	276
Shell Green Cemetery	3	—	412	—	1	—	1	—	1	11	418	11
Shrapnel Valley Cemetery	4	—	594	—	—	—	—	—	—	85	598	85
Skew Bridge Cemetery	130	—	126	—	—	—	—	—	—	351	256	351
Twelve Tree Copse Cemetery	37	—	1097	—	—	—	—	—	—	2226	1134	2226
V Beach Cemetery	12	—	204	—	—	—	—	—	—	480	216	480
Walker's Ridge Cemetery, Anzac	1	—	75	—	—	—	—	—	—	16	76	16
Totals:	**692**	—	**8,277**	**5**	**6**	—	**4**	—	**1**	**13,387**	**8,980**	**13,392**

Left: The Anzac Commemorative Site was conceived to cater for the increasing number of visitors attending the traditional dawn ceremony held each year on Anzac Day in Ari Burnu Cemetery. Also the new memorial area will form an important part of the new Battlefield Heritage Zone which has been set up on the Gallipoli peninsula. **Right:** Two of the ten illustrative panels: the charge of the 3rd Light Horse (top) and New Zealand soldiers resting during the attack on Chunuk Bair (bottom).

POSTSCRIPT

On Anzac Day 2000, the 85th anniversary of the landings, over 5,000 Australians and New Zealanders gathered at the traditional site for past Anzac Day dawn services at Gallipoli to see the Prime Ministers of both countries unveil a new monument on the beach.

Located 300 metres north of Ari Burnu, it was the spot occupied by elements of the 11th and 12th Battalions on April 25, 1915, and one of the main evacuation beaches nine months later. With its low stone walls and paths to the beach, the new memorial incorporates ten information panels of special significance to Australians and New Zealanders. These begin with a map of Gallipoli and then show the Anzac landing by George Lambert; the charge of the Australian 2nd Infantry Brigade at Krithia by Charles Wheeler; a blindfolded Turkish officer being led through Anzac lines to discuss the truce after the attack of May 19; stretcher bearers; the charge of the 3rd Light Horse at the Nek, also by George Lambert; New Zealanders resting during the assault towards Chunuk Bair on the night of August 6; the evacuation from North Beach, and Turkish artillery. The final panel depicts an Australian officer visiting a comrade's grave.

At the ceremony to dedicate the new memorial on April 25, Helen Clark, Prime Minister of New Zealand, said: 'They came as British colonial troops, they left as New Zealanders'. The Australian premier, John Howard, added: 'We come to observe not only a dawn, but a dusk. For dusk has all but fallen upon that greathearted generation of Australians who fought here. The shadows gather on a time and a world in which our nation's spirit was born.'

INDEX

Note: page numbers in *italics* refer to illustrations.